THE LORDS OF

one effort more and Scotland's free
lord of the isles my trust in thee
Sir Walter Scott

This book is dedicated to the memory of my grandfather,
Murdoch Campbell

THE LORDS OF THE ISLES

A HISTORY OF CLAN DONALD

Raymond Campbell Paterson

BIRLINN

This edition first published in 2008 by
Birlinn Limited
West Newington House
10 Newington Road
Edinburgh
EH9 1QS

www.birlinn.co.uk

ISBN13: 978 1 84158 718 9
ISBN10: 1 84158 718 4

British Library Cataloguing-in-Publication Data
A catalogue record for this book is available from the British Library

Typeset by Initial Typesetting Services, Edinburgh
Printed and bound by Antony Rowe Ltd, Chippenham

CONTENTS

FOREWORD

That is the mark of the Scot that he stands in an attitude to the past unthinkable in Englishmen, and remembers and cherishes the memory of his forebears, good and bad, and there burns alive in him a sense of identity with the dead, even to the twentieth generation.

Robert Louis Stevenson

At the height of the Middle Ages – while elsewhere in Scotland great nobles were building castles to protect themselves from the English or their own neighbours – a unique political institution was taking shape amongst the Gaelic people of the west. This was the Lordship of the Isles, the highest expression of the organisational genius of Clan Donald. At a time when the King of Scots himself was forced by his enemies to take refuge in France, the Lord of the Isles was able to live in peace and safety among his own kin. The Lordship provided the Gaels of Scotland with a political unity and cultural focus that was never to be equalled. It represented a tradition that stretched back to the days of St Columba and the ancient kingdom of Dalriada.

At one point almost a third of Scotland was under the control of Clan Donald. This did not come about by accident, but by great skill in politics, diplomacy and war. Above all, it came about because of the loyalty and affection the Lordship inspired among its people, not just those of Clan Donald but also the other confederate clans. Until the years preceding the final collapse of the Lordship in 1493, the Island chiefs faced no serious internal challenge to their authority, a record that might have been envied by many of the kings of Scotland.

This book sets out to tell the story of Clan Donald, before, during and after the demise of the Lords of the Isles. I am sure there are many who will consider this to be a dangerous enterprise, for clan history tends to have a very poor reputation among serious historical scholarship, often deservedly so. This is a great pity, for there is much to be learned from the institution of clanship. However, one thing should be made clear at the outset. It has been said many times but it deserves repeating: the image of a clan as a distinct group of people all bearing the same name, wearing the same tartan and living in a clearly defined area is an appalling parody of the truth.

Scottish clans were complex institutions; they changed and modified through time. Patronymics, for instance, only started to be adopted during the course of the thirteenth century, when the descendants of Donald, grandson of Somerled, became the Macdonalds. But even here there are problems. There are times when the very name 'Macdonald' has something of the dignity of a royal title, reserved solely for the chief of the kin.[1] In the only extant Gaelic charter granted by the island chiefs, Donald, Lord of the Isles, signs himself simply as 'Mc Domnaill'.[2] For centuries afterwards it was only the blood descendants of the Lords of the Isles who bore the name. As late as 1615, when the last chief of the Macdonalds of Dunyveg was expelled from Islay, the very heart of the old Lordship, few of the leading tenants of the island were called Macdonald. The greatest of all the war chiefs of Clan Donald was only ever known to his Gaelic contemporaries as Alasdair MacColla, after his father, Coll MacGillespic. Only non-Gaelic outsiders referred to him as Alexander Macdonald. Surnames were largely unknown among the common people of the Highlands and Islands until the early eighteenth century, when clanship was already in decline. Many then simply adopted the surname of their chief, implying a kinship that only ever existed in legend.

Even the names of the chiefs of Clan Donald present us with additional problems. They were to be variously known as McConneill, MakConnell, McDhonnell, and MacDonell.[3] In the course of 1660, the chief of Glengarry changed the spelling of his name from Macdonald to Macdonnell, subsequently adopted by the rest of his kin. Coll of the Cows, the infamous chief of the Keppoch branch of Clan Donald, signed himself, according to his mood, as McDoniell or McDonell, although on at least one occasion he signed himself simply as MacDonald.[4] For the sake of simplicity the spelling Macdonald will be used for all branches of the clan, with the exception of the Macdonnells of Antrim and, from the period of the Restoration onwards, the Macdonnells of Glengarry.

From beginning to end, Clan Donald was a conservative institution, attempting to work out its destiny in the context of a Gaelic world. In this lay both the seeds of greatness and destruction. It was the failure to understand or accept the growing power of the Scottish and subsequently the British state that brought about its steady decline from the late fifteenth century onwards. The principal beneficiaries of this decline were other Highland families, like the Mackenzies and, most notably, the Campbells, who, possessing none of the great independent traditions of Clan Donald, were able to exist comfortably in both a Highland and Lowland world. There were, of course, exceptions to this and the Macdonnells of Antrim, arguably the most successful branch of the clan to emerge from the ruins of the Lordship, built up a considerable power in the early seventeenth century.

Any account of Clan Donald clearly has to spend time considering the growing rivalry between the Macdonalds and the Campbells. Too much can be made of this, however. The rivalry was certainly real enough, and became especially intense in the middle of the seventeenth century, but there are times when the two families enjoyed reasonably friendly relations. It would have been almost impossible, for example, for the Macdonalds of Dunyveg to consolidate their hold in Antrim without the active co-operation of Clan Campbell. In the popular imagination, however, the relations between the two clans will probably always be viewed through the prism of Glencoe. But the facts surrounding the infamous massacre are far more complex than a simple clan feud. Even the best popular histories of the event spend much time explaining the motives of Robert Campbell of Glenlyon, while ignoring those of Captain Drummond and his fellow Lowlanders, who proved themselves to be far more brutal in their conduct. John Campbell, Earl of Breadalbane, continues to be viewed by many as the chief villain of the piece, but he was one of the few men to express open outrage at the horror of the massacre and the damage it did in the Highlands.

In writing this history I am happy to acknowledge my debt to the Reverends Angus and Archibald Macdonald, whose three-volume *Clan Donald* continues to be a mine of information and will probably never be surpassed as a work of genealogy. It is, however, now a fairly dated work, in both its overall structure and its interpretation of events. Moreover, it shares some of the weaknesses of traditional clan history, failing at points to maintain critical distance. The more recent *Clan Donald* by Donald Macdonald follows closely in the steps of the Reverends Angus and Archibald, so closely that he inevitably duplicates some of their chief errors.

Finally, a brief word on the sources used. As far as possible I have drawn on contemporary records and chronicles of the events described. Unfortunately, for much of the history of Clan Donald, especially the time of the Lordship of the Isles, there are few internal records, and almost all accounts of the period are written by outsiders, who were often hostile to the Gaelic world. It is not until the reign of Charles II that the first native accounts were set down in the *History of the Macdonalds* by Hugh Macdonald of Sleat and *The Book of Clanranald*. Both of these works are deeply informed by the politics of their time and are best treated with some caution, especially the garrulous Hugh Macdonald. Nevertheless, in setting down ancient traditions they help to fill some important gaps in the history of Clan Donald, adding flesh, at points, to brief contemporary records. It is thanks to Hugh Macdonald that our knowledge of the period just prior to the fall of the Lordship is not a total blank.

In conclusion, let me stress that this book attempts to unravel the story of Clan Donald against the background of Scottish history as a whole. As such it is essentially a political history rather than a work of genealogy. I have avoided the usual approach of describing the rise and fall of the Lords of the Isles, followed by an account of the individual branches of the clan, which inevitably involves some repetition. Rather, I attempt to knit the threads together in an overall pattern, highlighting individual elements only when it seems necessary to do so. It is my sincere hope that the end product will help to illuminate one of the great stories of Scottish history.

RCP
Edinburgh, 2000

1

THE KINGDOM OF THE SEA

For the people of the west the sea is a highway, not a barrier. Even today there are parts of the Highlands virtually inaccessible by land, but in the early centuries of the Christian era, when land routes were both difficult and dangerous, traders, missionaries, pirates and settlers were carried by sea to all parts of western Scotland. They came in boats made of animal hide stretched over a wickerwork frame, and powered by sail or oar. Some of these craft were sturdy enough to withstand even the heaviest seas. The boat that brought St Columba to Iona in 563 is said to have been some sixty feet long.[1]

In the centuries before Columba made his famous voyage, the Scots, a Gaelic-speaking people of Irish origin, had been settling on the islands and mainland of what is now called Argyll – the Coast of the Gael. In the third century AD, perhaps the year 258, an Irish prince by the name of Cairbre Riada landed in western Scotland. Riada is reputed to have been a son of Conar, High King of Ireland, and he already ruled a small kingdom in Ulster known as Dalriada – 'Riada's share'. The new frontier in Argyll was also to be called Dalriada.[2]

For the next 200 years the history of the Scots' settlement in the west is shrouded in darkness, but with the arrival in 500 AD of a fresh wave of immigrants led by Fergus MacErc, the kingdom of Dalriada takes on a more definite shape. Dalriada could only be firmly established in an almost permanent state of war with the Picts, the native people of what the Romans once called Caledonia. Sometimes the Scots gained the advantage, and at other times the Picts. One king of Dalriada, Aedan MacGabrain, is said to have fought the Picts for thirteen years without a break.[3] Clearly an ambitious man, he is also said to have fought with the Britons of Strathclyde and the Angles of Northumbria, whose kingdoms had emerged out of the ashes of the Roman Empire. In the year 741 Dalriada suffered a devastating defeat at the hands of the Picts, but managed to survive, perhaps because of a fresh transfusion of blood from Ireland. Before the end of the century all the peoples of what was soon to become the kingdom of Scotland were faced with a new and terrifying threat from a totally unexpected direction. In 795, Iona, the spiritual heart of both Dalriada and Pictland, was desecrated by a group of savage seamen who arrived in sleek wooden boats: by this action the Vikings announced their arrival on the stage of Celtic history.

With their magnificent longships, far superior to the Gaelic skin boats, the Vikings established almost total domination of the western seas. Coming first as raiders and then as settlers, they gained control of a large swathe of territory from the Shetlands to the Isle of Man and the east coast of Ireland, where Dublin was founded as a Viking base in 841. The Hebrides were so heavily penetrated that the Irish annalists began to refer to them as Innse Gall – 'the islands of the strangers'.

The ancient link between Scotland and Ireland was almost completely severed, and Dalriada itself became a dangerous frontier territory. In response, Kenneth MacAlpin, the last King of Dalriada, moved the centre of his power eastwards, when he united the Picts and Scots in the Kingdom of Alba or Scotland.

It is at this point, in the midst of a new dark age, that we obtain sight of an ancestor of Clan Donald. In 835 Kenneth MacAlpin, while still King of Dalriada, and under obvious pressure from the Norsemen, summoned fresh help from Ireland. For the last time in history the Irish answered the call of their Scots cousins, and a force under Godfrey, son of Fergus, managed to obtain a hold on at least some of the Western Isles.[4] Godfrey seems to have maintained his position, and died in 852 as a chief of Innse Gall.[5] His name is of Norse origin and suggests that, even at this early date, there was some racial and cultural convergence between the Vikings and the Gaels. It has been argued that this kind of convergence is far too early, and that the story of Godfrey was added to the sources in the early seventeenth century.[6] However, a thirteenth-century Gaelic poem in praise of Angus Mor Macdonald appears to confirm his authenticity;[7] and as late as the mid sixteenth-century Clan Donald was on occasions called Clan Godfrey.[8]

Godfrey's immediate successors were unable to maintain their position against the rising Viking tide. But the Norsemen were never able to establish the complete cultural domination of the southern isles – or Sudreys – that they did in the Nordreys of Orkney and Shetland. In the process of intermarriage between the Vikings and Celts a new warrior race emerged before the end of the ninth century. This was the *Gall-Gaedhil* or 'foreign Gael'.[9] The language of these people was to be Gaelic rather than Scandinavian, or a dialect of it. The great Somerled, the descendant of Godfrey MacFergus, was destined to come of this stock.

The tenth century was one of great political confusion, with various Scandinavian dynasties competing for supremacy in the Irish Sea world. In the 980s one Godfrey Haroldson established a new kingdom of Man and the Isles and was the first man to be called *ri Innse Gall* ('the King of the Hebrides');[10] but this new power proved unstable, disappearing on the death of Godfrey in 989.

The next figure of importance in the story of Clan Donald is another Norseman by the name of Godred Crovan. Almost nothing is known about the background of this man. One of the Irish annals refers to him as Gofraid mac mic Arailt, which suggests some kinship with Imar mac Arailt, a Viking king of Dublin.[11] A Norse warrior of the old school, Godred fought with the Norwegian King Harald Hardrada at the Battle of Stamford Bridge in 1066, escaping the carnage to establish, in 1079, a second dynasty of Man and the Isles which proved more enduring than the first. Godred, who lives on in Manx tradition as King Orry, died on Islay in 1095.[12] Ranghild, his granddaughter, was to be the wife of Somerled, and the mother of a new breed of Island chiefs.

Soon after the death of Godred Crovan the King of Norway began to take an interest in the Norse communities to the west. For some time there had been only the loosest association between Norway and the Western Isles. Godred Crovan seems to have established a fully independent state, never acknowledging the supremacy of Norway. This appears to have provided the pretext for King Magnus' descent on the Isles in 1098. Magnus – soon to acquire the nickname 'Barelegs' because of his fondness for Scottish dress – was a man with a tidy mind. No sooner had he established firm control over the kingdom of Man and the Isles than he decided it was time to agree a clear demarcation with the Scots. The Isles were geographically part of Scotland, but their political status had remained uncertain since the arrival of the Vikings. The rulers of Scotland, busy building up their power in the east and south, never seem to have given the matter much attention. Now, seemingly with the agreement of Edgar, King of Scots, Magnus established his authority to all Isles round which a ship could sail with its rudder set.[13] Magnus is also said to have laid claim to the Kintyre peninsula by having himself hauled across the narrows at Tarbert in a ship with himself at the rudder. This is almost certainly a fiction, and if not the trick was never formally recognised by the Scots. Two years after Magnus' expedition the diocese of Sodor – the south Isles – was established under the authority of the Archbishop of Trondheim. All the territory ceded in the treaty of 1098 is included, with the exception of Kintyre.[14] Thirty years later the authority of the King of Scots in the area appears to have been well established.[15]

It is doubtful if Edgar had sufficient authority in the west to enter into a meaningful treaty with Magnus Barelegs; but it at least established a precedent that Scots authority extended to the Atlantic shores. Magnus was obviously a man of limited strategic vision, for once the authority of the Scots kingdom was established in fact as well as in theory, it would be virtually impossible for the remote kings of Norway to prevent further expansion into the Isles. As it was the kingdom of Man was soon to discover how vulnerable it was to the aggression of a determined leader in control of mainland Argyll. Magnus left no lasting impression. After his death in 1103 no King of Norway was to repeat his exploits until Hakon IV came on his ill-fated expedition of 1263.

Magnus had re-established his authority in the Isles by no gentle means, and seems to have fallen particularly hard on the family of Somerled. At this period, not long before his birth, it would appear that his grandfather, Gilla-Adomnain, and his father, Gillabrigte, lost their lands in the Isles.[16] Gillabrigte is said in Macdonald tradition to have taken refuge in a cave in Morvern, and, as a result, acquired the nickname of *na h-Uamh*a – 'of the cave'. It is in stories like these that history and tradition come close to one another, although they never quite manage to meet.

After the death of Magnus the dynasty of Godred Crovan managed to reassert itself in the Isles, first in the person of his son, Lagman, and after his death by his brother, Olaf. In the Norse sources, Olaf is known as *Bitling* or *Klining* from his diminutive stature, but in Gaelic tradition he appears as Olaf the Red.[17] He proved himself a competent ruler, and the Isles settled down to a lengthy period of relative calm. It was during the reign of Olaf that Somerled grew to manhood, and established a power base in Argyll. Before discussing the career of Somerled it is important to consider some of the changes within the kingdom of Scotland, destined to have a considerable impact on his life and death.

After the union of the Picts and Scots under Kenneth MacAlpin, Scotland continued to evolve as an essentially Celtic kingdom. However, by the eleventh century this was beginning to change. Succession to the throne by primogeniture – the right of the first born – was beginning to be favoured after the death of MacBeth over the old Celtic practice of tanistry – succession by cousins. The Canmore dynasty was increasingly subject to English influences, especially after the marriage of Malcolm III to Princess Margaret. At first this extended to matters of church government and organisation, but after the Norman Conquest of England in 1066 the new continental practice of feudalism made a gradual appearance in Scotland. Slow at first it began to accelerate in the twelfth century during the reign of David I and his grandson,

Malcolm IV, particularly after David allowed a large number of Norman French to settle in Scotland, including the family of FitzAlan, the ancestors of the house of Stewart.

There had initially been some conservative reaction to this process. But after the deposition of Donald Ban, arguably the last Celtic King of Scots in the cultural if not the racial sense, it continued until the old ways were more and more confined to the fringes of the kingdom – Galloway, Moray and Argyll. Against this background, Somerled emerged not only as the paramount leader of the Gaelic–Norse world, but as the last great defender of the old Celtic tradition against feudal innovation.

Considering his historical importance, we know very little about the early life of Somerled, and much of that is drawn from tradition.[18] While his father, Gillabrigte, had a purely Gaelic name, Somerled, meaning Summer Voyager or Viking, would appear to have the mixed origin of his *Gall-Gaedhil* ancestors. By the 1140s he had built up sufficient power in the Isles to be a figure of some reckoning. The *Book of Clanranald* claims he cleared the 'Danes' from the mainland; although in terms of the treaty between Magnus and Edgar there should have been no official Norse presence in the area.[19] There certainly seems to have been some local resistance to him, from what source is difficult to say, but he soon established his mastery over the districts of Lorn, Kintyre and Knapdale.[20] His reputation spread beyond his own world, and he is referred to in the *Melrose Chronicle* as the *regulus* or Lord of Argyll.[21] Sometime before the year 1134 his sister married the enigmatic figure of Malcolm MacHeth, who may have been descended from the Scottish royal house, or more likely had connections with the Celtic earldom of Moray. MacHeth, a claimant to the Scottish throne, was certainly sufficiently important to be kept as a state prisoner by David I for over twenty years.

Apart from this politically ill-advised alliance, there is nothing in the record to suggest that Somerled enjoyed anything but good relations with David. A body of men from the west Highlands took part in David's invasion of England in 1138, and fought at the Battle of the Standard, which clearly could not have happened without Somerled's approval. There is, however, absolutely no evidence to support the view that he accompanied them in person.[22] It probably suited his purpose that David was preoccupied with events in England, allowing him to consolidate his own power in Argyll without outside interference.

Olaf the Red, King of Man and the Isles would, by the 1130s, have been well aware that a new power had grown up on his eastern flank. The potential threat this represented to his sprawling island kingdom could not be ignored, and he clearly wished to have the Gaelic chief as an ally, rather than an enemy. Sometime before the middle of the century, Somerled married Olaf's daughter, Ranghild. This union was one of the most politically significant in the Gaelic–Norse world. Through it, Somerled acquired a direct interest in the fate of the Isles. It also, in time, gave rise to a new warrior race, which the author of the *Manx Chronicle* was later to lament as the cause of the downfall of the kingdom of Man.[23]

Somerled's marriage alliances extended his influence not just in the west but throughout the Atlantic world. He already had connections with the Celtic lords of Moray. Through his father-in-law's marriage to Afreca, daughter of Fergus of Galloway, he was linked with the semi-independent Celtic principality of south-west Scotland, which shared many of the features of his own lordship in Argyll.[24] It has also been suggested that through an aunt of Somerled by the name of Biadok, he may have had a link with Harold Gillie, King of Norway.[25] We must picture him at this stage of his life at the centre of a Celtic–Norse world. His links with Ireland, Man, Galloway, Moray and Norway were far more important politically and culturally than his links with the feudal kingdom of Scotland. But for as long as Olaf and David were alive the whole delicate structure was held in balance. Soon these two important elements were removed from the equation.

When David died in 1153, he was succeeded by his grandson, the under-age Malcolm IV, in accordance with the laws of primogeniture. This appears to have produced a Celtic backlash, when the sons of the imprisoned Malcolm MacHeth rose in revolt, supported by their uncle, Somerled.[26] Unfortunately, we possess almost no evidence on the course of this rebellion: but it appears to have lost momentum when Somerled was diverted by a crisis in the Isles.

The prolonged period of peace and stability in the kingdom of Man came to an end when Olaf the Red was murdered by his nephews. His son, Godred, who had been in Norway at the time, returned to avenge his father's death and take his place on the throne. But it seems that Godred II, once established, began to act in a tyrannical fashion, alienating some of the chiefs of the Isles.[27] One of them, a Norseman by the name of Thorfinn Ottarson, came to Somerled and suggested that he set up his son, Dougall, the grandson of Olaf the Red, as King of the Isles. Somerled agreed and immediately prepared for war with Godred.

Before considering the outcome of the struggle, it is worth pausing to consider the implication of these events. We know that Somerled's family had an interest in the Isles, long before his marriage to Ranghild, going right back to the days of Godfrey MacFergus. His own father and grandfather were displaced either during the rise of Godred Crovan or at the time of Magnus Barelegs' expedition. Somerled himself may or may not have had a valid claim to the Isles; but his sons, as offshoots of the kings of Man, most certainly did. There is also the political dimension. If Somerled was prepared to challenge primogeniture in Scotland, why not also challenge Godred's right to succeed Olaf? But the Norse rulers could never be ousted from their island kingdom for as long as they dominated the seas, as they had for 300 years. We have to picture Somerled not simply reacting to events, but making lengthy preparations to challenge the naval power of the Vikings. Shipbuilding and seamanship are, after all, not skills that can be learned in a season. Somerled was the first of his race to realise the importance of Norse ship technology in dominating the Isles. By 1156 his preparations were complete, when the Gaelic galleys or birlinns took to the sea ready to take on the longships.

The two sides met off the coast of Islay and fought a bloody battle throughout the night of Epiphany – 5–6 January.[28] Since a battle could not be fought in total darkness it has been reasonably suggested that the actual date might have been 12 January – the night of the full moon – and that Epiphany was simply the nearest reference point in a time before calendars existed.[29] It is sometimes claimed that the Battle of Epiphany was indecisive, but this is not an accurate reading of the outcome. Somerled appears to have fought the Norsemen to a standstill, for the following day Godred, perhaps fearing for his own safety, agreed to partition his kingdom.

We do not know from contemporary records what form this partition took. The division of the Isles only became clear the following century. It has been deduced from this – with a reasonable assumption of accuracy – that Somerled and his sons obtained possession of the island groups south of Ardnamurchan, including Mull, Jura and Islay, and Godred retained control of the Outer Hebrides and Skye, as well as the Isle of Man. This was a remarkable achievement. Somerled had prevailed over the Norsemen, and laid the foundations for centuries of Gaelic sea power. More than this, he had effectively recreated the vanished kingdom of Dalriada. His ambition, once awakened, was not so easily put to rest. A simple glance at the map will show how unstable the Epiphany treaty was. Godred's kingdom had been fatally weakened by his concessions to Somerled, whose block of territory projected like a wedge into the Atlantic, cutting Man off from the Outer Isles. The final showdown came in 1158, when Somerled chased Godred out of his remaining possessions.

After his final defeat, Godred travelled around looking for allies against Somerled, appearing at various points in the courts of England, Norway and Scotland. It was probably to forestall any intervention on his enemy's behalf that Somerled launched a diplomatic offensive, first securing peace with Malcolm IV. Malcolm, by now well aware of Somerled's growing power in the west, prepared the ground for this in 1157 by releasing the long imprisoned Malcolm MacHeth, Somerled's brother-in-law, and creating him Earl of Ross. The two sides appear to have made their final peace sometime before Christmas 1160.[30] Unfortunately, the exact date of this agreement cannot now be determined, but it may have been early in the season. Somerled appears to have felt secure enough in the course of the year to visit King Inge in Norway to obtain confirmation of his right to hold the Isles.[31]

Nothing more is recorded of Somerled's activities until the dramatic events of 1164, when he rose in his final revolt against Malcolm IV and met his death in battle at Renfrew. The sources give no explanation for his conduct, but it is best seen against the background of his own role in a conservative Gaelic world and the steady expansion of the Scottish feudal state.

In growing to manhood, Malcolm was proving himself to be an aggressive and capable monarch, ready, like Somerled, to seize any opportunity to consolidate his power. Galloway was overwhelmed by 1161, and Fergus, Somerled's kinsman, taken as a captive to Edinburgh, where he died later the same year. Two years later Moray came under attack. Worst of all, from Somerled's point of view, the FitzAlan family, now the High Stewards of Scotland, were starting to push their feudal power to the shores of the Firth of Clyde, with their headquarters at Renfrew, dangerously close to his own domains. Not wishing to share the fate of Galloway or Moray, it would appear that Somerled launched his own pre-emptive attack.[32]

Somerled's army came from all parts of the west, including Kintyre, the Hebrides, Argyll and even a party of Vikings from Dublin. It was carried to Renfrewshire, according to the sources, almost certainly with some exaggeration, in an armada of 160 ships.[33] We have no information on the opposition the Islemen met, or who was in command; it remains a distinct possibility that it was a body of feudal knights under the command of Walter FitzAlan, the High Steward himself. In the battle that followed Somerled, one of his sons by the name of Gillabrigte, and many others were slain, before the survivors escaped back to the ships. The contest is dramatically described in *Carmen de Morte Sumerlidi*:

> Here a marvel! To the terrible, the battle was terrible. Heather and furze-bushes moving their heads; burnt thyme and branches;

brambles and ferns, caused panic, appearing to the enemy as soldiers. Never in this life had such miracles been heard. Shadows of thyme and ordure [smoke] were bulwarks of defense. And in the first cleft of battle the baleful leader fell. Wounded by a javelin, slain by the sword, Somerled died. And the raging wave swallowed his son, and the wounded of many thousand fugitives; because when this fierce leader was struck down, the wicked took to flight; and very many were slaughtered, both on sea and on land.[34]

We might obtain clues to the actual course of the Battle of Renfrew if we project forward to King Hakon's campaign in the Clyde estuary 100 years later. This showed the limits of a seaborne infantry force against knights ready to attack from good defensive positions.[35] Somerled's Islemen were simply not used to this kind of warfare, and appear to have been overwhelmed in a relatively short space of time. It is clearly a tribute to the power of the armoured warrior that Ranald, Somerled's son, had a seal made with a galley on one side and a knight on the other.[36]

Later Macdonald tradition insists that Somerled was not killed in battle, but was assassinated by his nephew or page, it is not clear which, whereupon his army, in dismay, fled back to their ships.[37] This requires us to reject all contemporary or near contemporary sources, Manx, Scots and Irish, some of them enemies of the Gaels, but not all. Moreover, it is difficult to see what advantage these annalists hoped to gain by hiding the true facts. The assassination theory emerged considerably later, at a time when the historians of Clan Donald were anxious to present a slightly different picture of their great ancestor. Soon after the execution of the Marquis of Argyll for treason in May 1661, his son, Lord Lorne, wrote a letter defending the record of Clan Campbell as champions of the crown back to the days of Somerled.[38] In possible response to this, Somerled is given a makeover in the *Book of Clanranald* as a man of peace out to subdue the king's enemies, as much a parody of the truth as the Campbell letter. Acceptance of Hugh Macdonald and the *Book of Clanranald* accounts also involve acceptance of the corollary: that the Islemen were so cowardly or panic stricken that they ran away, abandoning the body of their greatest leader.

Where Somerled is buried is also a matter of debate. The authors of the late nineteenth-century history of *Clan Donald* maintain that it was always clan tradition that he was buried at Saddell Abbey in Kintyre, but this is simply not true.[39] Hugh Macdonald quite clearly says that he was buried on Iona.[40] The connection between Somerled and Saddell is extremely tenuous, resting on no firmer foundation than a reference in a thirteenth-century list of Cistercian houses to a 'Sconedale', seemingly in existence in 1160. But all documentary references to Saddell confirm that Somerled's son, Ranald, founded the abbey.[41] Moreover, it appears not to have been fully completed until the early years of the thirteenth century – suggesting 1190 as the date of foundation, rather than 1160 – forty years after Somerled's death. There is a deeper point to be considered here, however: Somerled was the representative of a conservative Celtic tradition, who had tried, unsuccessfully, to restore the full dignity of the Columbian church.[42] It would seem more fitting that he is buried among his ancestors, Norse and Gael, on Iona, rather than with the French Cistercians.

Some time after Somerled's death, when genealogy became a medieval cottage industry, his descendants created a lineage for him going back to semi-legendary Irish heroes like Cholla Uais and Conn of the Hundred Battles. The authenticity of this is almost irrelevant, becoming part of a mythic tradition important not just in the formation of clans but of states themselves. But in the violent unpredictable world that Somerled grew up in, one took power not because of one's descent, important as this was in conferring legitimacy, but because of one's military and political abilities. Godred Crovan had been able to establish the dynasty on Man that was to last almost 200 years with no great claim to royal lineage. Somerled was another such. Whatever his ancestry he was the man of the moment, the kind of man who creates dynasties without necessarily descending from them. In recording his death, the *Annals of Tigernach* refer to him as *ri Innse Gall*.[43] He was the first of his race to bear this title.

The defeat of the Islemen at the Battle of Renfrew might have formed a prelude to a more sustained counter-offensive by the Scots, but Malcolm probably lacked the necessary naval power. At the very least Walter FitzAlan must have been rewarded for his services, or those of his feudal vassals, by some kind of territorial grant, possibly the island of Bute.[44] In any case, Somerled's attempt to stop the westward expansion of the Stewarts was a failure. By 1200 the family were firmly established on Bute, beginning the construction of Rothesay Castle not long after.[45] Malcolm IV died in 1165. William the Lion, his brother and successor, was too preoccupied with English affairs and successive revolts by pretenders to the Scottish crown to give much attention to the affairs of the Isles, which were left to their own devices for some considerable time.

The period that follows the death of Somerled is one of considerable confusion in the west. Godred II returned from exile in Norway and managed to re-establish the kingdom of Man in at least part of his old dominion, against the resistance of Somerled's three surviving sons, Dougall, Ranald and Angus, collectively known as the MacSorleys. In accordance with Celtic practice, Somerled's remaining territories were divided between them, although how these lands were apportioned is not recorded. The *Chronicle of Man* hints that there may have been some subdivision prior to Somerled's death, although no details are supplied.[46] Reading backwards from the next century, when the picture becomes a little clearer, the following inference can be made: Dougall, most likely the eldest of the three, appears to have received the heartland of Somerled's old kingdom in northern Argyll, including the island group of Mull, Coll and Tiree; Ranald received Islay, Jura and Kintyre; Angus is more of a problem, as his family was wiped out early in the thirteenth century. He is thought, however, to have received the mainland territories north of the Ardnamurchan peninsula around Moidart, as well as some of the islands, including Rhum and Eigg, and possibly Bute, Arran and Skye.

One thing at least is certain: the division was not amicable. Besides the struggle with Godred II, Somerled's family was involved in its own civil war. In 1192 Ranald was defeated in battle with Angus, although where it was fought and over what issue is not recorded.[47] Ranald, in a charter granted to Saddell Abbey, assumed his father's full title of King of the Isles, Lord of Argyll and Kintyre – on what authority is not known – and in a charter granted to Paisley Abbey he is referred to more modestly as Lord of the Hebrides.[48] Neither of these documents can be dated with any accuracy, so we have no way of knowing which comes first. It has been reasonably argued that the decline in Ranald's status may be a consequence of his defeat at the hands of Angus.[49] There are, however, dangers in reading too much into this, as a cleric writing in Ranald's territory in Kintyre would clearly be much more deferential than one writing in Stewart Paisley. Ranald also appears to have been involved in a struggle with his brother Dougall over possession of Mull.[50]

In 1210 Angus MacSorley and his three sons were killed in battle with the men of Skye, presumably as part of the ongoing struggle with the Norse dynasty of Man, into whose orbit the island then fell. His claim to Bute is said to have passed to the Stewart family by the marriage of his granddaughter, Jane, to one Alexander FitzAlan, although there are no details of this beyond traditional accounts.[51] Bute, as we have seen, was already in Stewart hands well before the death of Angus. His remaining territories were divided amongst his brothers and their descendants.

Considering the importance of Ranald in the history of Clan Donald, we know virtually nothing about his life. Even the date of his death is uncertain. According to the *Book of Clanranald* he died in 1207, although it has been suggested that it might have been as late as 1227 and as early as 1191.[52] There is no mention of him in the annals after the 1190s, which suggests that he might have been killed in the battle with Angus, or he could conceivably have retired from public life, leaving affairs to his two sons, Donald and Ruari. It is about this time that patronymics begin to make their first appearance in the Isles; the descendants of Ranald's brother, Dougall, became the Macdougalls, while Ranald's own sons became the descendants of the Macdonalds and the Macruaris. Donald was established on Islay, the heartland of Ranald's domains, while Ruari obtained lands in Moidart and some of the northern Isles.

Like his father, almost nothing is known of the life of Donald of Islay, beyond a few brief references in the chronicles. But he achieved a permanent memorial, not in his deeds or renown, but in his name, for he founded one of the lasting dynasties of Scottish history and a legacy that echoes round the world wherever those of Scots descent are to be found. His own son, Angus Mor, was the first MacDonald in history.

Affairs in the Isles had been free from outside interference for some time, but by the early 1220s this began to change. The later years of King William the Lion and the early years of his successor, Alexander II, had been troubled by Celtic pretenders to the throne, who appear to have received some assistance from the house of Somerled. In retaliation, Alexander led expeditions to the west in 1221 and again in 1222, indicating that the Scots state now possessed a naval arm absent during the days of Somerled. This was the first time a King of Scots was able to push so far to the west, and provided a clear indication of what was to come. One immediate result appears to have been the expulsion of Ruari from Kintyre in favour of Donald, suggesting that it was the former who had been giving support to the king's enemies.[53] Alexander's continuing interest in the west was confirmed by the construction of the new burgh of Dumbarton. It seems to have been about this time, moreover, that Stewart power spread to Cowal, with the construction of a castle at Dunoon. Further to the north, the new castle at Eilean Donan appears to date from the time of Alexander's expedition.[54] Soon after this, the Norwegians, long absentee landlords of the Isles, began to acquire a new interest in the area.

For decades after the death of Magnus Barelegs, the Norwegians had been too preoccupied with their own internal affairs to bother much about the Western Isles, still nominally under their control. This began to change in the thirteenth century, during the reign of Hakon

IV. For the year 1228–9, it is recorded in *The Saga of Hacon* that the kings of Somerled's race were unfaithful to their Norse overlord, although the reference is to the Macdougalls, rather than the race of Donald of Islay.[55] An expedition was sent west in 1230 under the leadership of one Uspak, possibly another son of Dougall MacSorley, to re-establish Norse authority. Uspak concluded his journey by attacking the Scots on Bute, either a dangerous provocation on his part, or a sign that Hakon wished to remind Alexander of the treaty of 1098. With the two kings moving steadily towards a clash in the Isles, the position of the semi-independent Gaelic and Norse lords was beginning to look uncertain. Much would depend on the side they chose to take.

In the 1240s Alexander, having achieved a final settlement of the Anglo-Scottish Border question, turned his attention once more to the Isles. His initial attempt to renegotiate the settlement between Magnus and Edgar was quickly rejected by Hakon, as was the offer to buy the Norwegians off. Hakon appears arrogant in his dealings with Alexander, never more so than when he created Ewan Macdougall 'king' in the Isles, although he may not have been fully aware of the political implications of this. Ewan certainly held a number of the Isles under Norwegian suzerainty, but he was also an important landholder in Argyll and a baron of Scotland. It was to humble Ewan and show his displeasure to Hakon that Alexander mounted his last expedition to the Isles in 1249. Ewan was quickly confronted by the simple lesson that it is impossible to serve two masters at once, but Alexander's sudden death on the island of Kerrera brought the campaign to a premature conclusion. During the minority of his successor, Alexander III, the western question was put on ice, but it was clearly only a matter of time before it would have to be addressed and settled. Against the growing power of the Scottish state the authority of a distant Norwegian monarch counted for very little. Ewan Macdougall, the chief target of the 1249 offensive, was among the first to learn this lesson, as his conduct in 1263 was to demonstrate.

Against this increasingly turbulent background, Donald of Islay flitted in and out of history, before disappearing altogether, and like so many of his kin we do not know with certainty the date of his death. There is an entry in the *Annals of Loch Ce* to the death of a MacSomhairle, King of Argyll, in 1247. This has been taken as a reference to Donald, but as neither he nor his descendants ever made a claim to such kingship, Ducan MacDougall would appear to be the more likely candidate.[56] Two years after this, though, his son Angus issued a charter for lands in Kintyre, suggesting that Donald was off the scene.[57] He is said to have left a second son, Alasdair, who, according to Macdonald tradition, was the progenitor of the MacAlisdairs of Loup, a branch of the clan settled in Kintyre. However, there is no certainty to this, as this name was not then usual among the Gaels. It has been plausibly suggested that their ancestor may in fact be Alasdair or Alexander Og, son of Angus Mor.[58]

At the height of his manhood, Angus seems to have enjoyed the freebooting lifestyle of his Norse ancestors, just as his father Donald did in his youth. He appears to have caused such trouble in the King of England's Irish domains that an order was issued in 1256 to keep him out for seven years.[59] But he was most certainly well respected in the Gaelic world, a poem being written in his honour sometime in the middle of the century, the first such in praise of a chief of Clan Donald:

> Though he came round Ireland; rare is the strand whence he hast not taken cattle: graceful long ships are sailed by thee, thou are like an otter, O scion of Tara.

> The House of Somerled, the Race of Godfried, whence thou art Sprung, who did not store up cattle, O fresh-planted orchard, O Apple branch, noble is each blood from which thou comest.[60]

Angus may have enjoyed the Viking life, but he was also a realist. Despite the failure of Alexander II's offensive in 1249, Angus clearly saw that the old Norse world was nearing its end. In his charter of 1249 bestowing the church of Kilkerran in Kintyre on the Abbey of Paisley, the gift was made 'for the weal of the soul of my lord Alexander, the illustrious King of Scots and of his son Alexander'. He also named his eldest son Alexander – Alasdair in Gaelic – the first authentic record we have of this name being used in the west.[61]

No sooner had King Alexander taken over the reigns of power in the early 1260s than he turned his attention to the west. Once again an embassy was sent to Hakon offering to buy the Isles, with no better result than in 1244. Alexander at once opted for less gentle methods; in 1262 the Earl of Ross, clearly acting with the king's approval, invaded the Isle of Skye, part of the kingdom of Man, and carried out many grim atrocities.[62] This act of provocation had the desired results. Man, sadly much diminished in power and status since the days of Godred Crovan, was in no position to defend itself against the Scots. King Hakon summoned his host to join him at Bergen in the summer of 1263. The last great Viking descent on the British Isles was about to begin.

Much had changed since the voyage of Magnus Barelegs in 1098. The Scottish state had extended its authority steadily to the west, and was now poised on the Atlantic shore, demonstrating the strategic weakness of the Isles. Hakon clearly hoped to kindle old loyalties, but his approach was greeted with far less enthusiasm than he expected. Of the MacSorley kindred, only the Macruaris willingly joined the king. Ewan of Argyll, not wishing a repetition of his experience in 1249, joined Alexander III. Angus of Islay agreed to support Hakon, but only under duress. He found himself in an impossible situation, risking either Alexander's displeasure or destruction at the hands of Hakon. Hakon was closer, so Angus sensibly capitulated, surrendering Islay to the king and immediately having it granted back. From the outer Isles the fleet sailed on, following in the wake of Somerled into the Firth of Clyde. It was already dangerously late in the season, with the autumn storms fast approaching.

Hakon's armada was essentially a huge bluff. Facing the dangers of adverse weather and shortage of supplies, the Norwegians needed a quick result. Alexander had to be made to give in or fight on Hakon's terms; but he was prepared to do neither. Knowing time was on his side, the King of Scots entered into negotiations with the enemy, spinning the talks out for as long as possible. At the very least, Hakon wanted Alexander to recognise the Norse claim to Bute, Arran and the Cumbraes, suggesting that the Scots were already well established on these strategically important islands. Alexander refused to consider the proposal. To try to speed matters up Hakon sent part of his force, the men of the Isles and Man, to raid the Stewart country of Lennox around Loch Lomond. It was led by Angus of Islay, Dougald and Alan Macdougall, and Magnus, King of Man. Angus and his kin would be pleased enough to take part in this raid, seeing it as part of the ongoing struggle against Stewart expansionism, started a century before by Somerled,[63] but it made no difference to the outcome of the campaign.

It was always open to Hakon, of course, to seek Alexander out. However, he faced the same problems that confronted Somerled in 1164: his army was essentially composed of infantrymen like the Viking armies of old, ill equipped to risk a contest with armoured knights fighting from castles and other fortified positions. In the end Hakon's bluff was called. It was not the Battle of Largs – little more than a series of indecisive skirmishes – which decided the outcome; rather it was the weakness that lay at the heart of the whole enterprise: it was impossible for a remote Norwegian king to force a permanent settlement in the Isles against the will of the Scots. It is best summarised by a laconic entry in the *Chronicle of Man* – 'Hakon, king of Norway, came to the regions of Scotland, but effecting nothing, he returned to the Orkneys.'[64] Before he left he granted Bute to one Rudri, possibly a son of Uspak who attacked the island in 1230, but most certainly not Ruari, son of Ranald MacSorley, as is sometimes maintained. Needless to say, it had no lasting effect. The death of Hakon on Orkney in December symbolised not just the end of Norwegian authority in the Isles, but the end of the Viking age itself.

The following year Alexander launched a counter-offensive against the MacSorleys and the kingdom of Man. Angus of Islay was quick to submit, surrendering his son Alexander as a hostage. King Magnus of Man also gave way to the inevitable, accepting Alexander III as his overlord. On his death in 1265 what was left of Godred Crovan's island state passed into Scottish hands. Dugald Macruari, the only one of Somerled's kin to show real enthusiasm for Hakon's enterprise, continued to hold out until his death in 1268. His courage clearly impressed the Irish annalists, who, in recording his death, refer to him as 'King of the Hebrides and Argyll'. It is impossible to say if he ever assumed that proud title himself.[65] Accepting the inevitable, King Magnus of Norway, Hakon's successor, agreed to surrender the Western Isles to the Scots. The Treaty of Perth, concluded in July 1266, guaranteed that there would be no reprisals against those formerly loyal to Norway.

In the years that followed Clan Donald, Clan Dougall and even Clan Ruari, the three great dynasties founded by Somerled, were steadily integrated into the Scottish state. Alexander summoned a council at Scone in 1284 to decide the succession, following the death of his son. Among those attending were Angus Macdonald, Alexander Macdougall and Alan Macruari, all described as barons of the realm of Scotland.[66] With the other nobles the MacSorleys agreed to recognise Margaret the Maid of Norway, Alexander's granddaughter, as heir to the kingdom. This was a remarkable development. The western clans were, in effect, recognising the feudal practice of primogeniture in its most advanced form – that an infant female should have rule over an ancient warrior society by right of birth alone. This seemed to confirm that the age of the Gaelic sea kings was finally over. Angus Macdonald's immediate successors, his sons, Alexander and Angus, had no grander title than *de Yla* – 'of Islay'.[67]

Two years after the Council of Scone Alexander was dead, followed not many years later by the little Maid of Norway, who never set foot in her kingdom. In the crisis that was soon to envelop Scotland, Clan Donald began its ascent to greatness.

2

LORDS OF THE ISLES

Like the other chief men of the realm, the MacSorleys took sides in the dynastic crisis that followed the death of the Maid of Norway, as the various claimants made their bid for the throne. Clan Dougall, by now the most powerful branch of the family, sided with John Balliol, while Clan Donald allied itself with the Bruces of Annandale. Interestingly, none of the western clans took the part of King Eric of Norway, father of the Maid, who also made a rather halfhearted bid for the legacy of his dead daughter, presumably because nobody took this seriously. As early as 1286, soon after the death of King Alexander, Angus of Islay entered into the Turnberry Band, allying himself with Robert Bruce – grandfather of the future king – and some other nobles, including James Stewart.[1] Although the Band was principally concerned with affairs in Ireland, it was formulated at a time of great political tension, when alliances, once made, were likely to be lasting.

Unable to settle the question of who should rule by any internal process, the Scots invited Edward I of England to settle the matter for them. With his tidy, legal mind, Edward attended to Scottish affairs with scrupulous fairness and much self-interest, insisting that he be recognised as the overlord of Scotland. Once this preliminary was out of the way, the matter was investigated, and, in 1292, John Balliol emerged as king.

This decision would certainly have pleased Alexander MacDougall, for he was allied to the new King John and his Comyn relatives through marriage, and would probably expect to be rewarded for his loyalty. He was not disappointed. When John's fist parliament met in February 1293, Alexander was appointed sheriff of Lorn, becoming the king's principal agent in the west. Angus Mor, in contrast, failed to appear at the February parliament. More than this, he appears to have ignored the summons of his Macdougall kinsman to perform homage to the new king. It is tempting to assume that he was following the example set by his Bruce allies, who refused to accept the outcome of the Great

Cause, or it may be that advancing years made him reluctant to leave his home on Islay. The fact that Alexander Macdonald, Angus' son and heir, also absented himself from Balliol's parliament provides a reasonable clue to the attitude of the family.[2] Balliol's appointment of Alexander Macdougall as sheriff of Lorn would have provided an additional cause of resentment, for the two families were involved in a bitter dispute over land. The struggle between Clan Dougall and Clan Donald for domination in the west was to run its course against the wider background of the coming Wars of Independence.

As with so many problems in life, it began with a marriage. Before the Great Cause had been finally settled, Alexander of Islay married Juliana Macdougall, either a daughter or a sister of the Lord of Argyll. This seems to have resulted in a dowry dispute, possibly over the island of Lismore.[3] It was serious enough to come before King Edward himself in the summer of 1292, when Angus Mor and his son, Alexander, swore to keep the peace in the Isles.[4] John Balliol's subsequent intervention only made matters worse.

Even before John Balliol was crowned King of Scots in November 1292, Edward of England is likely to have had the measure of the man. In the years that followed, determined to exercise his rights as overlord to the full, he made John's life intolerable. Among other things Edward reserved the right to hear appeals from Scottish courts, bypassing that most fundamental prerogative of a sovereign crown. Included among those appeals was one from Alexander and Juliana Macdonald in 1295, claiming that John had occupied part of Lismore and was refusing to surrender it to them, indicating that he had taken Alexander Macdougall's part in the dispute.[5] The matter appears to have remained unsettled when war broke out between Scotland and England the following year.

In the midst of these dramatic events Angus Mor of Islay died, possibly in the year 1294, after a long and eventful life, covering a period of huge political change in the Isles.[6] Besides Alexander, his successor, and Angus, he had a third son, Iain, known by his Gaelic nickname as *Sprangaich* – 'the Bold' – the founder of that branch of the Macdonald tree known as the Macians, who appear to have settled in Ardna-murchan in the fourteenth century, during the reign of David II.[7]

Tired of the timidity of their spineless king, the barons of Scotland took charge of affairs, allied Scotland with France and declared war on England. Edward invaded, won the Battle of Dunbar and deposed his client king: Scotland was now to have a status in his empire no greater than that of Wales or Ireland. He could make and break kings; but he could not break the people – the Wars of Independence were soon firmly under way.

Clan Dougall had done well in King John's reign. Besides the additional powers Alexander of Argyll had obtained, giving him an advantage over his Macdonald cousins, the Macdougalls had considerably extended their power by defeating the Campbells of Lochawe in battle sometime in the mid-1290s. Although Alexander, along with the other barons of Scotland, swore allegiance to Edward of England in the summer of 1296, it is clear that he was not trusted, possibly because of his family associations with the deposed John Balliol. He was held prisoner for a time at Berwick, and no sooner was he released in the early summer of 1297, than he began to organise disorders in the west. If Clan Dougall was Edward's enemy, then Clan Donald was his friend.

We have to tread carefully here. The struggle between the Macdougalls and Macdonalds forms a subtext to the bigger story of Scotland's war of liberation, but it should not be seen in simple political terms. At a time when patriotism was still an ill-defined idea, and when noblemen whose families had been Scots for many generations changed sides with bewildering frequency, it is hardly surprising if the Gaels of the west should see events very much in their own terms. The Isles had only been part of Scotland politically for a short period of thirty years before the wars with England began. The process of integration had been reasonably successful over this time, but now it had been arrested, with dramatic and unforeseen consequences that only started to become clear by the middle of the following century. Remote from the main area of struggle, the Gaels, whether they belonged to Clan Donald or Clan Dougall, would follow the path that offered them the greatest advantage.

Free from all restraint, Alexander of Argyll apparently tried to extend his power in a war with his Macdonald kin. Alexander of Islay was soon under such pressure that he was forced to write to King Edward, begging him to instruct the nobles of Ross and Argyll to help him keep the peace.[8] He also told Edward that Alexander Macdougall and his son John were actively encouraging the lawless Macruaris, apparently allowing them to revert to their old Viking ways. Alexander was joined by his brother, Angus Og, in the struggle with their Macdougall and Macruari kin.

We now have a mystery and, to make matters worse, this has been complicated by a false trail laid down in the seventeenth century by Hugh Macdonald, which has misled generations of historians. After 1297, Alexander vanishes from the records of the time. When a chief of Clan Donald next appears it is Angus, not his brother. So what happened to Alexander? According to Hugh Macdonald, he remained loyal to the English when the rest of Clan Donald embraced the cause

of Robert Bruce after the murder of John Comyn in 1306.[9] The
Macdougalls became consistently pro-English after the murder of their
Comyn kinsman, and as Alexander's wife, Juliana, was a Macdougall,
this is cited as a further reason for his opposition to Bruce. All the past
bitterness over Lismore appears to have been forgotten. Alexander
fought against Bruce, was finally captured and died in prison in 1308:
but he receives no mention in John Barbour's epic poem, *The Bruce*,
either as an enemy or a friend, although many lesser individuals appear.
The truth, long overlooked, is contained in an entry in the *Annals of
Ulster*, where it is recorded that in January 1299, 'Alexander MacDomnaill,
the person who was best for hospitality and excellence that was in
Ireland or Scotland, was killed, together with a countless number of
his own people that were slaughtered around him, by Alexander
MacDubhghaill.'[10] It has been argued that this refers not to Alexander,
but to his uncle and namesake, a brother of Angus Mor.[11] However,
this Alexander, a son of Donald of Islay, must have been at an advanced
age in 1299, hardly likely to be taking up arms. As the above entry
coincides with the total disappearance of Alexander of Islay, the evidence seems fairly conclusive.[12]

Angus Og first appears as the head of Clan Donald in the autumn of
1301, when he is found engaging in naval operations on behalf of the
English off the coast of Bute and Kintyre.[13] He receives no further
mention until 1306, one of the most dramatic years in Scottish history.
It is quite likely that Angus remained loyal to Edward while the
Macdougalls counted themselves among his enemies, but in 1305
Alexander of Argyll submitted to the English king. In doing so there is
no evidence that he lost Lismore or any other territory to the Macdonalds.
At this point Angus' attachment to Edward is likely to have been
considerably weakened. He soon broke away altogether.

In February 1306, Robert Bruce murdered John Comyn, a leading
rival, and rode at once to Scone where he was crowned King of Scots.
This outraged King Edward, who at once mobilised his army, and it
also outraged Comyn's kinsmen, including the Macdougalls of Argyll.
Men who had hitherto always fought on the patriotic side, now ranged
themselves permanently on the side of the English.

In the summer of 1306 the English defeated King Robert at the Battle
of Methven near Perth. In retreating westwards what was left of his
little army was intercepted and mauled by the Macdougalls under
Alexander's son John Bacach – 'the Lame' – at the Battle of Dalry near
Tyndrum. This second defeat all but finished the cause of Robert Bruce.
Escaping with difficulty, he took to the heather, as a descendant of his
was to do 400 years later. His cause survived because of the help he

received from Neil Campbell of Lochawe and Angus Og of Islay, both confirmed enemies of Clan Dougall. Angus Og's support was particularly important because it gave Robert access to the naval power of Clan Donald, which was to prove crucial in the coming months and years. John Barbour describes Angus' reception of the royal fugitive:

> Angus of Islay then was sire
> And lord and leader of Kintyre,
> The king right gladly welcomed he
> And promised him his fealty,
> And offered freely out of hand
> Such service as he might demand,
> And for a stronghold to him gave
> Dunaverty, his castle safe,
> To dwell therin as he might need.
> Right thankfully the king agreed
> And gladly took his fealty.[14]

Dunaverty, close to the Mull of Kintyre, was too vulnerable for the king to remain there for long. In the winter of 1306–7 he took refuge in the Isles – it is not absolutely certain where – no doubt carried from place to place in the birlinns of Clan Donald. He was also aided at this time by Angus kinswoman, Christiana Macruari.[15] Although the details are scanty, it is reasonably certain that Angus and Christiana provided some of the soldiers and all of the galleys that enabled King Robert to make his descent on the coast of Ayrshire in early 1307, beginning a campaign that climaxed at Bannockburn seven years later.[16] Clan Donald's naval strength brought about a decisive shift in the balance of power in the western seas. In preparing for what was to be his final campaign, Edward I arranged for supplies to be sent from Ireland, issuing strict instructions that the ships keep clear of the coast of Ayrshire and Galloway, presumably because Angus' birlinns were patrolling the area.[17]

Edward I died in July 1307, just short of the Scottish Border. His son, the far less capable Edward II, was initially too preoccupied with English affairs to bother much about the war in the north, and this gave Bruce time to consolidate his hold on Scotland by wiping out his domestic enemies one by one. Alexander Macdougall was the first to come under the shadow of the angry king. Bruce's northern advance was aided by a fleet of galleys on Loch Linnhe, which could only be supplied by Angus. Under threat from both land and sea, John Bacach was forced to seek a temporary truce, allowing the king to proceed to the northeast and wipe out the Comyns of Buchan. After this he turned his attention back to Argyll, breaking the Macdougalls at the Battle of the Pass of Brander in 1308.[18] Both Alexander and John eventually took refuge in England, their power in Scotland completely destroyed. The principal beneficiary of this was Clan Donald.

Victorious throughout Scotland, King Robert summoned his first parliament, which met at St Andrews in 1309. We are now faced with what is, perhaps, one of the greatest puzzles in the history of Clan Donald. The man who represented the family at St Andrews was not Angus Og, but one Donald of Islay. The existence of this individual has been so problematic that it has even been suggested that the name is a simple clerical error, and that it really was Angus who was at St Andrews,[19] but there is simply too much evidence that confirms Donald of Islay was a real person.[20] Geoffrey Barrow has argued that Donald was a brother of Angus, but neglects to mention that Donald in turn had a brother by the name of Godfrey: this seems to extend Angus Mor's progeny just one step too far.[21] The matter will never be solved satisfactorily, but it may be that Donald was the son of Alexander Og, Angus' brother, and had succeeded to the chieftainship of the clan by the old Celtic practice of tanistry.[22] This suggests, perhaps, that Angus only enjoyed temporary control of the clan, or that he was never more than a war chief, much like Donald Balloch in the fifteenth century, but this view is contradicted by John Barbour's account. It is possible to speculate endlessly on this question without reaching a definite conclusion. All that can be said is that until the emergence of Good John of Islay, first Lord of the Isles, later in the century, much of the story of Clan Donald is shrouded in obscurity.

By 1314 Robert Bruce had established a dominant position in Scotland. The English were reduced to holding a few strongholds, including Stirling Castle, the most strategically important in the land. It was to try and break the Scots' siege of Stirling that Edward II advanced north with a great army in midsummer, meeting King Robert just south of Stirling near the Bannock Burn, where the English suffered one of the worst defeats in their history. Robert took the Scots reserve under his personal control during the battle. This division comprised the Gaels from his own native earldom of Carrick and the men of the Highlands and Islands, under the command of Angus Og.[23] It was not until the battle was at its height that the king committed Angus and his men, in support, it is thought, of his brother, Edward Bruce, who commanded the division fighting on the right of the Scots army. The Highlanders fought with great courage, and in reward Robert is said to have promised that Clan Donald would always stand on the right, the position of honour. This is a late tradition, however, which finds no support in contemporary evidence. Clan Donald always fought bravely, regardless of the part of the field on which they stood. The tradition was only ever to acquire importance in the context of the last Jacobite Rebellion, when it became the basis for an enduring myth about the clan's performance at the Battle of Culloden, the circumstances of which will be explored in a later chapter.

King Robert was sufficiently impressed with the fighting prowess of the Gaels to take them on his later raids into England. In 1322 the Highlanders and Islanders performed an important role in defeating the English at the Battle of Old Byland in Yorkshire.[24] Above all, however, it was Clan Donald's naval power that gave the king a crucial tactical advantage in extending the war against England. The Isle of Man was taken from English control in 1313, greatly improving the Scots position in the Irish Sea, and in 1315 Edward Bruce opened up a second front in Ireland, almost certainly carried there in transports provided by Angus. Given their ancient associations with Ireland, it was inevitable that Clan Donald found itself deeply committed to the war on the island.

Considering the vital contribution Angus and his kin made to King Robert's cause they would naturally expect to be well rewarded; and so they were, receiving much of the old Macdougall inheritance. This included Lochaber, Ardnamurchan, Morvern, Duror and Glencoe. One Alexander of Islay, possibly an unrecorded son or nephew of Angus, received Mull and Tiree. Yet the relationship between Angus Og and Robert Bruce was not quite as straightforward as nineteenth-century historians have suggested. Angus was not a selfless patriot, but a man true to the traditions of his race. It would appear that he was not entirely trusted by the king, for, despite his extensive land grants, he was effectively frozen out of the new family power structure emerging in the west.[25] Land in Kintyre, which Angus might have hoped to receive, went instead to Robert Stewart, the king's grandson, thus completing the westward expansion of the Stewarts that had begun at the time of Somerled. Although Angus became Lord of Lochaber, the area was incorporated into the earldom of Moray, held by Thomas Randolph, the king's nephew. Much of the Macdougall land in Argyll went to Neil Campbell of Lochawe, also related to King Robert by marriage. While elsewhere in Scotland castles were destroyed to prevent them falling into the hands of the English, Tarbert Castle was rebuilt, a royal garrison placed in Dunaverty, Angus' chief stronghold in Kintyre, and Dunstaffnage, at the very heart of the Macdougall lordship, was placed in the hands of the Campbells. The king clearly had his own strategic interests at heart, and he knew enough of the history and traditions of the area to ensure that the key to the west was kept firmly in royal hands. It has to be said, however, that official policy had the effect of alienating Clan Donald, as the next reign would demonstrate.

Like so many of his ancestors, the date of Angus Og's death is unknown. He appears to have been off the scene by 1318, for in that year there is a reference in the Irish annals to the death of Alexander Macdonald at the Battle of Dundalk, who is described as King of Argyll.[26] This appears to be the Alexander of Islay, who received grants of land from Robert Bruce in Mull and Tiree. He fell alongside one Macruari, who is described as King of the Isles. Although the chiefs of Islay did not tend to be recorded as kings of Argyll – which argues against the assumption that Alexander is yet another missing son of Angus Og – they would certainly be known of old as kings of the Isles. If a Macruari could be accorded this title, it must be assumed that Angus was already dead. His eventual successor – Good John of Islay – did not die until 1387, so it is a reasonable assumption that there was some kind of power struggle in the west at this time, which allowed Clan Ruari to take the lead from Clan Donald. They appeared still to be dominating the affairs of the Isles as late as 1325, when another Ruari was forfeited for treason.[27] John of Islay, Angus' oldest son, does not make his appearance as head of the clan until several years after this.

Apart from John, Angus had only one other son, whose existence has been established with any degree of certainty.[28] This was another John, most usually known by his Gaelic name of Iain, who was born of an extra-marital liaison that Angus had with the only daughter of Dougal MacHenry or Henderson of Glencoe. Iain, sometimes known as Iain Abrach – 'John of Lochaber' – was to inherit the lands of Glencoe. From him the Macdonalds of Glencoe, the smallest branch of the family, were to be known as Clan Iain Abrach, and their chiefs as MacIains. Successive generations of Clan Iain Abrach came and went, largely unnoticed by history, until they came to tragic prominence in 1692.

On his death in 1329, King Robert was succeeded by his infant son, David II. Although King Edward III of England had been forced to concede Scottish independence the year before in the Treaty of Northampton, he was clearly unhappy to do so, an unhappiness shared by a group of Anglo-Scottish nobles with Balliol and Comyn associations. These men had been disinherited for taking the wrong side in the Wars of Independence, and were looking for ways of reversing the verdict of Northampton. With the tacit encouragement of Edward, they brought Edward Balliol, son of the long-dead King John, back

from his exile in France. With Balliol at their head, these men invaded
Scotland in 1332, defeating the Regent Mar at the Battle of Dupplin
Moor. Edward Balliol was then crowned at Scone as King of Scots.
Not long afterwards, the Bruce loyalists drove out his party. Edward
III was then forced to declare his hand in the summer of 1333, when
he inflicted a devastating defeat on the Scots at the Battle of Halidon
Hill near Berwick. Balliol then returned to claim his kingdom, and
David II was sent to France for safety.

Against this background, John of Islay took charge of Clan Donald.
So far his family had remained uncommitted to the new civil war
between the adherents of Bruce and Balliol, but he was soon to be
actively courted by both sides. Given the naval and military strength
he was able to draw on, John's support would be a tremendous advantage. But John was a man who throughout his life would always look
to his own advantage, and after the Battle of Halidon Hill he was
clearly inclining towards the Balliol party. In 1335 Thomas Randolph,
Earl of Moray and acting regent for David Bruce, came to see John at
Tarbert Castle, but failed to persuade him to drop his pro-English lean-
ings.[29] Edward Balliol, now under increasing pressure from the patriotic
party, subsequently made John an offer that was simply too good to
refuse.

Although Robert I had been wary of inflating Macdonald power in
the west, Edward Balliol was so desperate for support that he granted
John vast new estates, without balance or reservation. At the expense
of the Earl of Ross, killed at Halidon Hill, and Robert Stewart, forfeited
for his continuing opposition, in September 1336 John received a grant
to Skye, Lewis, Kintyre and Knapdale, as well as a new charter confirming all his existing lands.[30] But while John was happy to take all
this there is absolutely no evidence that he did anything to support his
beleaguered benefactor, who was driven out of Scotland for a second
time.

Clearly aware of the real power behind Balliol's shadow kingdom,
John subsequently wrote to Edward III, seeking confirmation of the
new land grants.[31] The significance of this letter is that he signed it
himself, for the first time, as *Dominus Insularum* – 'Lord of the Isles'.
This politically important step has been obscured by the insistence of
traditional historians that the chiefs of Clan Donald were always known
by this title. In the past, they had been awarded a variety of honours,
the most prestigious of which was *ri Innse Gall* – 'King of the Hebrides'.
There is no evidence, however, that Angus Mor or Angus Og ever
used, or were accorded, any regal or semi-regal title. It is particularly
significant that John called himself Lord of the Isles in a letter to Edward

III, who, among his other titles, was known as *Dominus Hibernie* – 'Lord of Ireland'; it is as if John were establishing himself in clear distance to his Balliol patron, and addressing the English king as an equal. This has to be seen as a significant step. The two men enjoyed good relations, and there is clear evidence to suggest that Edward saw John as an independent prince, quite different from the other supporters of Edward Balliol.[32]

Having shown his hand so clearly, John was formally declared a traitor after David II returned to Scotland in 1341. As relations with England remained bad, however, David could not afford to face such a powerful enemy on his northwest flank, so the two men reached an accommodation. John lost Kintyre and Knapdale, which were returned to Robert Stewart, the king's nephew and heir, and the Isle of Skye was returned to the earldom of Ross, but he kept all the other territories, both mainland and insular, granted to him by Balliol and Edward III. Some years earlier, John had married Ami Macruari, sister and only relative of Ranald Macruari. As Ranald had no heir, John thus acquired a direct interest in the extensive holdings of the family. This included the Lordship of Gamoran on the mainland, which embraced Knoydart, Moidart, Arisaig and Morar, as well as the islands of Uist, Barra, Eigg and Rhum.

In 1346, as David was preparing to invade England, Alan Macruari was murdered near Perth at the instigation of William, Earl of Ross. The circumstances of this crime remain fairly obscure, but appear to have involved a dispute over land. One thing at least is clear: it was John of Islay, not William of Ross, who benefited. He at once laid claim to the inheritance of Clan Ruari on behalf of his wife. It was to be some years, though, before this considerable extension to the power of Clan Donald was officially recognised. It has been suggested that John might have been involved in the murder of his brother-in-law, in that Ross was also linked to him by marriage, and no attempt was ever made to avenge the murder of his kinsman.[33] The evidence, though, is highly circumstantial.

After the defeat of the Scots army at the Battle of Neville's Cross near Durham in October 1346, and the capture and lengthy imprison-ment of David II in England, there was little anyone could do to stop John extending his power. He had effectively recreated the ancient kingdom of Somerled, a remarkable achievement. His position was now so secure that he was even prepared to allow his Macdougall kinsmen to resettle in Lorn, although very much in a subordinate posi-tion to the Lordship of the Isles. It is often maintained that feudal law was alien to the Gaelic way of life, but, as John's career clearly demonstrates, this is quite simply not true. He brought together the threads of an inheritance, divided at the time of the death of Somerled in accordance with ancient Celtic custom. In future, although younger sons were to receive an inheritance, the Lord of the Isles remained the feudal superior of the whole. Primogeniture was also to become the standard basis for inheritance in the Isles, rather than tanistry, which continued to be practised in the Gaelic lordships of Ireland. Although John's second son, also called John, was declared to be the 'Tanist' during the lifetime of his elder brother, Donald, it was Donald's eldest son, Alexander, who succeeded to the Lordship, rather than his uncle or cousin. Above all, John instituted the practice of issuing feudal charters, very much in the same fashion of any other king or noble of the medieval state.

Unlike his father, Angus, or his son, Donald, John of Islay was not a warrior, and it is doubtful if he ever fought in battle.[34] He was, rather, the greatest politician and diplomat Clan Donald ever possessed, managing to steer their affairs through difficult and turbulent times, never committing himself too far to one side or the other. He played a clever game, consolidating his power within the feudal state, while bringing back together the old patrimony of Somerled, now established on a more secure legal basis. John was clearly gifted with acute political sense, always knowing which way to jump, and always landing on firm ground. While his ancestor, Somerled, had died fighting a rearguard action against feudalism and the house of Stewart, John was comfortable with both, entering into a marital alliance which was to bring political and territorial benefits to his family.

In 1350 John took as his second wife Margaret Stewart, daughter of Robert Stewart, regent of the kingdom during the absence of David II, and heir to the throne. There is no good evidence that his marriage with Ami Macruari was ever annulled, so it is reasonable to assume that she died sometime prior to this.[35] This new alliance proved to be lasting, and John failed to respond to Edward III's attempts to bring him back to his side. After David II was ransomed in 1357, John continued to align himself with the Stewart party, often in conflict with the interests of the king, who continued with his refusal to recognise John's assumption of the Macruari inheritance. Along with some of his fellow nobles, John rebelled against David, and was among the last to submit to royal authority in 1369. But he was too well established in his island kingdom to suffer any real harm.

After the death of the childless David in 1371, John's father-in-law succeeded to the throne as Robert II. This brought almost immediate benefits. As well as confirmation of the Macruari inheritance, he received a grant to the Stewart lands in Kintyre. John also attempted to make the most of his kinship with the royal family, which required some delicate handling within Clan Donald. Ranald, his oldest son by his first marriage, was persuaded to give up his claim to the chieftainship in favour of Donald, the oldest son by the second marriage, and now grandson of the king. As a reward for this concession, Ranald was allowed to inherit the Macruari lands of his mother, and in the process founded that branch of the family known as Clanranald.

John had established great power and influence for himself, always managing to balance several competing interests. His manipulation of the clan leadership shows that he saw good relations with the royal house of Stewart as the key to the future prosperity of the Isles. He had, in the past, enjoyed good relations with the English, but never allowed himself to be drawn too far down an anti-Scottish course. His successors were less judicious: John's legacy created an understandable arrogance, and relations with the English became increasingly treasonable. John created a semi-regal power in the west, but never claimed full sovereignty, or never acted as if he did. As Alexander II and Alexander III had proved, the Isles were always vulnerable to a powerful Scottish state. In seeking an illusory sovereignty, his successors were destined to ruin the Lordship.

John died in 1387, greatly lamented by his kin. The *Book of Clanranald* records the event with some poignancy:

> Having received the body of Christ and having been anointed, his fair body was brought to Icolumcille [Iona], and the abbot and the monks and the vicars came to meet him, as was the custom to meet the body of the kings of Fionnghall, and his service and waking were honourably performed during eight days and eight nights, and he was laid in the same grave as his father.[36]

For his generosity to the church he was known as Good John of Islay. Godfrey, the second son of his first marriage, established *Soil Gofraid* – 'the seed of Godfrey' – seemingly supplanting the family of Ranald from their inheritance for a time. Alan MacGorrie, the son of Godfrey, was executed by James I at Inverness in 1427, and thereafter *Soil Gofraid* went into decline. By his second marriage John had two other surviving sons, John and Alasdair. John received lands in Islay around Dunyveg Castle. Through his marriage to Marjory Bisset, he acquired title to the Glens of Antrim, and established Clan Iain Mor, sometimes known as Clan Donald South. His brother Alexander obtained lands in Lochaber. He is often confused with his more famous son, Alasdair Carrach, who fought at the battles of Harlaw and Inverlochy, becoming the progenitor of the Macdonalds of Keppoch, sometimes known as Clanranald of Lochaber.[37]

The death of John was followed three years later by the death of Robert II. He and John had enjoyed a good working relationship. Nevertheless Clan Donald were still political outsiders, very much as they had been during the reigns of John Balliol and Robert I. Despite his great territorial power and his family connection with the king, John never obtained public office, unlike Gillespic Campbell, who became royal lieutenant in Argyll.[38] This failure to integrate the island chiefs more thoroughly into the kingdom was probably a reflection of a growing hostility in the Lowlands to the Gaels or the 'Wild Scots', as they were sometimes known at the time. Soon, the division was to grow still wider.

3

THE REID HARLAW

Ranald of Gamoran, eldest son of Good John of Islay, was loyal to the memory of his dead father. Against the wishes of at least some of his kinsmen, he elevated his younger half-brother, Donald, to the full dignity of the Lordship of the Isles. The *Book of Clanranald* records the ceremony, which appears to have had all the force of a royal coronation: 'On the death of his father he [Ranald] called a meeting of the nobles of the Isles and of his brethren at one place, and gave the sceptre to his brother at Cill Donan in Eigg, and he was nominated Macdonald and Donald of Isla.'[1]

It appears from this that while the men of the Isles belonged to the great Clan Donald in the widest sense, the name 'Macdonald' itself has the dignity of a royal title, conferring some special power and status on its holder. Beyond Donald of Islay himself it seems certain that its use would be conferred upon only the immediate blood kin. The ceremony of appointing the new Lord of the Isles is also quite unique in medieval Scotland, and would have amazed even the most powerful among the Lowland nobles. Hugh Macdonald provides us with a little more detail of the general process involved. 'There was a square stone, seven or eight feet long, and the tract of a man's foot cut thereon, upon which he stood, denoting that he should walk in the footsteps and uprightness of his predecessors, and that he was installed by right of his predecessors.'

This is an ancient ritual, which can be traced back at least as far as the kingdom of Dalriada. On the Hill of Dunadd in Argyllshire a footprint can still be seen, carved in the living rock, where the earliest Kings of Scots walked in the paths of their ancestors. Hugh Macdonald continues by saying that the Lord of the Isles was then clothed in a white habit to show his innocence, and then: 'He was to receive a white rod in his hand, intimating that he had the power to rule, not with tyranny and partiality, but with discretion and sincerity.'[2]

We must now picture the Lordship close to its height. It embraced all the leading families of the Western Highlands and Isles. This included the Macleans, Mackinnons, Macduffies, Macquarries, Macmillans and Mackays of Ugdale, Maceacherns, Macnicols, Camerons, Mackintoshes, Macleods and Macneils.[3] The Lord of the Isles also had his own dynasty of lawyers – the Morrisons – and doctors, the Beatons. Fitting his status, he had many fine castles, like other great nobles, and Ardtornish in Morvern was a particular favourite. But the real political heart of the Lordship was not a castle or fortified town, but the palace complex at Loch Finlaggan on Islay. Here, on two islands in the Loch, Good John of Islay established the administrative centre of the Lordship; it was not a stronghold like Dunyveg or Ardtornish, but a residential mansion, where the lord met and conferred with the chief men of his dominions in safety and security.[4]

It can be concluded from all of this that the Lordship of the Isles had a status far grander than, say, the Lowland House of Douglas, but it would be wrong to suggest, as it often is, that it was an exclusively Celtic institution. From Finlaggan and elsewhere, the Lords of the Isles issued charters, very much in a way that would have been recognised throughout Europe in the feudal age. This had the effect of conferring lands on the principal vassals of the Lordship, who, in turn, pledged loyalty and service to their overlord. This worked very well, as long as there was land to give: but in a very real sense the history of the Highlands is the history of the struggle for land, and when there was no more to be had, the tensions induced were to tear the Lordship apart. Clanship and blood could do nothing to save it from destruction.

Not only was land held by feudal tenure, but primogeniture was established as a basis for succession. The circumstances surrounding the elevation of the second Lord of the Isles were slightly unusual. However, after this, until the end of the Lordship in 1493, each chief was succeeded by his eldest living son. There was to be no more talk of tanistry.

Donald was proud of his Stewart kinship as well as his Gaelic inheritance. On his official seal the traditional Macdonald galley is surrounded by the royal tressure of the Stewart kings,[5] yet the blend between the two proved a little more difficult than Good John of Islay may have anticipated. In 1389, a mere two years after John's death, John Stewart of Carrick, the eldest son of Robert II, lodged a formal complaint in parliament that his sister, Margaret, the widow of John of Islay, was being badly treated by her sons. The dispute appears to have centred on the disposal of lands that Margaret held jointly with her late husband. No settlement appears to have been reached, and the matter dragged on for some years. In 1394 it became so bad that John, now King Robert III, ordered his brother, Robert Earl of Fife, to take their sister under his protection.[6] This went hand in hand with another dispute involving the Earl of Moray and Alexander, the youngest brother of the Lord of the Isles, who was firmly established as Lord of Lochaber by 1398.[7] Moray claimed that Alexander was blackmailing him; in angry response, Alexander seized Urquhart Castle. To resolve these problems it was decided that David, Duke of Rothesay, the eldest son of the king, and his uncle, Robert, formerly Earl of Fife and now Duke of Albany, should lead an armed expedition against the Isles. Nothing came of this, but it deserves to be noted as the first reference to a proposal that was to become such a feature of Stewart–Macdonald relations in the centuries to come.

Clan Donald was in no position to counter any external threat at this time, for it was divided by a serious internal dispute, and again the matter concerned land. John Mor Tanister, eldest brother and designated successor to the as-yet-childless Donald, had received lands in Islay and Kintyre. However, unhappy with his share of the family inheritance, he rose in rebellion, under the malign influence – so says Hugh Macdonald – of the Green Abbot of Finon.[8] The rising failed, and John fled first to Galloway and from there on to Ireland. The story of the Green Abbot is, perhaps, a little dubious. It is certainly true, though, that John and Donald had a serious quarrel. In a letter written from Armagh in February 1395, John offered his services to the English king, Richard II, saying that he had been banished to Ireland by his brother.[9] It was probably during this period that John married Marjory Bisset, heiress to the Glens of Antrim. By February 1401 he was being referred to in official documents as Lord of the Glens; and from this point forward John and his descendants became the Macdonalds of Dunyveg and the Glens. This additional territory seemingly put at rest his discontent over his Scottish inheritance, and he was reconciled with his brother sometime before 1401.[10] John's marriage to Marjory was one of the most important in Macdonald history, for it established the family on a firm basis in Ireland. In time, the Macdonnells of Antrim were to become the most powerful part of the clan to emerge from the ruins of the Lordship of the Isles. Antrim also became a useful bolthole for John's descendants when matters became too hot in Scotland, as they did from time to time.

By far the greatest land dispute of these years concerned the earldom of Ross, a huge northern territory stretching from Skye to Inverness. This was a complex affair, involving a mixture of national politics, family ambition and dynastic rivalry. While the Bruce dynasty had proved itself economical in the production of children, so much so that it died out altogether in 1371, the reverse was true of the Stewarts.

Robert II had many children, all of whom had to be provided for, by a steady accumulation of honours and territory. Beginning with the earldom of Atholl in 1342, they spread steadily northwards, obtaining Strathearn in 1357, Menteith in 1361, Caithness in 1375, Buchan in 1382 and the old Macdougall Lordship of Lorn by 1390.[11] The important earldom of Mar fell to them in 1405, when Alexander Stewart, the thuggish son of a thuggish father, arranged the murder of the previous incumbent and forcibly married his wife. At the same time the Stewart tide was already lapping against the shores of Ross.

Donald could not remain indifferent to these developments. For one thing Ross, standing on the northern flank of the Lordship, and projecting into the Isles, was of vital strategic interest. For another, his wife, Mariota Leslie, was the sister of Alexander Leslie, Earl of Ross, who died in 1402 leaving as his heir a disabled girl by the name of Euphemia. The contest between the Macdonalds and Stewarts over Euphemia's legacy was to result in one of the most savage battles in Scottish history.

Matters might have been different if the king had been a stronger man, but Robert III was one of the worst rulers in Scottish history. Unable to control events, he let events control him. For much of his reign, national affairs were under the control of his brother Robert, Duke of Albany, a ruthlessly ambitious man. In 1402 his chief rival, David Stewart, Duke of Rothesay and eldest son of the king, was removed from the scene, dying in mysterious circumstances at Albany's castle in Falkland. No sooner had Alexander Leslie died than Albany seized hold of little Euphemia, his granddaughter. Completely ignoring the rights of Donald's wife, Albany assumed responsibility for the girl's affairs. In response to this clear provocation, Donald appears to have staked his own claim by sending Alexander on a raid into Elgin.[12] Albany ignored this, and, in 1405, assumed the title 'Lord of the Ward of Ross', clearly a preliminary to the complete absorption of the area. Alexander Stewart acquired the earldom of Mar the same year by murder and rape, excused only by the fact that he was Albany's nephew. One can only smile at the many traditional accounts of the events leading up to the Battle of Harlaw, which depict it as a clash between Highland barbarism and Lowland civilisation, when Donald must have felt that he was about to be boxed in by a kind of Stewart mafia.

Matters deteriorated still further in 1406. Prince James, the only surviving son of the king, was taken prisoner by the English while on his way to France: ostensibly to escape the tender care of his uncle. This was followed soon after by the death of Robert III. Albany, in no hurry to see the return of his nephew, settled in for a period of prolonged personal rule. For Donald, this was an alarming development. Albany now seemed to hold all the cards, and was likely to put pressure on Euphemia to surrender her rights to Ross. Worse than this, he had clear ambitions to take the throne itself. It was Robert of Albany who was about to swallow Scotland, not Donald of Islay.

Donald's contacts with the English over this period must be viewed against this background, rather than the usual assumption that he was preening himself as an independent prince.[13] His opposition was not to Scotland as such, but to the growing power of the Albany Stewarts. In August 1406 Hector Maclean, Donald's nephew, was given permission by the English to come and speak with the captive King James.[14] Five years later, just prior to the Harlaw campaign, Donald's chaplain, John Lyon, had talks with King Henry IV.[15] Sadly, we do not know the outcome of either of these discussions. It has been suggested that James and Henry supported and encouraged Donald's planned attack on Albany, but the evidence is just too scanty.[16] What is certain, though, is that Donald and James, for their own differing reasons, conceived an informal alliance against the Albany Stewarts, which continued after the king's return in 1424.

Soon after John Lyon met Henry IV, Donald made his move. Euphemia of Ross was still alive, and had not yet surrendered her rights, but this was only a matter of time. With the Albany Stewarts in possession of Skye and the rest of the earldom, Donald clearly saw himself facing the same kind of danger that his ancestor Somerled had prior to the Battle of Renfrew. Summoning his vassals and kin – most likely by the old Gaelic method of the fiery cross – Donald is said by Walter Bower, the only contemporary chronicler of the event, to have gathered an army of 10 000 men.[17] One should not take this suspiciously round figure too seriously, as there is no way of knowing exactly how many men Donald had, and medieval chroniclers invariably inflate the size of armies. Advancing rapidly across country, the army of the Isles met no resistance until it arrived at Dingwall, where a force of Mackays loyal to Albany was quickly swept aside. Donald continued his march into Moray by way of Inverness, plundering the surrounding countryside as he went. It must have given him particular satisfaction to lay waste to the estates of Alexander Stewart, Earl of Mar.[18]

Donald had now established his right to Ross by sheer force. His conduct from this point forward has been subject to endless speculation, much of it ill informed. Walter Bower says that he aimed to sack Aberdeen and establish his authority south to the River Tay.[19] It is also claimed that he simply intended to establish his right to the Aberdeenshire lands pertaining to the earldom of Ross, although why he needed

to take his whole army to achieve this simple aim is difficult to say.[20]
The reality is his formidable army could only be kept in the field for a
short season, and harvest time was coming fast. If the conquest of
Ross were to be made secure, Donald would have to launch a pre-
emptive strike to destroy the Lowland force that Mar was gathering to
the south-east. The suggestion that he aimed at the throne of Scotland
itself is totally without foundation. If anything, the Harlaw campaign
was designed to end Albany's royal pretences rather than advance his
own.

Marching by way of Enzie, Strathbogie and Garioch, the Highland
army came on, finally camping on the evening of 23 July 1411 at the
Water of Urry near its junction with the Don at a place called Harlaw.
That evening, the nervous citizens of Aberdeen could see the light of
the great fires of Donald's army in the night sky. It was perhaps now
that Lachlann Macvuirich, founder of a long dynasty of Clanranald
poets, recited his famous *brosnachadh* – incitement to battle – to the
watchful ranks of Clan Donald:

> O children of Conn, remember
> Hardihood in time of battle:
> Be watchful, be daring
> Be dexterous, winning renown;
> Be vigorous, pre-eminent;
> Be strong, nursing your wrath;
> Be stout, be brave,
> Be valiant, triumphant,
> Be resolute and fierce.

It continues like this for some time, before reaching an explosive
crescendo:

> O children of Conn of the Hundred Battles,
> Now is the time to win recognition,
> O raging whelps,
> O sturdy bears,
> O most sprightly lions,
> O battle-long warriors
> O brave, heroic firebrands,
> The Children of Conn of the Hundred Battles
> O children of Conn, remember
> Hardihood in time of battle.[21]

Donald chose his position well. His camp stood on the summit of a
moorland plateau, secured on the right flank by the valley of the Ure

and on the left by a marshy hollow, bisected by the Lochter Burn. The camp could only be approached by a long slope, at the brow of which the Ure was crossed by a bridge at Howford.[22] This was a sensible precaution against surprise attack, but it also suggests that he may not have been confident that he had the advantage of numbers. Nevertheless, he appears to have felt safe enough not to take the precaution of posting sentries.[23]

Two miles to the south Alexander, Earl of Mar, had concentrated his own forces at Inverurie. An unpleasant and unscrupulous man, he was, nevertheless, a competent soldier who had learned his trade in arms from his equally unscrupulous father and namesake, Alexander, the infamous Wolf of Badenoch. He gathered around him the Lowland levies of Angus and the Mearns, under the command of Sir Alexander Ogilvy, Sir James Scrymgeour, constable of Dundee and hereditary standard bearer of Scotland, Sir Alexander Irvine, Sir Robert Melville, Sir William Abernethy and many other barons and their retinues. In addition, a group of citizen soldiers came from Aberdeen under the command of the provost, Sir Robert Davidson. The core of the army was a body of professional armoured knights; Donald's army, in contrast, was composed of infantrymen, armed with bows, battleaxes and spears. In this regard, at least, the coming Battle of Harlaw resembled the Battle of Renfrew. As with the Highlanders, we have no way of knowing the exact size of Mar's army, although the usual assumption that he was outnumbered by a factor of ten to one is almost certainly wrong.[24] Rather than fight from a defensive position, which significant weakness in numbers would demand, Mar opened the battle, suggesting that the two armies were more evenly matched.[25]

Without waiting for all his forces to gather, Mar began his attack early in the morning of 24 July, with a rapid advance towards the Highlanders across Howford Bridge. Not expecting such boldness, Donald appears to have been caught unawares, but his army was quick to recover from the initial surprise, seizing their arms before rushing on the enemy. The two forces appear to have met in a terrible frontal collision on the top of the plateau between Balhaggardy and Harlaw, where a monument was erected just before the outbreak of the First World War. Donald's army was divided into three divisions: Hector Maclean of Duart commanded the right, Calum Beg Mackintosh had the left and Donald himself the centre. The Lowland vanguard, commanded by Scrymgeour and Ogilvy, met the onslaught with level lances and spears, while Mar and the rearguard came on in support. Mar's men appear to have adopted the schiltron formation of tight bodies of spearmen, used against the English in many previous battles.

John Major, a Scottish historian, writing in the following century, provides us with a vivid description of the Battle of Harlaw:

> The wild Scots rushed upon them in their fury as wild boars will do; hardly would any weapon make stand against their axes handled as they knew to handle them; all around them was a very shambles of dead men, and when, stung by wounds, they were yet unable by reason of the long staves of the enemy to come to close quarters, they threw off their plaids and, as their custom was, did not hesitate to offer their naked bellies to the point of a spear. Now in close contact with the foe, no thought is theirs but of glorious death that availed them if only they might at the same time compass his death too. Once entered the heat of the conflict, even as one sheep will follow another, so they, and hold cheap their lives. The whole plateau is red with blood; from the higher points to the lower blood flows in streams. In blood the heroes fought, yea knee deep.[26]

The historian has quite clearly been carried off by his creative imagination, but his account conveys something of the naked courage of both armies. There appears to have been no military subtlety to Harlaw, no great skill in tactics and disposition. It was very much a battle in the old sense, a saga-like struggle fought in the northern world in ages past, resolving itself into a series of heroic encounters. Less well protected than the Lowlanders, many Highlanders fell dead against Mar's wall of spears, including Maclean of Duart: but Lowland casualties were also heavy. Scrymgeour was slain, as was Provost Davidson of Aberdeen, surrounded in death by many of his fellow townsmen. One baron by the name of Lesley was cut down with all six of his sons. As a proportion of his army, Mar's casualties are said to have been even greater than those of Donald, but he did not break or abandon the field. In the end the bloody struggle seems to have exhausted both sides. Donald disengaged and drew off by nightfall, while Mar's men, now exhausted and too badly mauled to attempt a pursuit, fell asleep in the field, surrounded by the groans of the wounded and the silence of the dead. It had been a savage and murderous day, long remembered in poetry and tradition as the 'Reid Harlaw'. Aberdeen schoolboys were still acting out the conflict in their games a hundred years later, and bones were being dug up as late as 1837.[27]

In recording the outcome of the Battle of Harlaw, the *Annals of Loch Ce* claim it as a 'great victory for MacDomhnaill of Alba over the Foreigners of Alba'.[28] As such, it has always been celebrated in Macdonald tradition. Even Denis Campbell, Dean of Limerick in the late sixteenth century, and a severe critic of Clan Donald, says that it was a victory for the Gaels.[29] Donald was only ever routed by the Lowland poets, often more colourful than accurate in their depiction of the battle. Yet a battle can only ever be measured by its results. The Germans in 1916 claimed the Battle of Jutland as a victory because the British lost more ships and men, and by this material standard they are probably right; but they still failed to break the naval blockade around their country. In 1715, Clan Donald, this time under the leadership of an Earl of Mar, swept away the enemy to their own front at the Battle of Sheriffmuir; but the Jacobite leadership failed in their objective of crossing the River Forth, and so they lost. One of the many Scots poems on the Battle of Harlaw makes a simple observation:

> On Monandy at mornin'
>   The battle it began;
> On Saturday at gloamin'
>   Ye'd scarce tell wha had wan.[30]

The timescale is exaggerated for poetic effect. The essential truth is not: Harlaw was a stalemate, a judgement confirmed in the accounts of both John Major and Hector Boece.[31] For Donald, that was as good as a defeat. If his objective was to sweep away Mar, prior to advancing on Aberdeen and then the Tay, he lost. If Mar's objective was to prevent him doing these things, then he won: his casualties may have been heavier than Donald's, but he still remained in place after a bloody day. Donald retreated not just to Ross, but all the way back to the Western Isles. Albany, with more to lose than most, treated the outcome with considerable relief. The families of the dead were allowed to succeed to their estates without incurring the usual feudal charges, a privilege that had in the past only ever been extended to those killed fighting against a foreign enemy.

It is difficult to know what Donald would have done if he had won an outright victory at the Battle of Harlaw. At the very least he would have established an undisputed title to the earldom of Ross; beyond that we cannot say with authority. By the nineteenth century, when racial categories were becoming increasingly popular, the battle tended to be viewed as a struggle for supremacy between Celts and Saxons, which appears to mean that one side spoke Gaelic and the other English or Scots, to be more precise. But many of the men in Mar's army were just as Celtic in ancestry as their Highland opponents, and many of their relatives would have spoken Gaelic, perhaps within living memory. Nevertheless, Harlaw marks an important point in the growing political and cultural separation of the Highlands and Islands from the rest of Scotland, a process started during the Wars of Independence; in time this was to bring destruction to the Lordship of the Isles and a fatal fragmentation in the power of Clan Donald.

Wasting no time, Albany raised a fresh army to exploit Donald's check at Harlaw. He advanced north to Ross, capturing the important castle of Dingwall. In the following summer the offensive resumed, as Albany made ready to attack Donald in the Isles.[32] Before this could happen Donald came to Lochgilphead and submitted to the Governor. No details of this treaty have survived, but Albany would have insisted that, at the very least, Donald give up his claim to Ross. Clan Donald historians have dismissed Donald's submission as a fiction by Bower (wrongly identified as John Fordun). But Bower lived through these events, and there is really no good reason why he should have lied. His account, moreover, finds some confirmation in the Exchequer Records of the time, which refer to Albany's expenses in taking an army to Loch Gilp 'for the pacification of the kingdom'.[33]

As if to confirm the outcome of the Treaty of Lochgilphead, Euphemia finally surrendered her rights in Ross to her grandfather in 1415, who, in turn, conferred the earldom upon his second son, John, Earl of Buchan. Buchan continued to enjoy the title until his death in 1424, fighting for the French at the Battle of Verneuil; after that it technically reverted to the crown: as late as 1430, James I was signing himself as King of Scots and Earl of Ross.[34] It is certain that Donald was never fully reconciled to this. In 1421 he is referred to in a supplication to Rome as 'Donald de Yle, Lord of the Isles and of the Earldom of Ross'.[35] In this regard, it is probably worth noting that Albany had died the previous year, and had been succeeded as Governor by his eldest son, Murdoch Stewart, a particularly ineffective individual. John Stewart, the titular holder of the earldom, was too preoccupied with affairs in France to bother much at Donald's provocation, assuming he ever knew.

It could be of some significance that Lochgilphead was part of the sheriffdom of Argyll, and thus under the control of Colin Campbell of Lochawe, a close associate of Albany. Colin was now too old to have taken part in Harlaw, or any other offensive action against the Lord of the Isles. It seems likely that he was acting as a diplomatic bridge between the two enemies, on the assumption that Donald would not have agreed to meet Albany on hostile territory, but with his attention firmly concentrated on Ross, Donald did not appreciate that something quite significant was happening in his own backyard: Clan Campbell was steadily taking on the role the Macdougalls once enjoyed in Argyll. As early as 1395 Colin Campbell was referred to as *Dominus de Ergadia* – 'Lord of Argyll' – a title that had only ever been held in the past by the descendants of Somerled. More than this, the Campbells now controlled much of the old heartland of Somerled's kingdom, prior to his expansion into the Isles after the Battle of Epiphany. Although themselves of Gaelic origin, they were increasingly able to bridge the gap between the Highland and Lowland world, developing a lasting alliance with the house of Stewart. In time, this was to be a serious threat to the political integrity of Clan Donald.[36]

The great events leading to the Battle of Harlaw have tended to overshadow other aspects of Clan Donald's history at this time; however, the family continued to extend and develop. Ranald, Donald's older half-brother, was firmly established in Moidart, where he set up his headquarters at Castle Tioram, a property formerly belonging to the Macruaris. By his marriage to a daughter of Walter, Earl of Atholl, he had two sons, Allan, who continued the main line of Clanranald, and from whom the various chiefs acquired their Gaelic title *Mac Mhic Ailein* – 'the son of Allan's son' – and Donald, who was to found the Glengarry dynasty. His son, Alasdair, was the first to settle in Glengarry, and from him the successive chiefs acquired their title *Mac'ic Alisdair*.

Donald died sometime prior to the return of James I in 1424; his son, Alexander, succeeded him. If Alexander hoped to benefit from his father's early alliance with the king, he was soon to learn how mistaken this was.

4

PRIDE AND DESTRUCTION

Good King James is one of the myths of Scottish history. Set against the increasing disorder and misrule that arose during the reign of Robert III and the governorship of Albany and his son Murdoch, it is almost inevitable that any strong man would be viewed favourably by posterity. So it has been with James I. But James was to Albany as Stalin was to Tsar Nicholas II: if cruelty, avariciousness, paranoia, high-handedness and deceit measure good rule, then James possessed these qualities in abundance.

His first task was to rid himself of his hated cousins, the Albany Stewarts, whom he justly blamed for the length of his English captivity. To accomplish this task he needed the support of his other senior noblemen, including Alexander of the Isles. There was one sure way of buying off Alexander: no sooner had Buchan been conveniently killed off at Verneuil, than James recognised Mariota of the Isles, Alexander's mother, as the heiress of Ross; by this Alexander became the Master of Ross.[1] In 1425 we find him sitting on the jury which condemned Murdoch Stewart to death, in long overdue fulfilment of a pact that may have been conceived in 1406.

Before the trial of Murdoch began his youngest son, James Stewart, rose in rebellion, burning the town of Dumbarton, no doubt making matters worse for his father. The rising failed, and Stewart fled to Ireland, where he subsequently married an unnamed woman of Clan Donald, and by this may have established some kind of understanding with John Mor Tanister, Alexander's uncle.[2] This might provide the key to another of the great mysteries of Clan Donald history – the murder of John Mor.

According to Hugh Macdonald, the king sent one James Campbell on a mission to John Mor, aimed at persuading him to take his nephew's place as Lord of the Isles.[3] John refused and was killed resisting arrest. This appears to have been after the execution of Murdoch Stewart, and we know, from subsequent events, that James was already considering a break with Alexander, who had now served his purpose. But why would he give the game away in this manner unless John Mor's co-operation could be guaranteed, which it most certainly was not? Even the identity of James Campbell has never been established. He may be connected with the Campbells of Lochawe, but there is no evidence to support this; Hugh Macdonald's tale is simply not convincing. He claims that Campbell came to see John accompanied, like a powerful nobleman, with a large following. But why would such an obscure figure be sent on such a delicate mission in such a public way? All we know of James Campbell from contemporary sources is Walter Bower's statement that he was hanged at Inverness in 1427 for the murder of John.[4] Hanging was the punishment of a commoner, not a man sent on diplomatic mission with a great number of attendants. It is possible that the king was involved in the murder of John Mor, and that Campbell was his instrument, but it appears more likely that John was killed because of his associations with the rebel James Stewart, rather than because he refused to betray his nephew. As with so many of these questions, the truth will never be known.

In 1427, sometime after the murder of John, the king summoned a parliament to Inverness to consider the problem of disorder in the Isles. Alexander came, not doubting James' good faith; but he was promptly arrested and thrown in prison, as was his mother. By this action James established a pattern of deceit and bad faith that was to characterise his descendants' relations with Clan Donald, down to the reign of James VI. Alexander came to Inverness clearly with the intention of co-operating with the king, and a great deal could have been achieved by this. Instead, James' high-handed approach ushered in a phase of intense disorder in the west, and brought about the Battle of Inverlochy, one of the most serious defeats ever suffered by a royal army in the Highlands. He managed to strip Alexander and his mother of their title to Ross; beyond that his Highland policy, like that of so many of his line, was a complete failure.[5]

Alexander was released after a short time in prison, but in a fury of wounded pride he advanced with his vassals on Inverness, destroying the scene of his recent humiliation in the spring of 1429. It was to be the sad fate of this Highland town that it was to be long the focus of Macdonald anger. In this his teenage nephew, Donald Balloch, son of John Mor, and now the new chief of the Macdonalds of Dunyveg and the Glens, supported him. It must be assumed that Donald was in possession of the full facts of his father's tragic death, for he remained an implacable enemy of the Stewarts for the rest of his life. The rebel James Stewart was still living under his protection in the Glens, and it seems certain that it was on Donald's suggestion that he be brought over to act as a pretender to the throne. Before this plot could be fully developed, James Stewart died.[6]

Enraged by Alexander's rebellion, James gathered his own forces, moving rapidly into Lochaber, where Alexander confronted him with 10 000 men – again that suspiciously round figure.[7] But there was to be no rerun of Harlaw. Meeting the Earl of Mar was one thing, the king quite another: the Camerons and Mackintoshes both deserted Alexander. Weakened in numbers and most likely demoralised, the rest of the army abandoned the field. With the king threatening to invade the Isles, as Albany had in 1412, Alexander was compelled to surrender. Once again he was imprisoned, this time to the castle of Tantallon in East Lothian, under the custody of the Earl of Angus. It was left to Donald Balloch and Alasdair Carrach, son of Alexander of Lochaber, to restore the broken pride of Clan Donald.

Soon after his success in Lochaber, James left the conduct of affairs in the north in the hands of the veteran Earl of Mar, the man who held the onslaught of Clan Donald at Harlaw. However, the rebellion rumbled on for two years without any kind of resolution. Finally, in September 1431, the royal army advanced into Lochaber under Mar and the Earl of Caithness, seeking a final confrontation and taking up a position close to the old Comyn castle of Inverlochy. Alasdair Carrach in Lochaber, lacking sufficient force to confront Mar and Caithness, took to the hills and there waited for the arrival of his cousin, Donald Balloch. Not far to the west, Donald and his brother, Ranald Bane, summoned their kin to meet them on the Isle of Carna in Loch Sunart. MacIain of Ardnamurchan and Alan MacAlan of Moidart and many others joined them there. From Loch Sunart the combined force sailed off, landing some two miles south of Inverlochy. Seeing them approach, Alasdair Carrach with his bowmen positioned himself on the flank of the royal army. Seemingly unprepared, Mar and Caithness were attacked from two sides. Before long their army crumbled under the pressure. Caithness was killed and Mar wounded, managing to escape from the field with some difficulty.[8] Over 900 of the royal army were killed. Donald, in contrast, is reputed to have lost under thirty men, although, once again, it would be dangerous to place too much reliance on these figures. One thing at least is certain: unlike Harlaw, the Battle of Inverlochy was a clear and unambiguous victory for the men of Clan Donald – but the result was just the same. Donald, like his namesake at Harlaw, retreated back to the Isles.

It might be thought that Donald Balloch's precipitate action could have placed Alexander of the Isles, still a prisoner of the king, in some considerable danger. After all the rebellion of James Stewart in 1425 only hastened the death of his father, Murdoch. Instead it only emphasised that the king's policy in the north, designed to bring disorder to an end, was a complete failure. If this was clear to James, it was also clear to the nobles of the realm, tired of expensive and fruitless campaigns in the Highlands. Parliament met in October 1431, the month after Inverlochy, but proved very reluctant to grant James funds for a fresh campaign.[9] He was left with no other option but to come to terms with Alexander if he was to have any hope of restoring order in the realm. So James finally brought to an end his four-year war with Clan Donald, caused by his ill-judged and arbitrary conduct. Alexander was pardoned and freed, although his mother remained at Inchcolm, under the gentle captivity of the scholarly Walter Bower. Unable to ride the northern torrent, James appears later in his reign to have made some concession to Alexander, who was referring to himself as Earl of Ross in January 1437, shortly before the king was murdered at Perth.[10]

There could, of course, be no reprieve for Donald Balloch; he fled to Ireland. Later a head was sent to James by Hugh Boy, chief of the O'Neils of Ulster, supposedly that of Donald. Honour satisfied, James did not pursue the matter further. This head, sacrificed for the greater good of the Gaelic world, was most assuredly not that of Donald Balloch, who lived to trouble the hated Stewarts for many years to come. Alasdair Carrach is said to have been forfeited by Alexander under pressure from the king; but there is no convincing evidence for this. Alasdair seems never to have been known as Lord of Lochaber, a title that had been bestowed on his father, Alexander of the Isles, suggesting that he may have been illegitimate. All that can be proved is that in 1443 and 1447 Alexander granted Malcolm Mackintosh, the Chief of Clan Chattan, land and titles in Lochaber.[11] These grants were confirmed in 1466 by John, Lord of the Isles, the son of Alexander, in a charter issued to Duncan Mackintosh and his heirs. At the time of the initial grant James I had been dead for some years, James II, his successor, was still a minor, and Alexander was a figure of some political importance in the north. He was thus clearly under no pressure when he granted the Keppoch lands to Mackintosh.[12] However, as Donald held on to his head, Alasdair and his descendants retained a firm grip of Lochaber. All Alexander's grant had achieved was the creation of a feud between the Macdonalds of Keppoch and Clan Chattan that was destined to last for over 200 years.

During the minority of James II Clan Donald ceased to be political outsiders. In 1438 Alexander was appointed to the important post of sheriff north of the Forth, which gave him considerable legal and administrative power. It also gave him control of Inverness, the capital of the Highlands, where he held many of his courts. This presumably caused the good citizens of that town some distress, considering Alexander's conduct in 1429. He appears to have owed this honour to his friendship with the Earl of Douglas, the dominant political figure at the time. This alliance with the Border House of Douglas was destined to bring ruin to the Lordship of the Isles.

While Alexander clearly forgave the Mackintoshes for their desertion at Lochaber in 1429, he was less magnanimous with the Camerons. Using his new powers, he forced Donald Dubh Cameron to flee to Ireland. His lands were then granted to the Macleans, who fared no better than the Mackintoshes in holding on to land against the will of those who lived there.[13] Matters only started to settle down later in the century, when the Cameron lands were granted to Celestine of Lochalsh, brother of John of the Isles, a good friend to the Camerons, who allowed them to settle in Lochaber as his vassals.

Under Alexander the power of Clan Donald reached its high tide. With Ross and all the Western Isles under his control, Alexander's power was greater even than that of Somerled. However, he appears to have lost his attachment to the heartlands of Clan Donald, basing himself towards the end of his life in the richer lands of Easter Ross, from where his later charters were issued, mainly at Dingwall or Inverness. This trend continued under his son, John. There were real problems in this for the political unity of the island kingdom. Ross, unlike the Macruari inheritance of Gamoran, was not clan territory, but a purely feudal acquisition. Most of the local families, the Mackenzies above all, never developed any real sense of attachment or loyalty to the chiefs of Clan Donald. In a sense the eastward shift of the Lord of the Isles mirrored the earlier eastward shift of the kings of Dalriada. Against this background, kinship ties began to unravel, an important factor in the crisis which enveloped the Isles after 1476.

It used to be said that Alexander entered into a bond of mutual alliance with his friends the Earl of Douglas and the Earl of Crawford in March 1445. Alliances of this kind were fairly common among senior noblemen, as can be seen from the earlier Turnberry Band, in which Robert Bruce of Annandale and Angus Mor Macdonald were both involved. However, Alexander's bond with Douglas and Crawford is assumed to have been a treasonable alliance against the king. The bond itself has not survived, and the only evidence that it was made in 1445 is contained in the Annals of Sir James Balfour, set down in the early seventeenth century.[14] But in the context of the time it simply makes no sense. James was still a minor, Douglas was a senior figure in the government of Scotland, and Alexander had a secure power base in the north. Neither Douglas nor Alexander was under any kind of threat. It seems likely that this famous bond was concluded, rather, sometime after 1450, when James was beginning his attack on the powerful Douglas family. This was also a time when John, Alexander's successor, had his own particular quarrel with the king.[15]

Alexander died in 1449 in Dingwall Castle and was buried at Rosemarkie in Easter Ross, rather than among his ancestors on Iona, a move that served to emphasise the changing nature of the Lordship. As well as John, his successor, he had two other sons – Celestine and Hugh. Celestine received the lands of Lochalsh, Lochcarron and Lochbroom in Ross. He also became the feudal superior, as we have seen, of the Cameron lands around Locheil in Lochaber. Hugh, the youngest brother, was in time to found the last great branch of the family: the Macdonalds of Sleat.

It is difficult to know what to make of John of the Isles, the man who was destined to preside over the ruin of a great inheritance. He appears to have an odd combination of qualities, sometimes assertive and arrogant, at other times weak and submissive. Hugh Macdonald says of him that he was 'a meek and modest man . . . more fitting to be a churchman than to command so many irregular tribes of people'.[16] Yet his wife, Elizabeth Livingstone, was to accuse him of trying to murder her while she was pregnant – hardly the action of a meek and modest man.[17] He started his rule as a lion and ended as a sheep, having in the process alienated almost everyone, including those who should have been closest to him.

One cannot help but feel a certain sympathy for John. Early in his career he was forced to marry a woman he did not love, for a promise that was never kept. He also appears to have been quite young at the time of his succession to the Lordship, perhaps no more than fifteen. His senior kin would have been responsible for guiding him. This included the formidable and intimidating Donald Balloch, who himself had succeeded to his inheritance as a teenager. Donald was a well-respected figure within the clan, although perhaps not the best role model.

John's marriage to Elizabeth was dictated by affairs of state, as were the marriages of most important people at the time. There was however one important difference between the marriage of John and Elizabeth: he came from a great landed family, the greatest in Scotland, and she did not. Elizabeth was the daughter of Sir James Livingstone, a powerful politician during the minority of James II, but in a conservative, land-based society, a figure of little real significance. John, with a large and hungry following at his heels, rich as he was, always needed more land. Sir James' power was purely personal, and his daughter would not normally have been considered a suitable match for the Lord of the Isles.[18] It seems he was persuaded to marry her after certain unspecified promises from the king. After Livingstone fell from power in the early 1450s, James refused to honour his promises. Instead of growing to love or at least respect Elizabeth, John came to loathe her.

Soon after his disgrace, Sir James fled Edinburgh in 1451and took refuge with his son-in-law. John rose in revolt and at once seized the royal castles of Inverness, Urquhart and Ruthven, perhaps less to show support for the Livingstones than to remind the king of his broken word. These events have usually been assigned to 1452 through a mistaken reading of the *Auchinleck Chronicle*, a sparse but important source for the reign of James II.[19]

The revolt of the Lord of the Isles came at a dangerous time for the king, who was involved in a dispute with the eighth Earl of Douglas, the most powerful noble in southern Scotland. We can probably date to this time the famous bond between Ross and Douglas, men who were hardly natural allies. There is absolutely no evidence that Ross, Douglas and Crawford, the other party to the bond, planned to depose the king, which has not prevented many historians making such a claim.[20] If this had been the intention James would presumably have taken much more direct action, rather than simply invite Douglas to Stirling in February 1452 to discuss the matter, and Douglas would hardly have put himself in the power of the king, even with a safe conduct. As it was James tried to persuade the Earl to break the bond, and, when he refused, murdered him in a fit of royal anger. If the bond had been so treasonable, the arrest and trial of Douglas would have served his ends much more effectively than this crude crime of passion.

John appears not to have been unduly disturbed by the fate of his ally, especially after the king restored the Livingstones to favour and condoned the seizure of the northern castles. James' struggle with the House of Douglas was now close to its height, so, even if he had wanted to, there was little he could do against John. In 1455 Inverness and Urquhart Castles and the lands pertaining to them were both annexed to the crown by Act of Parliament, although John's occupation remained undisturbed. Accepting the inevitable, James agreed to award him a life grant in the properties, as well as additional lands in Glenmoriston.[21] Donald Balloch's famous raid on Inverkip, Arran and the Cumbraes, all properties belonging to the king, appears to have taken place in the summer of 1454, which probably helped to focus the royal mind. Having secured his own interests, John did nothing to prevent the final downfall of the Douglases in 1455. Instead he obtained title to some of the northern lands of the disgraced Border magnates.[22]

For the remainder of the reign John appears to have enjoyed reasonably good relations with the king, so much so that he joined him in the Borders in 1460 to make war on the English. With England distracted by the murderous dynastic conflict later known as the Wars of the Roses, James prepared to retake Roxburgh Castle, which had been in English hands since the days of Edward Balliol. This was the first and only time a Lord of the Isles took part in the ancient Border wars. According to the chronicler John came 'witht ane great companie of men all armit witht haberiunes bowis and exis and promissit to passe ony farther in the boundis of Ingland that he and his companie sould pace ane leage myle befor the rest of the oist and to tak upoun thame the first dint of the battell'.[23] John was never given the opportunity to fulfil this rash promise, for James was killed in early August when a cannon accidentally blew up. James III, yet another minor, became king, and John returned with his men to the Isles; soon after he received a proposal which was to bring about his ruin.

So far, John had done rather well. He had survived the ruin of his Douglas ally and increased his own already extensive territories. Had he died at this point he might be well remembered in the annals of Clan Donald. But he now took a fatal step, the consequences of which were to betray the essential weakness of his character. In England the Yorkists under Edward IV had chased the Lancastrian Henry VI from the country. Henry took refuge in Scotland, where he was well received. This was particularly dangerous for Edward IV, for there was still considerable support for the House of Lancaster in the north of England. It made sense, therefore, to create trouble for the Scots in their own backyard. The ninth Earl of Douglas, brother of the man killed at Stirling, had been in exile in England for some years. He was now dispatched on a mission to the Lord of the Isles, the sometime ally of England.[24] On 19 October 1461, John, surrounded by his chief vassals at Ardtornish Castle, authorised his kinsmen, Ranald of the Isles and Duncan, Archdeacon of Ross, to open negotiations with the representatives of the King of England. This was a dangerous move, for while John's predecessors had contacts with the English, they had never committed themselves too far. Moreover, the English had never made any real attempt to assist the Lordship when it was in difficulties with the crown of Scotland. It should have been perfectly clear that Edward was trying to create a diversion. Sadly, for the Lord of the Isles, it was not.

John's representatives accompanied Douglas to London, and, on 13 February 1462, they concluded the terms of an alliance, once pompously described as the Treaty of Westminster–Ardtornish, that envisaged nothing less than the conquest and partition of Scotland. John agreed to become the vassal of Edward in return for his aid in subjecting all of Scotland north of the Forth.[25] Furthermore, John and Donald Balloch were to receive a regular English subsidy in peace and war. John's negotiators, possibly under the guidance of the Earl of Douglas, appear all along to have danced to an English tune, for the treaty is a remarkably vague document, considering the risks John was prepared to take. It says nothing about the nature, scale and timing of the promised English support: indeed, no questions appear to have been raised about Edward IV's ability to mount an invasion of southern Scotland. Northumberland, after all, was still an area strong in Lancastrian sympathies, and was soon up in arms against the Yorkist king. But for Edward, the alliance with the Lord of the Isles was a brilliant diplomatic coup. He achieved maximum results at minimum expense, laying out only as much bait as was necessary to create a major diversion in northern Scotland.

Even before the Westminster agreement was concluded, the men of the west were in arms, under the leadership of the veteran Donald Balloch and Angus Og, John's illegitimate son, who thus made his dramatic entry on to the stage of history.[26] It is of some interest that John, who had been in arms only two years before, took no part in the coming campaign, which might suggest that it was Donald Balloch who was the driving force behind the whole enterprise. Advancing eastwards, the two commanders captured the castle of Inverness. Here they issued proclamations ordering the inhabitants of the north to acknowledge Angus Og as the lieutenant of the Lord of the Isles under pain of death. Crown taxes were to be paid to Angus, and all those within his jurisdiction were to deny the authority of James III.

Beyond this, sad to say, we know nothing, not even how the rebellion was brought under control. It most certainly had the effect Edward desired. With rebellion in the north and the potential of an English attack from the south, the Scottish government was soon to drop its politically embarrassing Lancastrian connections. Negotiations were entered into, and Edward ordered Douglas to abandon his attacks on the Border, at the same time leaving John to face the consequences of his treason. Without the promised English support, the rebellion of the Lord of the Isles, potentially of extreme danger, had no more than local significance, and was over by the time of the Anglo-Scots truce of 1464.[27] John, presumably by now aware how worthless the Westminster agreement was, backed down and admitted that his seizure of the Inverness customs had been illegal.[28] No further action was taken against him – for the present.

It is worth pausing to consider why this should have been so. After all, even if, as it is generally assumed, the Scots government did not as yet know of the secret Westminster agreement, John's actions had been highly treasonable. Not only had he wrongly seized royal revenues, but he had effectively usurped the powers of the sovereign, declaring moreover that all those who continued to acknowledge James III would be put to death. The simple explanation is that the king had not yet come of age, and Scotland was subject to the factional struggles that inevitably attended royal minorities. But there is more than this. The Lord of the Isles had proved himself a useful tool of the English king. Edward was clearly not so simple-minded that he would abandon John to the fury of the Scots. For James, timing was crucial. In 1475, now enjoying full royal authority, he made his move. He was in a position to do so because, first, he had entered into a lengthy peace with the English, and second, Edward IV soon had his hands tied preparing for a new war with France. Against this background, it may be that the full nature of John's secret negotiations had been known all along. Given the status of the evidence, though, this can never be more than supposition.

Throughout the 1460s John's personal and political problems appear to have been getting worse. His marriage to Elizabeth broke down beyond recall. In 1463 or 1464 she petitioned the Pope to admonish John for ejecting her from her lands and for continuing a liaison with an unnamed adulteress.[29] We cannot say who this woman was, but it is not beyond possibility that she was the mother of Angus Og. Elizabeth, fearing for her safety, eventually sought the protection of the king.

John also appears to have broken with Donald Balloch and his family. The *Annals of Ulster* note that, in 1465, the forces of John slew Angus, the son of Donald.[30] Unfortunately, the details given are too sparse to allow us to form a judgement about the nature and circumstances of this feud. It is certainly beyond doubt, though, that tensions over land were becoming ever more pronounced at this period, causing a steady alienation between John and his own immediate kin in Clan Donald. In 1466, as we have seen, in confirming earlier charters, he granted Duncan Mackintosh of Clan Chattan lands in Lochaber, including those occupied by the Keppoch Macdonalds. His own son, Angus, was unhappy about further land grants made to the Macleans in Morvern.[31] Under pressure to satisfy everybody, John ended by satisfying nobody. In about 1469 he tried to provide for his younger brother, Hugh, by granting him land in the Sleat peninsula on Skye, which opened a prolonged conflict with the Macleods. The Lord of the Isles found himself in a desperate position: if he gave lands to his kin, he lost his allies; if he gave land to his allies, he angered his kin.

The tensions of this time are well illustrated in a story told by Hugh Macdonald.[32] A feast was held at Aros on Mull for the chief kin and allies of Clan Donald. John Macdonald, the tutor of Moidart, was given the task of seating the principal men according to their rank. After seating the ancient septs of Clan Donald, including their bards and physicians, he turned to the Macleans, Macleods and Macneils, all standing, with the words 'Now, saith he, I am the oldest and best of your surnames here present, and will sit down; as for those fellows who have raised up their heads of late, and are upstarts, whose pedigree we know not, nor even they themselves, let them sit as they please.'

It is impossible to say if this gratuitously offensive spectacle ever took place, but it provides a taste of the growing rivalry within the Lordship, later to erupt in the rebellion of Angus Og and the Battle of Bloody Bay.

Slowly disintegrating from within, the Lordship was faced with a great external threat in 1475. John of the Isles was summoned by the Scottish parliament to answer for his various acts of treason all the way back to 1451, which included, of course, his supposedly secret alliance with England.[33] Preferring to shut himself up in the Isles, he made no answer, and was duly forfeited on 1 December 1475. Colin Campbell, the first Earl of Argyll, was given a commission to invade John's territory with fire and sword. A similar commission was granted to the Earl of Huntly, chief of the Gordons. Huntly was quick to take action, capturing Dingwall Castle, the Lordship's eastern headquarters, before the end of March 1476. Faced with this show of force, John appears to have lost heart and formally submitted before parliament in July.[34] In a spectacle that had clearly been prearranged, he surrendered all his lands and titles to the king. James pardoned the offender but stripped him of the earldom of Ross, as well as lands in Kintyre and Knapdale. He was then created a peer of parliament with the title 'Lord of the Isles'.

In reality John was not too badly handled when one considers the extent of his treason, far greater than that of the ruined house of Douglas. Although he lost most of Ross, he at least retained the Isle of Skye, which for long had formed part of the earldom, and thus kept hold of all of the Western Isles. He was still, by far, the most powerful landholder in Scotland. Yet he had lost much more than mere land. As Gaelic Lord of the Isles he enjoyed a unique status, one far greater than any feudal title and still resonant with the old honour of *ri Innse Gall*. Only the king could now confer his title. Caught thus within a feudal net it lost much of its resonance and splendour, giving its holder a status considerably less than that of an earl or a duke.

Angus Og also did not do too badly out of the forfeiture and regrant of 1476. Although a bastard, and thus not allowed to succeed to his father's estates under feudal law, he was declared to be John's heir by favour of the king. He is also said to have married a daughter of the Earl of Argyll soon after. But Angus and his kin were not reconciled to the territorial losses, particularly the loss of Kintyre and Knapdale. The success of the Lordship had depended on steady territorial expansion. After this expansion came to a standstill in 1463 tensions had started to build up. Now it was contracting, so matters became still worse. In this crisis Clan Donald turned away from John of the Isles to his more militant son, Angus, who was to act as a lightning conductor for the family's sense of frustration.

The loss of Kintyre and Knapdale was an early source of trouble, and John was summoned once more on a charge of treason in April 1478.[35] He clearly convinced the authorities of his innocence, for we find in 1481 that he received a life grant of his former estates in Kintyre and Knapdale. It is certainly of some interest that no mention is made in these charters of Angus, his son and designated successor, suggesting that the government was now aware of where the real threat came from.

From the uncertain light cast by contemporary record the story of Clan Donald now slips into a period of almost total darkness. The only clues we possess to the vital events of the 1480s are contained in the Exchequer Records and the traditional accounts set out 200 years later. Even the chronology is uncertain. Macdonald tradition is probably correct, though, in dating the start of Angus Og's rebellion to about 1481.[36] This would certainly be the best time, for Scotland had been at war with England since 1480 and James III, an unpopular king, was temporarily removed from power in 1482.

With the support of the old core of Clan Donald, Angus began his rising by deposing his father. John, according to Hugh Macdonald, was even ejected from his home, spending the night under the shelter of an old boat! However, while Angus was supported by his Macdonald relatives, John was able to rally the other clans of the Lordship to his cause. Sometime during the course of the 1480s, we cannot be more precise than that, the two sides met in a naval conflict in a sheltered area to the north-west of Tobermory in Mull, forever after called Bloody Bay. John's fleet is thought to have been under the command of Hector Maclean of Duart, supported by the Macneils and Macleods, all insulted at the feast of Aros.[37] The Battle of Bloody Bay was a complete victory for the birlinns of Clan Donald, and was possibly the last naval battle of its kind ever fought in the Isles. These sturdy vessels served thereafter chiefly as troop ships, carrying the soldiers of Clan Donald to the endless wars in Ireland. What happened to John after this is not certain; it may be he simply retired to one of his homes, perhaps in Kintyre, where he spent some time in obscure retirement. Angus went on to seize Duntulm Castle on the Totternish peninsula in Skye from the Macleods, and soon after he adopted the title of Master of the Isles and Lord of Totternish.

With Angus now in charge, and the Macdonalds victorious over the confederate clans, attention was turned towards Ross. Hugh Macdonald's story that Angus was provoked into action by Kenneth Mackenzie of Kintail's insulting treatment of his sister is probably best disregarded.[38] What is true is that Angus and the rest of his clan had been deeply angered by his father's cowardly submission in 1476, and were determined to restore the full power of Clan Donald, including the earldom of Ross. With the country distracted by events in the Borders and the political crisis that continued until the murder of James III in 1488, Angus virtually had a free hand in the north. Official records show that the revenues of Ross were seriously disrupted in the mid-1480s, most likely the period that Angus established control.[39] Mackenzie resistance was swept aside at the Battle of Lagebrad, fought sometime between 1481 and 1483.

With Angus now at the height of his power, this seems to be the appropriate point to discuss the case of his son, Donald Dubh – Dark Donald. Despite his importance in the story of Clan Donald, Donald Dubh is a rather obscure individual. Even some of the facts of his life are not completely certain. His mother is thought to have been a daughter of the first Earl of Argyll, but there is no contemporary record of her marriage to Angus. Even her name is a source of considerable confusion. In Campbell tradition there is reference to one Isobella 'Lady of the Isles', although the nature of her connection with Angus is not specified.[40] She is unnamed in Macdonald tradition, but elsewhere appears variously as 'Mary', 'Margaret', or 'Katherine', sometimes under two separate names in the same source.[41] Donald Dubh was later declared to be illegitimate by the Scottish government, the 'bastard and unlawful son of Angus of ye Isles'.[42] This is assumed to have been a crude attempt to undermine the support he received in the Gaelic world, although concepts of legitimacy and illegitimacy were not nearly as important here as they were in the rest of feudal Scotland. It may, however, be of some significance that, after the death of Angus Og, Alexander of Lochalsh, John's nephew, was appearing as the heir to the Lordship without mention of Donald. Later, Alexander's own son, Donald Gallda, was proclaimed Lord of the Isles, again without any apparent reference to the rights of Donald Dubh. Later still, a descendant of Hugh of Sleat claimed the title while Donald Dubh was still alive. As for the oft-repeated tale that Colin Campbell colluded in having his own grandson declared illegitimate, Argyll died in 1493 and the first references to Donald as a bastard do not appear until early the following century.

Hugh Macdonald tells us that the Earl of Atholl crossed to Islay in galleys provided by Argyll and kidnapped Donald, handing him over to his grandfather. He was then held in custody by the Campbells 'until his hair got grey'.[43] In fury, Angus then charged into the country of Atholl, and took the earl and his countess prisoner, forcibly removing them from the sanctuary of the Chapel of St Bride. But why should the Earl of Atholl have agreed to act in such a way with no apparent profit to himself, and why did he take refuge in a chapel and not the nearby castle of Blair Atholl? Why, moreover, did Angus ignore the imprisonment of his son and charge off in the opposite direction? We know that the Macdonalds of Glencoe were able to rescue Donald in 1501, apparently with some ease, suggesting that he was not held with any great rigour. The story simply makes no sense. It is not until a century later that the first account of the Atholl raid appears, and there is no mention of Donald Dubh. Bishop John Lesley attributes the raid to one Donald and dates it to 1460. The *Chronicle of the Frasers* dates it to 1464, under the leadership of Donald of the Isles.[44] This would appear to suggest that it was Donald Balloch and not Angus Og who was responsible for the exploit, years before the birth of Donald Dubh. Most important of all, the evidence suggests that Angus never knew that he had a son.

Hugh Macdonald's account is wrong in two important respects: first, we know that the Campbells only held Donald Dubh until 1501. After his recapture he remained a state prisoner until he escaped from Edinburgh in 1543. Second, the *Book of Clanranald* quite clearly says that he was born *after* the murder of his father, when his mother presumably took refuge with her Campbell kin, an account later confirmed by Donald himself in a letter to Henry VIII.[45]

Angus' career finally came to an end in 1490, when he was murdered by Dairmaid O'Cairbre, an Irish harpist.[46] The motive for the crime is not explored in contemporary accounts, but it is quite possible, as Hugh Macdonald suggests, that his Mackenzie enemies were responsible. As for Dairmaid O'Cairbre, he was tied between horses and pulled apart.

Later clan tradition depicts Angus as a violent and unstable individual; but he was well respected at the time. The *Annals of Loch Ce* describe him as the best man in Ireland or Scotland, and a poem in his praise was written shortly after his death:

> No wonder that my spirit fails, to see the lord of Islay
> My well-being is grown heavy and strengthless, since
> My king is dead.[47]

Angus was probably the last great leader of Clan Donald in the tradition of Somerled. With his death a heroic age seems finally to end, and soon after the Lordship itself crashed to its ruin.

With the death of Angus, the almost forgotten figure of John, Lord of the Isles, made a reappearance, but he appears to have been firmly under the guidance of his nephew, Alexander of Lochalsh. Alexander tried to re-establish Macdonald control of Ross, presumably lost after the death of Angus, but he was soundly defeated by the Mackenzies at the Battle of Park. In 1493, James IV, tiring of John's obvious incapacity to control disorder among his kin, finally brought the Lordship of the Isles to an end. It ended, oddly enough, with a whimper rather than a bang. Few, it seems, were prepared to defend John. There was no tragedy to his final years. As a silent, pathetic figure, he lived as a pensioner of the king, dependent on him for his clothes and pocket money, finally drifting out of history, apparently unlamented even by his own kin. The high noon of Somerled had sunk to a dismal twilight. Most of the standard histories of the clan even manage to get the date and place of John's death wrong: he died not in Paisley in 1498 but in Dundee in 1503.[48] There is also some uncertainty over his place of burial. At his own request, he is said to have been laid to rest in the tomb of his royal ancestor, Robert II, in Paisley Abbey; but Robert II was buried at Scone, not Paisley, where the tomb of Robert III is located.

If John himself was little regarded, the loss of the Lordship was soon keenly felt, giving rise to one of the saddest of all Gaelic poems. It is called *Ni H-eibhneas gan Chlainn Domhnaill* – 'It is no Joy without Clan Donald'. A few verses give something of the flavour of this great lament.

> It is no joy without Clan Donald; it is no strength to
> Be without them; the best race in the round world,
> To them belongs every goodly man.

> The noblest race of all created, in whom dwelt prowess
> And terribleness; a race to whom tyrants bowed,
> In whom dwelt wisdom and piety

> A race kindly, mighty, valorous; a race the hottest in
> Time of battle; a race the gentlest among ladies,
> And mightiest in warfare.

> A race whose assembly was most numerous, the best in
> Honour and esteem; a race that makes no war on
> The church, a race whose fear it was to be dispraised . . .
>
> For sorrow and for sadness I have forsaken wisdom and
> Learning; on their account I have forsaken all things:
> It is no joy without Clan Donald.[49]

It was one of the great tragedies of history that the Lordship of the Isles was never able to achieve a working compromise with the Scottish state. Despite periodic conflicts, the Lordship, until its final years, was a force for order and stability in the Highlands and Islands. Its collapse ushered in the *Linn nan Creach* – 'the Age of Forays' – a period of anarchy and instability that was to last for over 200 years. It was a sign of the times that Finlaggan was abandoned in about 1494: in the new era chiefs would require more secure accommodation.

5

SEARCH FOR LOST GLORY

The abolition of the Lordship of the Isles did not in itself bring about any major revolution in the patterns of land ownership in the Highlands and Islands. It simply meant that those who formerly held their lands from the Lord of the Isles now held them from the king. Given the ease with which John, the last lord, was removed, it seems that few were sorry to see him depart, but it would need time and patience for the vassals of the Isles to develop a new relationship with the king. Time and patience, sadly, were qualities that James IV did not possess in abundance. In the years to come the branches of Clan Donald held together by pride of race, but even the vassal clans developed a new enthusiasm for the vanished Lordship when faced with royal mismanagement.

The fate of the Lordship appears to have been tied up with the factional politics of the time. Colin, the first Earl of Argyll, had been Chancellor of Scotland until his death in 1493: thereafter the post went not to his son, Archibald, but to the Earl of Angus. The Campbells still held considerable power in the west, and with Donald Dubh in their hands, it was always open to them to extend this power still further.[1] The abolition of the Lordship followed by a personal visit to the area by the king, still legally a minor, offered Angus the best way of arresting Campbell ambitions.

James began the task enthusiastically enough. He came to the Highlands in person shortly after the abolition of the Lordship to receive the submission of the chief landholders.[2] Alexander of Lochalsh, John of Dunyveg and the Glens, Maclean of Lochbuy and Duncan Mackintosh of Clan Chattan all came to pay him homage. Alexander of Lochalsh, in view of his relationship to John of Islay, might have been considered politically dangerous, but James received him well and conferred upon him the honour of knighthood. A similar honour was bestowed on John of Dunyveg. How far the king saw this as a personal project, and how far he was acting under the guidance of

Angus, is difficult to say. A few years later he was to pull the whole delicate structure down by an act of astonishing insensitivity, suggesting he really knew nothing of the politics of the Gaelic world.

James returned to the Isles twice in 1494. In April the old royal castle of Tarbert was restored, and in July a garrison was placed in the former Macdonald stronghold of Dunaverty in Kintyre. This was too much of a provocation for Clan Iain Mor. Despite his recent knighthood, Sir John of Dunyveg and his son, John Cathanach, laid siege to the castle as soon as the king sailed off. According to tradition, the castle was taken and the new governor hanged before the eyes of the king (who had not yet sailed over the horizon). Given the timescale involved, this does not seem very credible.[3] Sir James was later summoned to appear for an unspecified treason committed in Kintyre.

There appears to have been some form of power struggle within Clan Donald at this time, perhaps connected with schemes to restore the Lordship. We have to step carefully here in order to disentangle myth from established historical fact. Before the end of the century, Alexander of Lochalsh is said to have invaded Ross, only to be defeated by the Mackenzies at Drumchatt.[4] He subsequently retired to the island of Oronsay, where he was surprised and killed by his kinsman, John Maciain of Ardnamurchan, acting on behalf of the king. The Maciains were one of the smaller septs of Clan Donald, and were doing quite well in their support of royal policy in the west. However – and this is where the water gets very muddy – the *Annals of Ulster* record that Alexander of Lochalsh was killed in 1494 in a battle with John Cathanach of Dunyveg.[5] Following this John's father, Sir John of Dunyveg, seems to have assumed the title of *ri Innse Gall*, or so he is referred to by the Irish annalist who recorded his death several years later.[6] Both men were subsequently captured by Maciain of Ardna-murchan either in 1494 or 1499, it is not clear which. They were certainly hanged in Edinburgh in 1499, and Maciain was well rewarded by the king with additional land grants on Islay. For the rest of the reign we hear no more of Clan Iain Mor in Scotland.

James continued his regular visits to the Isles over these years. In May 1495 he sailed to Mingary Castle in Ardnamurchan, where he received some of the principal gentry of Clan Donald, including John Hughson of Sleat, Donald of Keppoch and Allan Macruari of Moidart, among others. However, a few years later the whole policy of pacifi-cation was in ruins, when the king, like Samson, pulled the building down around his ears.

One of the features of feudal law was the right of the sovereign to revoke all land grants made when he or she was a minor, which, by the standards of the day, was any time before their twenty-fifth birthday. James was twenty-five on 17 March 1498. Before this date he issued a revocation annulling all previous charters, including those granted so painstakingly in the Isles over the previous five years. All those affected could then have their rights restored by fresh charters – issued of course at a price. Those who refused to pay were threatened that they would become mere tenants at the will of the king.[7] But for the men of the Highlands and Islands, unused to such practices, it gave all the appearance of simple deception.[8] It was James IV who gave the Islanders their first taste of arbitrary feudalism, forcing them to face a terrible reality: that the lands that had been held by their forebears for many generations could be taken away by the scribbling of an Edinburgh lawyer. The sudden awareness of the arbitrary nature of Stewart kingship created the conditions that led to the first rebellion of Donald Dubh.[9]

In 1498, a few months after his disastrous revocation, James sailed back to the Isles, setting up court at Kilkerran Castle in Kintyre. This time few came to pay homage, and he left in early August, never to return. Clearly tiring of his continual efforts in the west and the obduracy of the Gaelic people, he introduced a new approach in 1499. Archibald Campbell, the second Earl of Argyll, was given the custody of Tarbert Castle, followed in early 1500 by the grant of a lieutenancy over almost all of the old Lordship of the Isles for a period of three years. This gave the Campbell chief authority second only to that of the king. He could make statutes in the king's name and take all necessary action against rebels, including granting remissions. Argyll was not the only one to benefit from the new policy. The Gordons of Huntly received extensive authority over the lands in Lochaber, which had formed part of the Lordship. Later, the Campbells and Gordons were to be joined by the Mackenzies, who became the third pillar of the Stewart establishment in the north. But it was the growing power of the Campbells that caused most resentment to the people of Clan Donald.

Argyll and his Campbells were well placed to take advantage of the new realities. During the latter part of the Lordship, when efforts were focused on the earldom of Ross, the Campbells had risen steadily in Argyll. Although they were, like the Macdonalds, Gaelic in origin, they had no great independent traditions to draw on, instead relying on a close partnership with the royal house. By the end of the fourteenth century they had taken almost all of the old Macdougall territory, and in 1457 Colin Campbell was created Earl of Argyll. As head of his kin he and his successors were also known by their Gaelic title of *Maccailein*

Mor – 'son of Great Colin' – after the founder of Clan Campbell. Perhaps alone of all the Gaelic peoples, they managed to bridge two worlds, equally at home in Edinburgh and the Isles. Above all, the Campbells acquired an astute understanding of feudal law, and were to make skilful use of it in extending their political authority. When the Lordship of the Isles was at its height, Clan Donald claimed the headship of the Gael. Now they faced a new challenger, whose sentiments are captured in a poem dating from the sixteenth century:

> A good charter is the headship of the Gael
> Whoever it may be that has a grip of it,
> A people's might at this time it has exalted
> It is the noblest title in Alba.

> *Giolla-easbuig* (Archibald), earl of the Gael,
> has grasped the charter of the headship of the people;
> in his charter it has ever been of right to rule
> a willing people without self seekers.[10]

Neither the Gordons nor the Mackenzies, ambitious as they were, ever made this kind of claim. The Campbells were Gaels: they saw a vacuum and they moved to fill it. There is nothing surprising or malevolent in this, for just as Clan Donald's power was built on the ruin of Clan Dougall, so Clan Campbell's power was built on the ruin of Clan Donald. Unfortunately, this has given rise to a tiresome and quite unhistorical school of denunciation, which has become one of the great clichés of Scottish history. The two families became rivals, and were destined to strike bitter blows against each other, but there is no basis for the view that sees Campbell plots behind the successive misfortunes of Clan Donald.[11]

James' new policy put the western chiefs on the defensive, and soon a new longing for the old Lordship of the Isles began to grow. Donald Dubh, the son of Angus Og and therefore a figure of some considerable political importance, was still in the custody of his Campbell relatives. We have no information on how they intended to make use of him, but he would clearly be of some use in advancing Campbell authority in the Isles. He was kept on the island castle of Inchconnell on Loch Awe, the ancient headquarters of Clan Campbell. In what gives all the appearance of a very well-executed plan, the Macdonalds of Glencoe rescued him in 1501, when he can have been no more than eleven years old. No details of this remarkable exploit have survived. Considering its importance, Inchconnell would have been well guarded, and not easily approached by hostile forces. Donald was only a child, and was probably kept with no great rigour. He was almost certainly not kept in a dungeon, as Donald Gregory suggests.[12] It is possible that he was taken from his guardians while exercising on the mainland. No sooner was he freed, than the Glencoe men handed him over to Torquil Macleod of Lewis, suggesting that it was he who was behind the whole exploit. It is also of some significance that James granted certain lands in Glencoe to Duncan Stewart of Appin before this, which would provide Clan Iain Abrach with the motivation to release the Lord of the Isles.

There are two points of interest in this rising in the Isles, the most serious in the reign of James IV. First, Donald was proclaimed Lord of the Isles, although his grandfather was still alive. John is likely to have been fairly elderly at this time, and there were probably few that would welcome his return. Second, and more important, this first drive to restore the Lordship came not from the men of Clan Donald, but from the confederate clans, principally the Macleods and Macleans, who fought on the side of John of the Isles at the Battle of Bloody Bay. These men clearly preferred the loose confederation of the Isles to the political uncertainty brought about by the king. It is likely that some of the branches of Clan Donald provided support, but Maciain of Ardnamurchan remained firmly on the side of James.

As soon as James discovered Donald's whereabouts he ordered Torquil Macleod to hand him over on pain of treason. Macleod ignored the summons. He was then declared to be a rebel and his lands were forfeited. Donald was also declared to be illegitimate, to little practical effect. Having failed to arrest the rebellion in its course, the government then gave Argyll, Huntly and Lord Lovat power to proceed against the insurgents in Lochaber and the Isles. There are few details on the actual course of events; Badenoch was raided around Christmas 1503, but beyond that there is nothing.[13] This area was under Huntly's jurisdiction, and inhabited chiefly by the Mackintoshes and the people of Clan Chattan, so it is quite possible that the Keppoch Macdonalds were involved. In response, Huntly advanced to the Atlantic shores, and by 1504 the castles of Strome and Eilean Donan were in his hands.[14]

The following year the rising began to collapse. Maclean of Duart was the first to submit, followed by Maclean of Lochbuy and Donald Macranaldbane of Largie, the only significant chief of Clan Donald mentioned in connection with the rising. Almost alone, Torquil Macleod held out to the end. He was besieged by Huntly in his castle at Stornoway, which fell in the course of 1506. After the capture of Stornoway Donald Dubh was carried south as a prisoner. We do not know what happened to Torquil, but he seems to have got away, dying several years later. As for Donald, this tragic and unhappy individual was taken south as a state prisoner, and remained in rigorous captivity for almost forty years, for no other crime than being himself.

Huntly did well out of the whole affair, obtaining jurisdiction of the northern Hebrides. Argyll, in contrast, seems to have suffered some political embarrassment. It was he, after all, who had allowed Donald to escape, and he was related by marriage to both Torquil Macleod and Maclean of Duart, which may have raised questions about his loyalties. Once his lieutenancy expired in 1503 it was not renewed for three years, and restricted to the Isles not under the control of Huntly. As the king was not willing or able to spend resources and time building up royal authority in the Isles, he was really left with no choice but to make use of the men on the spot. However, it was not the restoration of Argyll but the continuing favour shown to Maciain of Ardnamurchan that was a source of future trouble. James would no doubt have lavished rewards on other loyal chiefs, but it was Maciain's breach of solidarity that made him all the more conspicuous.

For the remainder of James' reign there was no further trouble in the west, and many of the men of the Highlands and Islands followed him to disaster at the Battle of Flodden in 1513, where they were cut down with Argyll and many others of their race. There really does not seem to be any basis for the oft-repeated assumption that James was popular with the Gaels. The revocation of 1498 had created a lasting sense of distrust, as did his appointment of powerful nobles as viceroys. His rule was almost certainly seen as a burden, judging by the speed with which it was thrown off after news of his death, and that of Argyll, reached the Isles. Once more the Gaels rallied to the banner of the Lordship, this time under the leadership of Donald Gallda, the eldest son of Alexander of Lochalsh.

Donald had spent his formative years at the court of King James, with the result that he acquired the nickname *Gallda* – 'the foreigner' – among his Gaelic kin.[15] Donald is said to have been a personal favourite of the king, and received the honour of knighthood on the field of Flodden. However, he never developed any lasting attachment to the House of Stewart. The new king, James V, was an infant, and Scotland faced a period of considerable uncertainty. By November 1513, Donald Gallda had been proclaimed Lord of the Isles and gathered a large force of men. With the aid of Alasdair Ranaldson of Glengarry, he captured Urquhart Castle and raided the nearby country of Clan Grant. In the Isles the rising was supported by Maclean of Duart, who captured the royal castle of Cairnburgh on Mull, while Macleod of Harris seized Dunskaith Castle on Skye. It was about this time that Clan Iain Mor made its reappearance in Scotland, rallying to Donald's cause under the leadership of Alexander of Dunyveg, sometimes known after his father as John Cathanachson.

Faced with this hostility in the Isles and the possibility of renewed English aggression, the new regent, John Stewart, Duke of Albany, had to tread with care. Commissions were issued to various men to bring the rebellion under control, although very little direct action appears to have been taken. In the end John Maciain of Ardnamurchan was appointed to open negotiations with the less intransigent among Donald Gallda's supporters. Colin Campbell, the third Earl of Argyll, was also important in this regard, using his influence to persuade all the principal rebels to submit. Even Sir Donald Gallda was sufficiently reassured by Argyll's guarantees of fair treatment that he made several appearances in Edinburgh. His dispute with Maciain of Ardnamurchan was submitted to arbitration and soon gave the appearance of being settled.[16] Matters proceeded so far that Albany felt confident enough to summon Donald to join him in 1516 for his planned invasion of England.

But contrary to appearances Donald Gallda had not abandoned his ambitions. He was entangled in a new intrigue, which appears to have involved negotiations with the English through the Border magnate Lord Home. After Home was executed for treason in October 1516, his followers took refuge with Donald in the Isles.[17] Soon after, Donald, pretending that he had been given a commission of lieutenancy in the Isles, persuaded a number of chiefs to support him with their armed followers, and then proceeded to ravage the lands that were supposedly under his protection. Maciain was expelled from Ardnamurchan and Mingary Castle, the principal seat of his family, was taken and destroyed. But the chiefs were now tiring of Donald. Once aware of his deception they began to abandon him. To try to restore their good standing with the government, Maclean of Duart and Macleod of Dunvegan attempted to capture the self-styled Lord of the Isles and hand him over to Albany. He managed to escape, but his two brothers were taken and sent to Edinburgh, where they were executed. In making his peace, Lachlan Maclean made an extraordinary proposal to the government: that it should take steps to seek out and destroy the last descendants of the Lord of the Isles, 'for as long as that blood reigns, the King shall never have the Isles in peace, whenever they find an opportunity to break loose, as is evident from daily experience'.[18]

By now all of Sir Donald's resentments were directed against Maciain of Ardnamurchan. Supposedly with the support of the Macleods of Lewis and Raasay and Alexander of Dunyveg, he met Maciain in battle at a place called Creag-an-Airgid or Silver Craig in Morvern sometime in 1518 or 1519. Maciain was killed, as were two of his sons, John Sunartach and Angus, along with a large number of his followers. Argyll at once demanded that the royal council pass sentence of forfeiture against Sir Donald. Oddly enough, this met with resistance from his fellow peers, forcing him to declare before parliament that he could no longer take responsibility for any mishaps that might in future arise from rebellion in the Isles. Argyll had built up a power base in the west at least equal to any of the old Lords of the Isles, and there were many that were clearly suspicious of his motives. The whole question was brought to an end, however, by the sudden death of Donald Gallda in 1519.

With the death of Sir Donald the direct line of Celestine of Lochalsh came to an end. Margaret, his sister, was married to Alasdair Ranaldson, chief of Glengarry, who laid claim to Sir Donald's Lochalsh estates. A formal claim was laid before the Lords of the Council in 1524. It was not until 1539, however, that Glengarry obtained a charter to the lands of Lochalsh, Lochcarron, and Lochbroom, with custody of Strome Castle.[19] This was to be a source of much future trouble with the Mackenzies, soon to be the dominant family in the old earldom of Ross.

The real beneficiary of the new peace in the Isles was Colin of Argyll. Once again enjoying a commission of lieutenancy, which was to become virtually hereditary in his family, he spent time consolidating his position by various alliances made with individual chieftains. These alliances, either through marriage or by means of a formal contract known as bonds of manrent, were a device allowing Argyll to advance his claim to the headship of the Gael. Soon he had connections with the Macleans of Duart and of Coll, the Macneils of Gigha and of Barra, the Stewarts of Appin, the Macleods of Dunvegan, the Mackinnons and Macquarries, as well as the Macdonalds of Largie and the Macalisters of Loup, two of the smaller branches of Clan Donald.[20] Argyll became the guardian of John Maciain's surviving children, and his brother, John, the first Campbell of the Cawdor line, was entrusted with the management of their estates. But by far the most important alliance created at this time was that between the Campbells and the Macdonalds of Dunyveg.

In 1517, before the death of Donald Gallda, Alexander of Dunyveg was pardoned. The Council was magnanimous enough to recognise his family had been forced into rebellion 'because thai have na heritage'.[21] Three years later, Alexander entered into a bond of manrent with John Campbell of Cawdor. In return for agreeing to become Cawdor's ally for a period of five years, Alexander received the island of Colonsay as well as an extensive grant of lands on Islay and Jura, formerly part of the Maciain inheritance. Alexander also gave a solemn pledge not to molest any of the Clan Maciain, several of whom lived on Islay. Two years later, presumably following the intercession of Argyll and Cawdor, Alexander received a further grant of lands on Kintyre from Regent Albany.[22] From being outlaws during the reign of James IV, Clan Iain Mor now began its steady ascent to greatness. For most of the remainder of the sixteenth century, the Macdonalds of Dunyveg enjoyed reasonably good relations with their Campbell neighbours, apart from one major interruption, which began in 1528. The cause of this was not Campbell perfidy, as is so often maintained, but once again the crass political insensitivity of a Stewart king.

In 1528, the young King James V finally freed himself from the tutelage of his hated guardian, the Earl of Angus, who had for some years dominated Scottish politics in succession to Albany. James' experience in growing up had not been very pleasant. He had a brooding, vindictive and suspicious side to his nature, inherited in part from his mother's Tudor relatives and from his own Stewart forebears, particularly James I, whom in many ways he resembled. His true attitude towards Highlanders may be deduced from his proposal in November 1528 to exterminate the men of Clan Chattan and dump their women and children on some foreign shore.[23] It was never carried out, but we see in this the ancestor of a Lowland thought-process that was, in time, to lead to the murder of the people of Glencoe.

Learning nothing from the experience of his father in 1498, one of James' first acts was to issue a revocation, clawing back all land grants made during his minority, including those to Alexander of Dunyveg. Argyll was then instructed to give effect to the revocation in the areas under his jurisdiction. This lead to the first serious clash between the Campbells and Macdonalds, and probably did much to end Argyll's painstaking attempt to have himself accepted as head of the Gael. Alexander rose in rebellion and was soon joined by the Macleans of Duart. In 1529 the two clans attacked the Campbell lands of Roseneath and Craignish, killing many of the inhabitants. Argyll and Cawdor responded by attacking their enemies on Mull, Tiree and Morvern. With matters getting out of hand, Campbell of Cawdor asked for extraordinary powers from the king to help deal with the emergency, including raising the men of the shires of Dunbarton and Renfrew and other places. Having stirred up a hornet's nest, James refused to grant this request, seemingly because he was suspicious of Argyll. Matters were still unresolved when the earl died in 1530; he was then succeeded by his son, Archibald.

Although the fourth Earl of Argyll received all his father's offices, including the lieutenancy of the Isles, James decided to bypass him and try the direct approach with the rebel chiefs. Offers of safe conduct were issued allowing the rebels to come to the king, with full protection from the Earl of Argyll. Although this met with an encouraging response, no definite conclusion was reached, and the king made ready to lead an expedition to the Isles in the spring of 1531. Parliament met on 26 April and passed sentence of forfeiture against all the rebels. Among those named was one individual described as 'Johane mordordach de ellanthoryn capitaneo de clanranald.'[24] With this John Moidertach of Clanranald makes his entry into history. He was to be quite a remarkable man, and it is as well to backtrack at this point to consider his origins.

Highland clans differed in one important respect from Lowland families: they were never reluctant to remove unpopular chiefs. In about 1513, Dougall MacRanald, the chief of Clanranald, was deposed and possibly murdered for unspecified acts of tyranny.[25] His uncle, Alexander MacAllan, replaced him. Alexander entered into a bond of manrent with John Campbell of Cawdor in February 1519, in which he is described as the Captain of Clanranald, the first occasion on which this famous title was used. From this point forward all chiefs of Clanranald used this designation, including John Moidertach, who succeeded his father in 1530. Although John enjoyed his inheritance for some time, with the full support of his clan, his succession was not beyond dispute. He had a kinsman, the son of an earlier chief by a second marriage to a daughter of Fraser of Lovat, and this man grew up among his Fraser kin, and came to be known among Clanranald as Ranald Gallda – 'the stranger'. When the opportunity came he attempted to replace John Moidertach.

John Moidertach was one of the principal supporters of Alexander of Islay. With the king threatening to come to the Isles, he and the other chiefs were in a position of great danger. Recognising this, Alexander at once opened up negotiations, offering to meet James at Stirling. Others followed his example, which effectively pulled the carpet from underneath the Earl of Argyll, a far less experienced man than his father. Alexander was restored to favour, and received a grant of his lands on Islay and Kintyre. Alarmed by his loss of influence, Argyll then adopted the dangerous tactic of alleging that Alexander had been guilty of various crimes. In the past, and in time to come, when threatened with Lowland courts Macdonald chiefs tended to hide away in the Isles. Argyll certainly hoped that Alexander would do this, which would then allow him to pursue the fugitive; instead, he called the bluff, and appeared in person before the council. It was Argyll, unable to back up his charges, who stayed in the west. But Alexander did not rest there. He immediately lodged his own counter-charges, claiming that Argyll had abused his position to advance his own interests rather than those of the king. Probably unbeknown to him, Alexander had selected just the right approach: James was always willing to harbour suspicions against his senior nobles. Argyll was summoned from the west and detained for a time in Edinburgh.[26] He appears never to have recovered his full authority in the Isles until after the death of James. Future Campbell chiefs were never again to make the third earl's attempt to have himself peacefully accepted as head of the Gaelic people. The acquisition of land was to become more important than the acquisition of ancient and vanished honours.

James was never close enough to any man to have personal favourites, but he was certainly willing to show a degree of political favouritism towards Alexander, allowing him to exercise some of the power formerly held by Argyll. There is, however, more in this than a simple desire to replace the Campbells with the Macdonalds. Alexander and the men of Clan Donald were useful to the king in his ongoing struggle with his uncle, Henry VIII of England. Alexander raised his kin and invaded Ulster, with the intention of creating trouble for the English and a diversion for James in the Border war of 1532, but despite this new association, there were always dangers for the Lowland authorities in placing too much trust in the Macdonalds, in view of their past traditions and ancient loyalties. We hear nothing over these years of the almost forgotten Donald Dubh, but the Lordship of the Isles remained far more than an empty memory.

The date of Alexander of Dunyveg's death is uncertain, but it seems to be sometime around 1539, the year a new claimant assumed the title of Lord of the Isles. Donald Gorme of Sleat was a descendant of Hugh, the youngest son of Alexander, third Lord of the Isles. The exact reason for Donald Gorme's rebellion is uncertain, as, indeed, is its timing. It may be connected with the death of Alexander and the failure of the king to make more substantial concessions to Clan Donald. In the absence of Argyll, moreover, royal authority in the Isles was not particularly strong, and it was into this obvious vacuum that Donald Gorme decided to step.

Much of the early history of the Macdonalds of Sleat or Clan Uisdein, as they are sometimes called, is fairly obscure. Apart from a few charter references, only Hugh Macdonald, the family historian, provides us with any clues. But much of his account is based upon conversations between people, unwitnessed and unrecorded at the time, and is clearly little more than an attempt to put some flesh on the bare bones of fact. It is not really until the early sixteenth century that the position becomes clearer, after Donald Grumach became chief.[27] By this time they were involved in a bitter dispute with the Macleods of Dunvegan over the Totternish peninsula, where they had apparently inherited the claim of Angus Og. Donald Grumach seems to have expelled the Macleods in about 1528. However, the struggle continued under Donald Gorme, who, in May 1539, invaded and occupied Totternish once again. To make the claim permanent, he moved the family headquarters from Dunscaith Castle in Sleat to Duntulm Castle in Totternish.[28] The Macleods appealed to the Privy Council, but before the matter could be settled, Donald took an even more dramatic step.

Taking advantage of the absence of Mackenzie of Kintail, Donald crossed to the mainland and laid claim to both the earldom of Ross and the Lordship of the Isles. After laying waste to some of the adjacent districts, he laid siege to the Mackenzie stronghold of Eilean Donan Castle. The garrison was under-strength and the castle would most likely have fallen to the insurgents, but for an unlucky accident: Donald came too close to the walls and was wounded by an arrow. In removing it he was unable to stop the flow of blood. He was taken to a nearby island by his followers and sheltered in a hut, where he died. As late as the nineteenth century, according to the historian Donald Gregory, local people would still point out the *Larach tigh Mhic Dhonuill* – 'the site of Macdonald's house'.[29]

The death of Donald Gorme brought this latest attempt to restore the Lordship to a sudden conclusion. However, the Isles appear to have remained in an unsettled condition, for we find that in the following year the king decided to come in person. In May 1540 he sailed with a small armada from the Firth of Forth, heading north, and then west from Orkney and south into the Isles, the first king to come this way since Hakon IV in 1263. The official reason given for the king's trip was to inspect the state of the fisheries, but he ended up, quite literally, as a fisher of men. From Stornoway south, he netted the rebellious chiefs, taking a particularly rich catch of Macdonalds at Totternish, including John Moidertach, and Alasdair of Glengarry and others 'quha allegit thame to be of the principalle bluide and lordis of the Iles'.[30] In the southern Hebrides, Hector Maclean of Duart and James of Dunyveg, the successor of Alexander, were also taken prisoner. Most of the chiefs were held as state prisoners until the death of James, including John Moidertach.

James' search for simple solutions to a complex problem made matters considerably worse. The chiefs came to see the king voluntarily and were forcibly detained, in yet another example of Stewart bad faith, which began with the 1427 parliament of Inverness. For his part in suppressing the rising, John Mackenzie of Kintail was granted the lands of Laggan and Invergarry and others belonging to the forfeited Alasdair of Glengarry. This simply laid the foundations for yet another murderous Highland feud, lasting some seventy years. With John Moidertach out of the way, Lord Lovat persuaded James to revoke all his previous charters and grant his lands to Ranald Gallda, who installed himself for a time as the head of Clanranald. John was never to forgive or forget the treatment he had received at the hands of the king, and after his release he was to be a source of almost continual trouble for successive governments.

James completed his exercise in December 1540, when parliament formally annexed the Lordship of the Isles inalienably to the crown; thus it resides to this day, among the many honours conferred upon the Prince of Wales. But the peace in the Isles was not to last. In 1542 the English routed the Scottish army at Solway Moss near Carlisle. James died soon after, reputedly of a broken heart, and his successor was his infant daughter, Mary. At only a week old, she was the youngest monarch ever to inherit the crown. Scotland, once again, faced a long royal minority. Given the factional struggle that inevitably followed, this was always a dangerous time. But the minority of Mary was more dangerous than most, for her great-uncle, Henry VIII, was soon seeking her as a bride for his own son, Edward. Many of the Lowland earls taken captive at Solway Moss were allowed to return home on the understanding that they would advance this aim. However, despite the best efforts of these men, Henry's overtures met with considerable resistance from many not willing to contemplate such a union. Henry responded with violence and the period known later as the Rough Wooing followed. It was during this that John Moidertach took to arms, but in a manner quite unconnected with Lowland politics. The Rough Wooing also provided the stage for one last attempt to restore the Lordship of the Isles.

6

A TIME OF TROUBLES

By the summer of 1543 the political situation was critical. For some time that great religious storm known as the Reformation had been raging in Western Europe. Henry VIII had himself broken with Rome in the 1530s. Now the tide was lapping against the shores of Scotland, the last Catholic power in northern Europe. The men taken at Solway Moss, most notably the Lowland Earls of Glencairn and Cassillis, had embraced the Reformed faith and the English alliance. Back home in Scotland they found themselves opposed by a national party, opposed both to the Reformation and to King Henry. This included among others the Earl of Huntly and Archibald Campbell, fourth Earl of Argyll. After his eclipse during the reign of James V, Argyll was now enjoying his own again. The outcome of the struggle clearly depended on who had control of the nation's affairs. There is no doubt that the best man for the vacant regency was Cardinal David Beaton, the chief minister of the late king. In the race to seize the reins of power he was, however, beaten by a far less capable individual – James Hamilton, Earl of Arran.

Arran is one of the puzzles of Scottish history. A man of no great principle or conviction, he gave the appearance of being on all sides, and none. As a policy maker he was bewilderingly inconsistent, ultimately serving no interest but his own.[1] The appointment of Beaton, a known political and religious enemy of Henry VIII, would most likely have been followed by an immediate English invasion at a time when Scotland was particularly vulnerable. Arran, on the other hand, looked as if he was prepared to do business with Henry and his Scottish fifth column. But in trusting Arran, Henry effectively threw away all the advantages he gained from his triumph at Solway Moss. When the truth became known, it was already too late.

Having lost his hand in one game, Beaton tried another. Fearful of the political and religious trend of Arran's policies in the early months of 1543, he brought home from France Matthew Stewart, Earl of Lennox. Lennox, like Arran, had strong blood connections with the royal house of Scotland, and believed that he had the better right to the post of governor. Beaton, of course, was well aware of the suggestion of illegitimacy in Arran's line, and used Lennox to remind the governor of this possible Achilles' heel. This was bad enough, but Argyll and Huntly had now taken up arms against him. Some kind of military diversion was clearly needed in the north and west, and it was to be provided by Donald Dubh.

By 1543 Donald, now in his fifties, had spent most of his unfortunate life in prison. The terms of this imprisonment were not gentle, if we can believe his own claim that he had been kept in chains.[2] This is certainly possible, for, as a pretender to the Lordship of the Isles, he was a prisoner of the greatest importance. Sir James Macdonald of Knockrinsay, last chief of the house of Dunyveg, was also to be kept in chains, although his political significance was far less than that of Donald. It would appear that Donald did not escape, as is usually claimed, but was deliberately released sometime during the course of the year. This cannot be proved, but it seems odd that the records are almost completely silent on the manner of his supposed escape: we do not even know the exact time of year. All that can be said with any certainty is that Arran, on the advice of Glencairn, later released all the Highland chiefs taken by James V in 1540, including John Moidertach of Clanranald. These men were freed to create a diversion against Argyll and Huntly, and so it remains a strong possibility that Donald Dubh was released for the same reason. In the short term the policy was remarkably successful, but in the long term it created a major political headache for Arran.

Donald knew his enemy. No sooner was he back in the Isles than he gathered some 1800 men and attacked the territory of Argyll, killing many of his men and carrying off much livestock. The two sides entered into a truce, but this seems to have been little more than a breathing space, allowing them to muster their forces for fresh blows.[3] Argyll was now too preoccupied defending his flank in the west to play much of a part in the political struggle elsewhere in Scotland. However, he was fortunate in at least one respect: the 1528 breach with the house of Dunyveg had now been mended, depriving Donald Dubh of the support of this most important branch of Clan Donald.

Unlike the other branches of their family, the Macdonalds of Dunyveg had not been badly handled by the late king in 1540, and thus harboured no deep-rooted resentments against the Scottish state. When Argyll's influence revived on the death of James V, he took pains to cultivate James of Dunyveg, Alexander's son and successor. In 1543 Argyll was given a ten-year lease of the old Maciain estates, including their extensive holdings on Islay, and these in turn were leased to James. In 1545, as Donald Dubh's rising was close to its height, James married Lady Agnes Campbell, Argyll's sister. At about the same time he received further extensive grants of land in Kintyre and Jura, along with smaller allotments on Arran, Gigha, Colonsay and elsewhere.[4] James was by now the biggest landowner on Islay, and enjoyed his territories not as a tenant or subtenant, but as a feudal baron with a charter from the crown. Apart from one brief interruption, the house of Dunyveg was firmly allied to the Campbells for some time, even supporting the fifth earl when he switched allegiance from the Catholic party to the Reformers later in the century.

With Argyll preoccupied with Donald Dubh, Huntly's problems were, if anything, even worse. Ranald Gallda had never been fully accepted by the people of Clanranald. Although he was to prove himself a brave and courageous man, the traces he has left in clan tradition are far from flattering. Highland chiefs were always expected to be lavish with their hospitality. However, when Ranald saw some oxen being prepared to celebrate his inauguration as chief, he is said to have remarked that chickens would have done as well, earning him the nickname of *Raonuill nan Cearc* – 'Ranald of the Hens'.[5] When John Moidertach reappeared in the summer of 1543, Ranald, with no local support, was forced to take refuge with his Fraser kinsmen. Lord Lovat at once prepared to defend his rights. True to his nature, John did not wait to be attacked – he carried his own war eastwards.

John summoned his kin and allies in the early summer of 1544. He was joined by the Camerons, the Maciains of Ardnamurchan, the Macdonalds of Glengarry and by Ranald Mor, seventh chief of the Macdonalds of Keppoch, from whom subsequent chiefs were to acquire their Gaelic title *Mac Mhic Raonaill* – 'son of Ranald's son'. The combined force then advanced east, carrying out an extensive raid in the districts of Abertarff and Stratherrick, the property of Lord Lovat, and the nearby estates of Urquhart and Glenmoriston, belonging to the Grants. Urquhart Castle on Loch Ness was also taken. This raid was more than a simple family feud; it was a major provocation to the government, and especially to George Gordon, the fourth Earl of Huntly. Gathering the levies of the north, including those of Lord Lovat and the Laird of Grant, Huntly advanced to meet the insurgents. Ranald Gallda came with the Frasers of Lord Lovat. But John now proved himself to be a guerilla leader of some genius. Rather than risking a battle with a stronger enemy force, he retreated right back to his own country, the almost impregnable territory known as the Rough Bounds, the area between Loch Sunart in the south and Loch Hourn in the

north, the very heartland of Clanranald.[6] Donald Gregory claims that
Huntly managed to advance right into Moidart to restore Ranald
Gallda, but there appears to be no evidence for this assertion, as the
authors of *Clan Donald* point out.[7] Surrounded by enemies, Ranald is
not likely to have felt very safe in Moidart. When Huntly returned to
the east, so too did Ranald Gallda.

No sooner had the enemy retreated than John advanced. Keeping
out of sight, he shadowed Huntly as far as the mouth of Glen Spean in
Lochaber. Here the enemy forces separated, with Huntly and the Laird
of Grant returning to Badenoch, while Lovat with Ranald Gallda returned to his own country, with no more than 400 men in all. This was
the moment John had waited for. Moving fast, he crossed to the north
of Loch Lochy in the Great Glen, ready to intercept the Frasers, marching along the southern bank. Seeing the danger he was in, Lovat sent
part of his force to take a nearby pass, which would offer some prospect
of retreat if things went wrong. He then prepared to engage the
Macdonalds and Camerons.

The Battle of Kinloch-Lochy began in the age-old Highland fashion
with a discharge of arrows. Once the missile weapons were exhausted,
both sides moved in to a terrible close-quarter engagement with
battleaxes and the huge two handed swords known as claymores. As
the grim struggle proceeded John's men began to prevail over their
Fraser opponents. Lovat attempted to disengage, but the men of
Clanranald had taken the pass through which he intended to make his
escape. Cut off, the Frasers fought to the death with savage courage,
and were apparently completely wiped out by their enemies. In noting
the outcome of the Battle of Kinloch-Lochy, Bishop John Leslie says
that it 'was reported that at this field thair was none of the surname of
the Frasers left levand that was cum to mannis age'.[8] Lord Lovat, his
eldest son, and Ranald Gallda were among the dead, along with several
hundred others. For days afterwards the Loch is said to have been red
with blood.[9]

The battle was fought in mid-July 1544, and the day is said to have
been so hot that both sides threw off their plaids, fighting in their
shirts. This supposedly gave rise to the Gaelic name for the battle of
Blar-na-Leine – 'the Field of Shirts', although this is almost certainly a
mistake for *Blar-na-Leana* – 'the Field of the Swampy Meadow'.
Highland armies at this time were still wearing chain-mail, as we know
from a reference by an English observer in Ireland in the year after the
Battle of Kinloch-Lochy.[10] This is supported in tradition by the tale
that the armourers of Clanranald and the Frasers laid blows on one
another to test the quality of their workmanship.[11] It was not until the

following century that Highland armies advanced into battle clad in plaid without body armour.

Huntly appears to have been unable to mount an effective response to this humiliation. Although he wasted the lands of some of the rebels, he made no attempt to penetrate the dangerous Rough Bounds. For some considerable time afterwards he took no more part in pacifying the north, drawn off by affairs elsewhere in Scotland. This allowed John and his allies to take revenge on the Grants of Glenmoriston, Huntly's allies, and a spectacular revenge it was. In April 1545 the Captain of Clanranald, aided by Cameron of Locheil and the chiefs of Glengarry, Keppoch and Glencoe, swept west and carried out a month-long raid in the neighbourhood of Urquhart Castle, carrying off a huge quantity of livestock and other movable goods. What could not be moved was burned.[12] In September 1545 John was summoned before parliament on a charge of treason. Secure in the Rough Bounds he ignored this summons and several others. Faced with such intransigence, the government was reduced to impotence.

While John was establishing his undisputed hold on Clanranald, the rebellion of Donald Dubh began to gather momentum in the west, greatly helped by the increasingly tense relations between Henry VIII and Governor Arran. In the summer of 1543, Arran finally abandoned his erstwhile support for the Reformed religion and the English alliance, allowing him to make peace with Cardinal Beaton. With no further use for Lennox, Beaton promptly dropped the frustrated nobleman. Although he remained a good Catholic, Lennox immediately started to intrigue with the Reform party and the English king. Henry, furious at the rejection of the treaty under which Mary and Edward were to be married, became increasingly violent. Edinburgh was destroyed in the spring of 1544 in a seaborne raid carried out by the Earl of Hertford. Henry decided to increase the pressure by using Lennox to make contact with the rebels in the Isles. Up to now, Donald Dubh's war had been little more than a local contest between him and Argyll. It was now to embrace the whole of the Isles and the rest of the Irish Sea world.

By the summer of 1544 Lennox was engaged in open rebellion, conducting naval raids in the Firth of Clyde on behalf of the English that included attacks on the Earl of Argyll and his ally James of Dunyveg. Yet it seems odd that no attempt was apparently made to exploit the potential offered by the rebellion in the Isles. Seemingly not until December 1544 did the English become fully aware of 'a new king in Scotland out of the Scottyshe Irysshe'.[13] The following year Lennox was appointed to open negotiations with Donald Dubh, much as the last Earl of Douglas had established contact with his grandfather, prior to the Westminster agreement of 1462. In May 1545 Donald had offered to enter the service of the English king. The full military potential of the rebellion in the Isles was clearly demonstrated the following August, when he arrived at Carrickfergus in Ireland with a force of 4000 men carried there in no less than 180 galleys[14] – and this was only half his strength, for another 4000 had been left in Scotland to create trouble for Argyll.

Under Donald Dubh, the old Council of the Isles had revived, which included all the chiefs of Clan Donald, including John Moidertach, no doubt something of a hero among his kin. The obvious exception was James Macdonald of Dunyveg and the Glens, but his brother Angus took part, suggesting that even he was hedging his bets. That James had not entirely given up on the ancient honours of his family was to be seen in the near future.

The Council of the Isles, acting in the name of Donald Dubh, appointed two plenipotentiaries to enter into negotiations with the English king under the guidance of the Earl of Lennox. A formal treaty was entered into. Among other things, the Islemen were promised a subsidy in return for supporting the cause of the English king. It is also stated that there should be no agreement with Argyll until Donald 'recovers the possessions which Argyll falsely took from him while he was in prison.'[15] It is difficult to know what this means, as Argyll had not taken direct control of any of the old Lordship, unless it is meant to indicate that he had usurped a general authority in the Isles. In confirming the terms of the treaty the Council of the Isles wrote to Henry in September, saying, 'it is to be remembered that we have always been enemies to the realm of Scotland, who, when at peace with the King (of England) hanged, hedit, presond, and destroed many of our kyn, friendis and forbears'.[16]

However, the rebellion, one of the greatest ever in the Isles and potentially of extreme danger to the realm of Scotland, was appallingly mismanaged. Lennox was clearly vital to its success, but instead of remaining to direct affairs in Ireland and the Isles, he was sent to join Hertford in the Border raids of September 1545, which did absolutely nothing to advance Henry's cause. By the time he returned Donald's army had largely disintegrated in a squabble over the distribution of the English subsidy.

It is a matter of some regret that in this last great act of his life we still get very little sense of the real Donald Dubh. His return to the Isles after such a long absence was greeted with great enthusiasm, judging by the number of men who rallied to his cause. Yet he still seems a very negative, almost insubstantial figure, of no great authority; it is as if his kin rallied to his cause simply for who he was rather than what he offered. It took the Earl of Lennox, a Lowlander, to give the rebellion any real sense of direction, and after he had gone it drifted out of control. The *Book of Clanranald* records the following: 'A ship came from England with a supply of money to carry on the war, which landed at Mull; and the money was given to Maclean of Dowart to be distributed among the commanders of the army; which they not receiving a proportion as it should have been distributed among them, caused the army to disperse.'[17]

Donald appears to have neither had the authority nor the charisma to hold the argumentative chiefs together. In this, perhaps, we can see the shade of his grandfather, John, last Lord of the Isles, rather than that of his father, Angus Og. Soon after Lennox returned, all hope of a fresh enterprise gone, Donald died of fever at Drogheda in Ireland, a tragic end to a tragic life. According to the *Book of Clanranald* he had no children; but we know that he had a bastard son, whom he commended to the care of Henry VIII.[18] Nothing more is recorded of this child, not even his name. He must therefore be presumed to have died at an early age.

It is sometimes claimed, on no sure evidence, that Donald nominated James of Dunyveg as his successor, but why he should have done so when James held aloof from his cause is not explained. The claim to the Lordship in the senior line should have passed to the Macdonalds of Sleat. However, the chief, Donald Gormeson was still a child, and it is unlikely that the family had fully recovered from the 1539 rebellion. But for James the opportunity was too good to let pass, despite his alliance with Argyll. Clearly excited by the prospect of a further English subsidy, he wrote to the Council of Ireland in January 1546 offering his services to Henry and describing himself as the 'heir of the Isles'.[19] He never received an answer. Although he obtained the support of the formidable John Moidertach and others of his kin, he achieved very little, beyond the rather pointless destruction of the little town of Saltcoats in Ayrshire. But lacking the general support enjoyed by Donald Dubh, and receiving no military or financial assistance from the English, his whole enterprise soon lost momentum. In the summer of 1546 he once again made his peace with Argyll and the government of Scotland. There was never again to be a serious attempt to restore the Lordship of the Isles. The chiefs of Sleat were, in time, to adopt the Gaelic title *MacDonuill na'n Eilean* – 'Macdonald of the Isles' – in reference to a vanished glory. Over time the families of the Isles began to drift apart, each looking to defend their own interests rather than seek a common cause. Before the end of the century the Macdonalds of Dunyveg were to become involved in a dispute with the Macleans of Mull which was to bring about their extinction.

Even after the submission of James of Dunyveg, the political situation in the north remained highly volatile. John of Moidart continued to defy the authorities from the security of the Rough Bounds. Alasdair Ranaldson of Glengarry had been forfeited for his own part in the Battle of Kinloch-Lochy and all his lands granted in life rent to James Grant of Freuchie, but this made little practical difference. He defied orders to give up Castle Strome to Grant, and was supported in his defiance by all his kin in the northern part of Clan Donald. However, the government enjoyed one small success when the Captain of Clan Chattan captured Cameron of Locheil and Ranald Macdonald of Keppoch, both of whom had fought on the side of John of Moidart against the Frasers. They were tried for high treason at Elgin and be-headed; both heads were then fixed to the town gates as a warning to the others.[20] If this was intended to have a sobering effect, then it failed in its aim.

The death of Henry VIII in January 1547 did nothing to ease the tension between Scotland and England. The sickly boy king, Edward VI, spurned bridegroom of Mary, Queen of Scots, now occupied the throne of England. His uncle, Edward Seymour, formerly Earl of Hertford and now Duke of Somerset, had himself appointed Protector of the Kingdom. His chief aim was to continue the Rough Wooing on behalf of his nephew. With Scotland facing a major invasion from the south, Arran summoned the country to arms, including the northern and western chiefs. Interestingly, he used the fiery cross, a device per-fected by the Lords of the Isles. But John of Clanranald and many others ignored the summons, not prepared to trust their wellbeing to the good faith of the Lowland authorities. There was little Arran could do in the circumstances, and even less after he was catastrophically defeated by Somerset at the Battle of Pinkie in September 1547. With the English in control of south-east Scotland, Arran made the best of a bad situation and pardoned the Highland deserters on fairly easy terms the following year.

It made little difference to John if the Lowland government frowned or smiled; he continued to go his own way. In 1552 he was summoned to meet the Regent at Aberdeen. He failed to come. Arran, a mild man, was probably sincere in desiring to be reconciled with the Highland chief, but after his experience at the hands of James V in 1540, John was not going to be drawn so easily. He was outlawed once again, and Huntly was authorised to proceed against him, with no better result than before. Two years later Mary of Guise, the Queen Mother, took over the direction of the country's affairs from Arran. The Rough Wooing had failed, her daughter Mary was safe in France – in time to marry the Dauphin Francis – so the Queen Regent was free to devote her time to dealing with the problem of law and order. At this time, the problem of law and order was John Moidertach and his kinsman, Donald Gormeson of Sleat, engaged in an ugly dispute with the Mackenzie enemies of his family.

In June 1554, soon after Mary of Guise assumed the regency, Huntly and Argyll were ordered to destroy Clanranald and the Macdonalds of Skye, as well as the Macleods of Lewis.[21] While Argyll was given a ship and artillery to deal with matters in the Isles, Huntly was given the task of attacking Clanranald from the mainland. This two-pronged attack was a total failure. Argyll probably lacked sufficient naval resources to push his offensive. Huntly failed for a simpler reason: the Lowland cavalry assigned to him refused to ride into the wild Highlands. Not willing to trust himself to the infantry of Clan Chattan, who blamed him for the execution of their chief some years before, Huntly abandoned the whole project. Furious at this, the Regent had him thrown into prison. The task of bringing the stubborn John of Moidart under control was then delegated to the Earl of Atholl.

Faced with a leader of John's ability, force and threats of force had been a clear failure, so Atholl decided on a less militant method. He was clearly a man possessed of a persuasive manner; for he managed to get John to agree to appear before the Regent in person, accompanied by two of his sons and some of his leading kinsmen. John had been defying the government for over ten years, so Atholl had achieved a minor diplomatic triumph. Mary of Guise, learning nothing from the actions of her husband, promptly threw this all away. She was gracious enough to pardon the past offences of the men of Clanranald, but then spoiled this by ordering that they be detained in the Lowlands for the time being. All escaped back to the Highlands, hotly pursued by the regent's furious and empty denunciations. It would not be so easy to tempt them back. John Lesley wrote of this: 'yit as the tod can not byd furth of his hoill, eftir thay had tareit thair certane space, thay brak thair wordis, and past secreitlie in thair awin contray, quhaire they streit up be thair counsall new troble agane . . .'[22]

In 1556 Mary came north in person, accompanied by Argyll and Huntly, to dispense royal justice. John Moidertach, however, remained secure, hidden by the mountains and guarded by his kin. Neither force, nor threats of treason, nor diplomacy and false promises would work for as long as John enjoyed the love and trust of Clanranald. Soon, her hands filled with the onset of the Reformation, Mary of Guise could devote no more time to the affairs of the north. Ten years later, after the return of Mary, Queen of Scots from France, the following problem was placed before parliament: 'be quhat means may all Scotland be brocht to universal obedience and how may Johne Moydart . . . be dantonit.'[23] Significantly, no answer ever seems to have been made. John finally died in 1584, defiant to the last. He deserves to be remembered as the greatest of all the captains of Clanranald.

Before continuing our narrative we have to pause for a time to consider one of the great puzzles of John Moidertach's time as chief. This concerns the Eigg Massacre, which is said to have occurred in 1577. In that year, the people of Eigg, a branch of Clanranald, mishandled some of the vassals of Alasdair Crotach, chief of the Macleods.[24] Seeking revenge, Alasdair sailed to the island with a great force. At the approach of the enemy, the Macdonalds all sought refuge in a cave by the name of *Uaimh Fhraing* – 'the Cave of Francis' – situated on the south-east of the island. Here they were discovered and the Macleod chief ordered a great fire to be lit at the mouth of the cave. All those within – almost 400 people – suffocated. Considering the enormity of this crime, involving as it did the murder of men, women and children, it is surprising that it receives absolutely no mention in the records of the time, existing only in tradition. However, it is certain there was a massacre on the island. For hundreds of years the bones of the slain remained as mute witness to the fact that some awful crime had indeed taken place, and no one was left to bury the dead. Sir Walter Scott visited the cave in 1814, helping himself to a skull, and thus beginning a tradition of ghoulish tourism.[25] Many skeletons were still to be found in the 1840s, when the geologist Hugh Miller came this way, although by this time all the skulls had been removed.[26]

There is nothing beyond tradition, strong as it is, to suggest that the Macleods were responsible for the massacre. However, we do know that, several years after 1577, Lachlan Mor Maclean of Duart was involved in a savage war with most of Clan Donald of the Isles. In this he used all means at his disposal, including employing a body of Spanish soldiers, who had sailed with the Armada of 1588. In January 1589 it is noted in the Privy Council records that, in the previous October, Maclean:

> accompanyed with a grite nowmer of thevis, brokin men, and sornaris of Clannis, besides the nowmer of ane hundreth Spanyeatis, come, bodin in beir of weir, to his Majesties propir ilis of Canna, Rum, Eg and the Ile of Elennole, and, eftir they had sorner, wracked, and spoilled the sadis haill Illis, thay tressonable rased fyre, and in maist barbarous, shameful and cruell maner,

brynt the same Illis, with the haill men, wemen and childrene
being thairintill, not sparing pupillis and infantis . . .[27]

It is not believable that the whole population of Eigg could have been
wiped out in 1577, only to recover and be wiped out again eleven
years later. Why, moreover, is there no mention of the Macleod atrocity
in the *Book of Clanranald*, a rich source of family traditions? Besides,
there are other problems with the traditional tale. Alasdair Crotach
had been dead for at least thirty years before the massacre. The
Macdonald dead are said to have included Angus, a son of John
Moidertach. The Clanranald chief was now quite elderly, but one has
to doubt if such a formidable warrior would have allowed this to pass
unavenged. Finally, considering the documented courage of the people
of Clanranald, are we to accept that they ran away from their enemies
to die in such a fashion?[28] Either the story of the Macleod massacre
has been exaggerated, or, what is more likely, it simply never happened.

Well before the death of John of Clanranald, the Reformation had
gained a firm grip on Scotland. But the whole question of religion was
complicated by other factors, notably land greed and power politics.
Mary of Guise defended the old faith, but she also defended the French
connection. Ever since the Rough Wooing there had been a steady
increase in the number of French troops in Scotland. For many, including
the Queen Regent's former ally, Archibald, Earl of Argyll, the French
were now as much a threat to Scottish liberty, and their own political
interests, as the English had ever been. Mary found herself faced with
powerful domestic opposition, organised in a body known as the Lords
of the Congregation. After Argyll's death in August 1558, his son and
namesake, Archibald, the fifth earl, became one of the leading figures
among these men. In looking for allies, Mary turned to the west. Sir
Ralph Sadler, an English diplomat, notes her attempts to woo James of
Dunyveg and the 'other Scottish Irishie' to create a diversion against
Argyll.[29] It seems fairly certain that James, like many others of his
family and kin, remained Catholic in conviction, but there were political
and territorial considerations to take into account. His family was
increasingly involved in building up their power in Ulster, and there
were already worrying signs of a growing dispute with the Macleans
over an area to the west of Islay known as the Rhinns. To maintain
their position the Macdonalds of Dunyveg would come to depend on
the goodwill and support of their Campbell kin. In October 1559 James
came west with 700 men to join the Lords of the Congregation.[30] The
following year the Reformers, with the support of the English, forced
the French to leave Scotland. Mary of Guise died in Edinburgh Castle,
her life's work undone.

At the start of the personal reign of Mary, Queen of Scots, it was not the power of Clan Campbell that was of most concern to Clan Donald of the Isles, but that of the Macleans of Duart, their allies of former days. Even before the end of the Lordship, the Macleans had established a strong presence in the west, with branches of the family on Mull, Coll, Tiree and the mainland districts of Ardgour and Morvern. With territorial power came political influence, and by 1517 the chief of Duart, the most important branch of Clan Gillean, could number the Macneils of Barra and the Macquarries of Ulva among his allies. We cannot be certain about the origin of the dispute between the Macleans and Macdonalds over the Rhinns of Islay. It might possibly have originated in some office the Macleans held under the Lord of the Isles, and we certainly know from reading Hugh Macdonald that family tensions were building up prior to the naval battle at Bloody Bay. It was an issue that simply refused to go away.

In 1506 the Laird of Duart claimed certain lands on Islay. Although it was disallowed, the claim resurfaced in 1542. Four years later, Hector Maclean renounced his alleged rights on Islay to James Macdonald, but in 1562 the two sides were in open conflict. Acting under some unidentified provocation, the Macdonalds of Dunyveg allied with the Macdonalds of Sleat attacked Tiree and Coll. Matters reached such a pitch that both James of Dunyveg and Hector Maclean of Mull were summoned to appear before the Privy Council in December 1563.[31] Hector failed to appear, and in April of the following year the matter was decided in favour of James.[32] The Macleans were never reconciled to this decision. Nothing happened for some years, though, after the death of Hector Maclean, and during the minority of the new chief; but in 1578 Lachlan Mor Maclean came of age. Clan Donald was now confronted with one of the most ruthless opponents it ever faced.

Prior to this Clan Iain Mor had achieved a power and prestige greater than any other branch of the family, either during or after the Lordship of the Isles. But in building a new empire in Ireland the Islay branch of the family pushed itself to exhaustion, and beyond that to ruin.

7

SORLEY BOY AND THE MACDONNELLS OF ANTRIM

From 1169, during the reign of Henry II of England, Anglo-Norman adventurers began to arrive in Ireland in increasing numbers. Soon they established a permanent hold of the old Viking kingdom of Dublin. Ireland had not embraced feudalism and was still divided into a number of petty kingdoms, where royal succession was decided on the basis of tanistry, in the ancient Celtic fashion. These chieftains lacked a professional warrior class, sufficiently skilled to counter the serious threat posed by the newcomers from the east. It seemed natural, therefore, to call on the aid of their cousins in the kingdom of the Isles. Over time a new Gaelic warrior class took shape, well able to meet both the English and native Irish in battle. These men were called *galloglaigh,* a word anglicised to gallowglas, meaning foreign serving man or mercenary. Clan Donald were one of the principal sources of *galloglaich*, and for centuries exported men from the Isles to the almost continuous wars in Ireland, a practice which only came to an end with the Union of the Crowns in 1603 and the subsequent Plantation of Ulster.[1]

The earliest reference we have to Macdonald *galloglaigh* is for the year 1264.[2] Thereafter they occur with increasing frequency. Many of these men found permanent homes in Ireland, not just in those areas adjacent to the Hebrides, but throughout the whole island. This was a natural process, for by the early Middle Ages the people of the Western Isles had more in common with their fellow Gaels in Ireland than their fellow Scots in Aberdeen. Ireland's demand for warriors also provided a much-needed outlet for the surplus military potential of Clan Donald and others. The sons of Alexander Og, chief of Clan Donald until his death in 1299, appear to have remained in Ireland, becoming prominent *galloglaich*. During the Wars of Independence, Clan Donald and their cousins of Clan Ruari provided, as we have seen, the troops and transports for the Bruce invasions of Ireland. There is even a reference in the *Irish Annals* for 1365 of a mysterious figure by the name of Somhairle Macdonald, described as heir to the lordship of Innse Gall and a prominent captain of the mercenary forces in Ulster.[3] By the beginning of the fifteenth century Macdonald warrior dynasties were firmly rooted in the provinces of Ulster, Connacht and Leinster.

The emergence of the Lordship of the Isles in the fourteenth century was important, not only for the internal politics of Scotland, but also for the politics of England and Ireland. Indeed, early English diplomatic contacts with the Lords of the Isles should probably be viewed as much in the context of Anglo-Gaelic relations than Anglo-Scottish relations. In 1404, for example, an Irish chief used a large force of men from the 'outer isles' to devastate the area around Downpatrick and Coleraine. Later the same year the English authorities in Dublin were worried that the colony would never recover from this, unless those who fled from the area were able to return in time for the harvest.[4] To try to establish some sort of peace, John Dongon, Bishop of Down, was authorised to open negotiations with Donald, Lord of the Isles. Negotiations continued until the spring of 1408, and although no formal agreement was reached, relations seem to have improved. Donald was now too preoccupied with the earldom of Ross in Scotland at this time, and was probably keen to get the support, or at least the goodwill of the English.

Although these early Clan Donald migrants established themselves as a permanent caste of professional soldiers, there was soon little to distinguish them from the native peoples in all other respects. The real beginnings of a separate Clan Donald power in Ireland came, as we discussed in an earlier chapter, with the marriage of John Mor Tanister, the brother of Donald of Harlaw, to Marjory Bisset, heiress to that part of north-east Antrim known as the Glens, in about 1399. The Glens embraced a substantial swathe of territory from Ballycastle to Larne, and included Rathlin Island. The location of this territory is also of some considerable importance. Because it was only a few short sea miles from Islay and the centre of Clan Donald power, a new territorial block could be constructed, in a way that could not if Marjory's inheritance had been in distant Leinster. From John onwards, the chiefs of Clan Iain Mor linked their Scottish and Irish territories as the Macdonalds of Dunyveg and the Glens. This bridge across two worlds was to be of crucial importance in relations with both England and Scotland. It also provided an important refuge for the Dunyveg chiefs, beyond the reach of the King of Scots, as Donald Balloch, John Mor's successor, had demonstrated after the Battle of Inverlochy. Donald Balloch managed to escape all the treacherous political currents of the time, dying at home in Islay in 1476, well respected as a chief and warrior among his people, just as his cousin John was leading the Lordship to its final disaster.

Until at least the end of the Lordship of the Isles in 1493, the Glens was little more than a personal holding of the chiefs of Dunyveg, whose tenants were mostly native Irish families. However, from about 1500 onwards, the people of the Isles began to settle permanently in the Glens. By the middle of the century the Macdonnells, as they are usually known in Ireland, were fully established as a permanent feature in a bewilderingly complex game of international politics, played out between them, the Scots, the English and the native Irish. This equation was made even more confusing by the regular intervention of the Campbells and Macleans, seeking to play their own hand. Before trying to make sense of this we have to say a few words about the history of England's involvement in Ireland.

Henry II, the first Plantagenet, is said to have obtained a mandate to rule Ireland from Adrian IV, the only English Pope. Thus from the Middle Ages, the King of England also claimed to be Lord of Ireland. English settlers moved steadily east and south from the initial base of settlement around Dublin, although this process was halted and then reversed at the time of the Bruce Wars. By the high Middle Ages English control was largely confined to the area around Dublin known as the Pale, with the rest of Ireland given over, in English eyes, to Gaelic savagery, and thus 'beyond the Pale'. This was particularly true of the ancient province of Ulster in the north, where English influence was only ever minimal. By the end of the Middle Ages this began to change, especially after the Tudors took the throne of England from the Plantagenets in 1485.

For England and the Atlantic powers like Spain and France the strategic focus shifted away from southern Europe and the Mediterranean to the New World at the end of the Middle Ages. This gave Ireland a greatly enhanced importance in English eyes. What had once been, so to speak, a barbarous backyard, now stood astride the vital sea-lanes to the west. For England, the picture became even more dangerous after the Reformation. While the new Protestant faith made headway in England during the reign of Henry VIII and his children, Edward VI and Elizabeth I, Ireland remained obdurately attached to Catholicism. This created a major strategic headache for the English, for it was always open to her major political competitors, the Catholic powers of Spain and France, to seek to make trouble in Ireland. To try to close this chink in her defensive armour, England under the Tudors set out to extend her control of Ireland.

In breaking his link with the Papacy, Henry VIII sought to define a new relationship by having himself declared King of Ireland in 1541. Irish chiefs were drawn into his net, initially in a fairly conciliatory way. In return for surrendering their lands to the king they received them back in a formal feudal grant, together with an English title, a process that James III might be said to have pioneered in his treatment of the Lord of the Isles in 1476. For example, Con Bacagh O'Neil, head of the most powerful native Irish clan in Ulster, gave up his proud Gaelic designation of 'The O'Neil' in return for the far less satisfactory English title of Earl of Tyrone. This was to cause tremendous friction within a conservative kin-based group, and was soon seen to be of limited political value. Having failed in the expressed aim of attaching the Gaels to the English throne, the so-called policy of surrender and regrant was replaced during the reign of Elizabeth I by one of outright conquest. For Elizabeth and her various Irish viceroys, there was no room for outsiders in Ireland; and by the 1550s the chief outsider was Clan Donald.

England probably had very little interest in John Mor's original acquisition of the Bisset inheritance in the Glens, for Ulster at that time was too far beyond its control. Besides, as the Gaels of the Western Isles had no strong attachment at that time to the Kings of Scotland, there was no great strategic issue at stake. This changed as the King of Scots established a firmer authority in the west from the time of James IV, and the English later began to probe north of Dublin. James V was probably the first King of Scots since Robert Bruce to appreciate the strategic importance of Ireland. This, in part, explains why he was prepared to set aside the alliance his father had made with the Campbells, in favour of Alexander Macdonald, fifth chief of Dunyveg and the Glens.[5] The two men enjoyed something of a symbiotic relationship; Alexander offered James a way of making trouble for Henry VIII in Ireland to counter English pressure on the Border, while James offered Alexander a way of extending his family's influence in Ulster. In 1532, with King James' approval, he crossed the North Channel with 8000 men, a force he used to push westwards into Tyrconnel and Connacht. The English Council in Dublin was so alarmed by these developments that it wrote to Henry VIII the year after:

> The Scottes also inhabite now buyselley a graet parte of Ulster, which is the King's inheritance; and it is greatlie to be feared, oonles thatin a short tyme they be dryven from the same that they, bringinge in more nombre daily, woll, by lyttle and lyttle soe far encroche in acquyringe and wynninge the possessions there, with the aid of the kingis disobeysant Irishe rebelles . . . that at lengthe they will put and expel the King from his hole seignory there.[6]

Alexander's power was based on the simple fact that he was able to ferry troops across the North Channel from Islay and Kintyre at very little notice, responding to each situation as it developed. The English gave the name 'redshank' to these new warriors from the Isles. Although similar to their *galloglaich* ancestors, the redshanks did not tend to settle in Ireland, remaining only for the campaigning season, before returning to winter in their homes in the Isles. They were to be a regular feature of warfare in Ulster until the end of the century.

By the time of the death of Alexander in 1539, Clan Iain Mor had experienced a dramatic reversal in its fortunes. Outlawed from Scotland under James IV, they were now established in a crucial strategic position, dominating both sides of the North Channel. Their position was further improved in 1545, when James Macdonald, Alexander's son and successor, married Lady Agnes Campbell, daughter of the third Earl of Argyll. This was another of the great political marriages in Macdonald history, ensuring that Clan Iain Mor would enjoy good relations with the Scottish government and Clan Campbell in the crucial years to follow, apart from a brief interruption in 1546.

Apart from James, Alexander had five other sons – Angus, Colla, Alasdair Oge, Donnell Gorme and the youngest, to whom he gave the name Somhairle. Called in Gaelic Somhairle Buidhe – 'Somerled the Fair' – he is more widely known as Sorley Boy. He was to grow into one of the greatest of all the leaders of Clan Donald, a worthy representative of his ancestor and namesake. But his skills, both military and diplomatic, were almost completely confined to the Irish theatre, which inevitably had the effect of weakening the family in Scotland.

It was to be one of the constant features of Tudor policy in Ulster that they sought to achieve maximum gains at minimum expense. Military effort was kept to a bare minimum for lengthy periods, and beyond a few garrisons, such as that at Carrickfergus, there was little English presence in the area. Henry VIII pursued a strategy that at times veered wildly between conciliation and threat in his attempts to persuade the O'Donnells and O'Neils, the chief Irish families of Ulster, to accept English authority. He met with some success, when the heads of both families submitted to the king by 1542. This allowed for a substantial reduction in the English garrisons in Ireland. But sadly for Henry, Clan Donald proved to be the main factor upsetting all his calculations. As long as they had the power to come and go at will, his position could never be completely secure. His support for Donald Dubh in 1545 was probably as much to do with shoring up his own position in the north of Ireland, as it was to do with creating trouble in Scotland.

Land hunger was always the driving force in the history of Clan Donald. Now well established in the Glens, the Macdonalds of Dunyveg turned their eyes west to the fertile territory known as the Route, held by the MacQuillins, an Irish family. This was probably inevitable: Alexander had left six sons, and since the Islay and Kintyre estates would eventually go to the descendants of the oldest son, James, the rest had to be provided for in some way.[7] Since the fall of the Lordship and the rise of the Campbells, Scotland offered few opportunities for territorial expansion. Ireland was different. Not only was the land richer than that of the Isles, but there was no dominant power. English control was at best nominal, and the leading Irish families were in constant competition with each other. James of Dunyveg enjoyed good relations with both the Campbell kin of his wife Agnes and, through the Earl of Argyll, with the Scottish government. With their eastern flank protected, the family was free to grasp the opportunities that Ireland offered.

For some time the English had viewed Clan Donald's growing interest in Ulster with alarm. They seemed to be acting as a bridgehead for further Scottish involvement in the area, especially worrying as this might at any time up until the late 1550s also have involved the French. Although the circumstances are not clear, it seems that Sorley Boy was taken prisoner sometime in 1550, in what was probably yet another English attempt to clear his family from the Glens. He was held for about a year in Dublin Castle. Clearly hoping to build on this minor success, Sir James Crofts, the English viceroy, ordered an attack on the Macdonnell position on Rathlin Island, but the whole enterprise went disastrously wrong. Rathlin was of great strategic importance, standing between Kintyre and the coast of Ulster; if the Scots could be dislodged, their position would be severely weakened. But James and his brother Colla were alert to the English manoeuvres: it was not they who were taken captive on Rathlin but the leaders of the English expedition, Sir Ralph Bagenal and Captain John Cuffe. This put Crofts in an embarrassing position, as the only way he could obtain the return of his officers was to order the immediate release of Sorley.[8]

Sorley signalled his return to Ulster by launching an attack on the English base at Carrickfergus in 1552. Walter Floddy, the constable, was taken captive, and only released after a heavy ransom was paid. It was reported at this time that Sorley was saying that the 'Inglische men had no ryght to Yrland'.[9] He was also taking a serious interest in the Route, along with his brother, Colla. Colla married Eveleen MacQuillin in early 1552, although the 'alliance' with her family was far from amicable, only serving to stimulate Macdonnell interest in their lands still further.[10]

For the English, affairs in Ulster went from bad to worse after the Carrickfergus raid. Among other things the policy of seeking accommodation with the old Irish chiefs, initiated by Henry VIII, was unravelling. They had hoped that the Earl of Tyrone would eventually be succeeded by his bastard son, Matthew O'Neil, Baron Dungannon. Instead it was his half-brother, Shane, Tyrone's legitimate son, who began to prevail in the internecine struggle that enveloped the O'Neils. Shane, one of the great figures of Gaelic Ireland, was far less compliant than his father and brother, and was soon a serious danger to English interests in Ulster. In supporting their own position, the Macdonnells were more than happy to enter into alliance with the troublesome Gaelic chief. Instead of reaching an accommodation with the Irish, the English began to consider a policy of outright conquest.[11]

The change in English policy was signalled in 1556 by the arrival in Dublin of a new Lord Lieutenant, Thomas Radcliffe, Lord Fitzwalter, the future Earl of Sussex. Fitzwalter came to Ireland with Sir Henry Sidney, who was appointed Treasurer. Sidney arrived in his new post with £25 000, an impressive war chest to be used against Irish rebels. It was Clan Donald, however, that was to be the chief target of the new policy. By 1555 they had completed their takeover of the Route. At about this time Colla was appointed governor of the area by his brother James, and was known as 'Captain of the Route'. This extension of the family's power could not be ignored.

Fitzwalter marched into Ulster in July supported by a small naval force, intended to block any attempt to reinforce the Macdonnells from across the North Channel. Much was promised of this effort, but little achieved. Fitzwalter claimed a victory when the two sides met at the pass of Ballohe M'Gille Corrough on the 18th, although he appears to have greatly exaggerated his battle report, later falsely claiming that James of Dunyveg had been killed.[12] The truth is that it did nothing to weaken Clan Donald's hold on the Glens. The true measure of Fitzwalter's success may be gauged from an act passed the following year by the Irish parliament in Dublin 'against the bringing in of Scots, retaining of them and marrying of them'.[13] This is a wonderful example of an occasion, when, for once, the pen proved no mightier than the sword.

In 1557 Fitzwalter, now Earl of Sussex, came north for a second attempt, faring no better than he had the previous year. He offered protection to Richard MacQuillin of the Route, ejected from his home by his rapacious neighbours, but this was only good for as long as the English remained. Colla remained in firm control until his death in May 1558. James then offered the Captaincy of the Route to his brothers Alasdair and Angus in turn. Both men refused. This was a difficult frontier posting, subject to hostility from the English and risings by the displaced MacQuillins.[14] The honour was then offered to the youngest brother, Sorley Boy, who had been closely associated with Colla in the subjection of the area. Believing himself equal to the task, Sorley accepted. For the MacQuillins this change of leadership offered them an opportunity, and they soon mounted a major challenge to the authority of Sorley. Colla, described by Sussex himself as the best of the brothers, left two sons – Gilliespic and Ranald. Gilliespic was to be the father of the infamous Coll Coitach, who, in turn, was the father of Alasdair MacColla, arguably the greatest soldier ever produced by Clan Donald.

Failure to establish effective control over Ulster was creating major strategic problems for the English government, especially after war broke out with France in the summer of 1557. French troops were still stationed in Scotland, and were thus capable of opening a front in Ireland with the help of Clan Iain Mor. To prevent this, Sussex mounted a third offensive. This time the main thrust would fall not on the Glens or the Route, but on the Scottish heartlands of James of Dunyveg. Mary, Queen of Scots and her French husband, Francis, had recently favoured James with a renewal of earlier land grants, as a reward for his continuing loyalty.[15] An attack on the Western Isles offered a way of preventing the continuing flow of Macdonald redshanks to Ireland, as well as stopping the French from using the area as a launch pad for their own invasion.

Sussex sailed from Dublin in mid-September 1558, landing towards the end of the month in Kintyre, near to the site of the future Campbeltown. From here his forces fanned out, destroying the adjacent countryside, including James' home at Saddell and the old castle of Dunaverty. Arran and the Cumbraes were also raided, but Sussex's plan to sail on to Islay was frustrated by bad weather. On his return to Dublin, he intended to finish the campaigning season with an attack on the Route, although in practice he achieved very little. Conciliation had failed; so too had force. In the face of the remarkable advance of Clan Iain Mor, English policy was shown to be impotent. The accession of Elizabeth I to the throne in November 1558 was followed by a temporary withdrawal from the contest, giving James and his brothers a free hand in Ulster. It came just at the right time.

Since the death of Colla in early 1558, Edward MacQuillin had been plotting to remove Sorley as Captain of the Route. His plans were complete by the summer of 1559, when he had mustered enough support from among his kinsmen to mount a direct challenge. In early July he attacked Sorley's camp near Bunnamairge, only to be repulsed with heavy losses. Sorley then set out in pursuit of his enemy, although he himself also suffered a large number of casualties in charging into the MacQuillin camp on the bank of the River Shesk. The MacQuillins retreated in good order to a place called Slieve-an-Aura. Hugh MacFelim, chief of the O'Neils of Clandeboy, arrived here with reinforcements. Not pausing to rest, Sorley advanced to the final confrontation on 13 July.[16]

Like all good soldiers, Sorley paid close attention to the terrain close to the enemy position. Noticing some marshy ground, he had this strewn with rushes under cover of darkness. This was a brilliant stratagem, because the worried Irish soldiers could hear their enemy working in the dark and assumed, wrongly, that the Macdonnells were covering the marsh, prior to launching an attack in the morning. Not willing to wait, they left their position at first light, intending to beat Sorley at his own game. But the rushes would not take their weight, and, stuck in the marsh, they were easy targets for the archers of Clan Iain Mor. Edward MacQuillin fell, as did Hugh MacFelim. The last serious challenge by the MacQuillins ended at the Battle of Slieve-an-Aura.

Sorley and James now enjoyed a unique position in the Gaelic world. Their assistance was sought both by the English and by Shane O'Neil, who had now overcome his brother Dungannon to take charge of his family's affairs. Although the English were worried by the steady advance of Clan Iain Mor, their greatest concern towards the end of the 1550s was over Shane O'Neil, who clearly aimed at nothing less than the recreation of the ancient power his family had once enjoyed in Ulster. Even Sussex was moved to suggest that the Macdonnells might be useful allies against Shane, and on his suggestion Elizabeth made overtures to James of Dunyveg in the summer of 1559.[17] At this time Sorley was prepared to make terms with the English in return for their recognition of his rights to the Route. But it was to take almost thirty years of torturous shifts and swings in policy before Elizabeth was willing to make this concession, which might have saved her considerable trouble and expense if agreed at the time.

Despite the success at Slieve-an-Aura, Clan Iain Mor was in a dangerous political position. Both the English and Shane O'Neil, looking at things from their own perspective, considered them to be outsiders. For the English they were Scots and thus subjects of a foreign prince; for O'Neil they were rivals in his aim to dominate Ulster. Only for as long as the Dublin authorities and Shane were enemies could Clan Iain Mor be safe in the complex dance of Irish politics. But in the 1560s this enmity was temporarily set aside, with disastrous consequences for the Macdonnells. Both the English and O'Neil had attempted to make use of the men of Clan Iain Mor; finally tiring of their neutrality, they combined to destroy them.

Sussex for a time continued to seek a military solution to the problems posed by Shane O'Neil, without decisive results. For the parsimonious Elizabeth, not willing to throw any more money into the bottomless bogs of Ulster, a deal with Shane offered a better prospect. After the failure of the latest attempt to pin Shane down, Elizabeth wrote to Sussex towards the end of August 1561, advising him of her intentions to open negotiations with the rebel chief. Matters proceeded so far that Shane was confident enough to leave his Gaelic heartland and come to London. This came at a very difficult time for Clan Iain Mor. James' relations with Argyll were no longer as strong as they had been, and the dispute with the Macleans over the Rhinns of Islay was becoming increasingly troublesome. The absorption in Irish affairs was beginning to weaken the family's interests in Scotland, a process that might conceivably be compared with the earlier obsession of the Lords of the Isles with the earldom of Ross.[18]

As well as seeking agreement with Shane, the English government was looking for other ways of weakening Clan Iain Mor. Donald Gorme of Sleat, who had his own deeply nurtured claim to the Lordship of the Isles, was clearly jealous of the success of his Islay cousins. He offered his services to Elizabeth in making war on the Antrim Macdonnells, even suggesting that he might attack James to make it easier for the English to expel Sorley from Ireland.[19] But the real crisis for the family came in September 1563, when Shane signed the Peace of Drum Cru with the English. In return for his co-operation against the Macdonnells, Elizabeth was even prepared to recognise Shane as 'The O'Neil', completely reversing the policy of her father. This was dangerously short sighted, for if Shane prevailed he was likely to pose an even greater threat to English interests than Sorley or James.

Shane was now free to take action against former allies in the Gaelic world. By the spring of 1565 he was ready to make a final push, having taken some preparatory steps the previous autumn. Not expecting an early assault, James had retired to Kintyre, leaving Sorley to keep an eye on Shane's movements. Shane made his move at just the right time: the traditional campaigning season had not yet begun, so most of Sorley's redshanks were back in Scotland. Outnumbering his enemy by a factor of two to one, Shane advanced to the border of Clandeboy in late April, taking Sorley by complete surprise.[20] Realising he faced something more serious than a raid, Sorley retreated to the north to organise his defences. Shane's wave then moved irresistibly forward. Sorley tried to stop it at Knockboy Pass, a strategic point that guarded the southern entry into both the Glens and the Route, but against sheer force of numbers it was a futile stand. Now in a desperate situation,

Sorley ordered that the signal fires be lit along the northern Antrim coast to alert his brother James, while he retreated with his remaining force towards Ballycastle. Meanwhile, Shane continued his advance.

James, like Sorley, was not prepared for this crisis. Although he reacted quickly to the pleading glow from across the North Channel, he sailed to Antrim with only such force as he could gather, leaving Alasdair Oge, his other brother, to follow on with reinforcements. Sorley and James finally combined their forces on 1 May, as Shane moved north from Red Bay Castle, a Macdonnell stronghold now in flames. The best strategy for the Macdonnell chiefs would have been to hold the vital port of Ballycastle, now the only point at which Alasdair Oge's anxiously awaited redshanks could land. However, there were clear dangers in being caught here with an inferior force between the Glens and the sea; and besides, Highland troops never fought at their best from a defensive position. To allow freedom of movement, Sorley and James moved south-west from Ballycastle into the valley of the River Tow, a place called Glentaisie. It was here that the two brothers prepared to make a stand, clearly hoping to draw Shane on and thus allow Alasdair Oge to make an unopposed landing. Tragically for them, Alasdair arrived too late.

The Battle of Glentaisie began early in the morning of 2 May. Few details of the encounter survive, but it almost certainly resembled John Moidertach's clash with the Frasers at the Battle of Kinloch-Lochy. After an initial discharge of bows and arrows, the two sides closed in a vicious hand-to-hand encounter, which lasted for most of the day. Heavily outnumbered, the Macdonnells fought with great courage, before giving way to the pressure of their enemy. In all some 300 to 400 Macdonnells were killed, including Angus Uaibhreach, the brother of James and Sorley. James himself was severely wounded and captured. Sorley also fell captive to the great O'Neil. Alasdair Oge arrived after the battle with almost 1000 redshanks, but with the situation now beyond recall, he retreated back to the Isles.[21]

Glentaisie was the most severe defeat Clan Iain Mor had ever experienced, and could possibly have led to their total disappearance from Ireland. But Shane acted with uncharacteristic moderation, breaking his promise to Elizabeth to kill and expel all of the Scots. He simply improved his strategic position by seizing Macdonnell strong-holds along the coast, including Dunluce Castle, thus preventing Alasdair Oge from seeking revenge in the near future. As for the captives, James was taken to the dungeons of Castle Corcra in Tryrone, while Sorley accompanied Shane on his continuing campaigns. Lady Agnes Campbell was soon busy pleading for her husband, and Mary,

Queen of Scots also strenuously sought his release, as did Argyll, Lady Agnes' nephew, who demanded it on behalf of the great lairds of the western Highlands and Hebrides.[22] But James, his wounds apparently untreated, lingered on in captivity for some two months before dying. His passing was recorded by the Irish annals: 'His death was very much lamented; he was a man distinguished for hospitality, feats of arms, liberality, conviviality, generosity, and the bestowal of gifts. There was not his equal among the Clan Donnell of Ireland or of Scotland at that time.'[23]

He left three young sons: Archibald, Angus and Ranald. Archibald was chief of Dunyveg until his early death in 1569, when Angus, the next brother, succeeded to the title. But for the immediate future the family's affairs were in the hands of Agnes Campbell and her brother-in-law, Alasdair Oge, both eager to revenge the death of James. Alasdair Oge was soon confident enough to return to Ireland, and in December 1566 it was reported to the Privy Council in Dublin that he had crossed the River Bann and killed at least sixty of Shane's men. As late as May 1567 he was seeking English help against Shane.[24] Alasdair was, in fact, destined to be the instrument of his dead brother's revenge, although it came in a manner he could never have anticipated, for it was Shane who brought about his own destruction.

Soon after his victory at Glentasie, Shane threw off his pretended allegiance to Elizabeth. After Sir Henry Sidney arrived in Ireland as the new Lord Deputy in January 1566, he sought to draw Clan Iain Mor into an alliance against Shane. This demonstrated the complete failure of English policy in Ulster; for they were now back exactly where they were some six years before, when Sussex was seeking an alliance with the Macdonnells. Beyond the temporary eclipse of Clan Iain Mor, the treaty with Shane had achieved precisely nothing. What is worse, it elevated an even greater enemy into a position of un-paralleled power. The problem for the English lay in the simple facts of geography: Islay and Kintyre were far closer to Ulster than Dublin or London. There could, therefore, never be a solution to the Irish problem without some kind of accommodation with Clan Donald.

Little by little the noose closed around Shane. Under pressure from Alasdair Oge in the east, he was defeated by his western Gaelic rivals, the O'Donnells, at the Battle of Farsetmore in May 1567. This reverse, quite as severe as the Macdonnells had suffered at Glentasie, brought Shane close to ruin. Having alienated almost everybody, he looked around for allies. Sorley had now been his captive for two years, and was the only ace left to the beleaguered chief. Using Sorley as an inter-mediary, Shane arranged to meet Alasdair Oge at Cushendun on the Antrim coast. His small party, Sorley included, rode to Cushendun in late May, where they were greeted not just by Alasdair but by a large force of Macdonnell redshanks. Several days' negotiation followed, with no apparent conclusion. Finally, on 2 June, the Macdonnells cut Shane to pieces, supposedly in the course of a drunken quarrel.

The circumstances surrounding the murder of Shane O'Neil are shrouded in obscurity. In these days when conspiracy theories take precedence over notions of family honour, it has become fashionable to see it as part of a carefully laid plot involving the English, rather than a simple revenge killing.[25] The evidence, however, is not conclusive. It does not appear to have been premeditated, for if Alasdair had murder in his heart he could have dispatched the virtually defenceless Shane as soon as he entered his camp. There is little doubt, however, that the Macdonnells had no love for Shane. Once it was clear that he had almost nothing to offer them in the way of any political advantage, he was of no further use. His death would clearly be welcome to the English, who might then be inclined to make the territorial concessions demanded by Clan Iain Mor. Shane, in short, was of greater service dead than alive. Set against these simple facts, there is really no need for secret agreements or hot Celtic passions.

Shane was buried at the monastery of Glenarm. Tradition has it that a friar came from Armagh to take the body of the dead chief back to his own country. In considering the request the abbot of Glenarm asked if the friar had brought the body of James of Dunyveg with him. On receiving a negative reply he said, 'then while you walk over the grave of my Lord James at Armagh, I will trample upon the great O'Neil at Glenarm.'[26]

The English were certainly grateful to see the end of Shane. William Piers carried his head to Dublin, where it was put on public display. Clan Iain Mor was to be thanked, and then sent packing. Once the inconvenient Celts were out of the way, civilised English settlers were to be planted in their place in eastern Ulster. Not willing to be disposed of so easily, the newly liberated Sorley set about building up the power of his family in the Glens and the Route, a task that was to occupy the remainder of his life. He was fortunate in two things: Turlough Luineach, the new chief of the O'Neils, was a far less formidable man than his cousin Shane; and the Earl of Argyll was willing to work with the Macdonnells.

Archibald Campbell, the fifth Earl of Argyll, was the key to the future prosperity of Clan Iain Mor in Ulster. Elizabeth and her advisers were certainly aware of this, and, in 1560, the price of English assistance to the Lords of the Congregation against the French included, among other things, the services of Argyll in restoring order in Ireland.[27] But with remarkable inconsistency, Elizabeth, distrustful of all Scots in Ireland, failed to make effective use of this weapon. Elizabeth also angered Argyll by her refusal to release Mary, Queen of Scots after she sought refuge in England. Rather than controlling the Macdonnells, he now supported them against the English government in Dublin. With Argyll's help, Sorley returned to Ireland in November 1567 with some 800 redshanks, Campbells and Macdonalds.[28] On landing he declared he would never be forced out of Ireland against his will. Argyll also provided support for the O'Neils and O'Donnells, completely frustrating English schemes for colonisation.

Sorley was now the dominant figure of Clan Iain Mor, in both Scotland and Ireland, although the Hebrides were really only of interest insofar as they could supply men to further his ambitions in Ulster. Agnes Campbell, Sorley's sister-in-law, was clearly worried by his intentions and how this would affect the rights of her children. She made her own overtures to Elizabeth, offering to accept an Irish husband of her choice, provided her children were allowed to enjoy their inheritance. If not, she added threateningly, 'as long as Clandonnell live they will not cease the prosecution of their title.'[29]

For some twenty years, Sorley tirelessly prosecuted his own title to the Route. All he wanted from Elizabeth was a formal recognition of his claim, but the English queen was prepared neither to do this nor to commit sufficient military resources to oust him. In 1573 Walter Devereux, Earl of Essex, was given a grant of Clandeboy, the Glens, the Route and Rathlin Island and just over 1000 troops to drive out the Scots and the native Irish. The task was beyond him. He simply could not pin down an enemy that had all the elusiveness of the mist. Towards the end of the year he was forced to concede that it might be best to offer Sorley citizenship in return for his services as a 'mercenary man and a soldier'.[30]

Essex made one last effort against Clan Iain in the summer of 1575, but once again Sorley merely fell back against superior forces. In frustration, Essex authorised an amphibious attack on Rathlin Island, where Sorley had sent his women and children for safety. Sailing from Carrickfergus on 20 July, the English force commanded by Captain John Norris landed on Rathlin two days later. Norris and his men cut down all they could find under the despairing eyes of Sorley, forced to watch the spectacle from the mainland. But the Rathlin Massacre achieved precisely nothing, simply marking a barbarous fullstop to a disastrous career. Soon after, Essex was recalled, although not for the behaviour of his troops on Rathlin, as is occasionally suggested.

In the years to follow the English changed their tactics with bewildering rapidity, often setting out to do one thing and then proceeding to do another. They attempted to make use of Turlough Luineach O'Neil against Sorley, but if Turlough occasionally roared like a lion he inevitably ended by bleating like a sheep. One last military effort was made against Clan Iain in 1584, after Sir John Perrot had been appointed Lord Deputy. But as so often in the past, the whole operation was hampered by a serious shortage of funds. Dunluce Castle was taken, only to be retaken after Perrot withdrew. The Lord Deputy then tried to divide Clan Iain by using either Sorley's brother, Donnell Gorme, or his nephew, Angus of Dunyveg, against him; but this came to nothing.[31] By early 1585, Sorley was once again in a dominant position in Ulster. In desperation, Perrot was reduced to plotting Sorley's assassination.[32] Finally, with little choice left to her, Elizabeth conceded what Sorley had been requesting for over twenty years: a charter for the Route.

Sorley, who had spent a good part of his life in arms, was now well advanced in age, and thus anxious to bring his long struggle to a satisfactory conclusion. He appeared before Perrot in Dublin in June 1586 and made his formal submission to Queen Elizabeth. In return, he received letters of citizenship, the captaincy of the Route and the constableship of Dunluce Castle. Angus of Dunyveg, his nephew and clan chief, received his own grant to the Glens, although the whole continued under the supervision of Sorley. Having achieved his life's purpose, Sorley lived out his remaining years in peace, dying at Dunanynie Castle in early 1590.

Donald Gregory wrongly assumed that Sorley usurped the rights of Angus and laboured exclusively for his own advancement.[33] In fact, the two branches of the family enjoyed good relations until Sorley's death. Angus was always willing to support his uncle, to the detriment, arguably, of his own interests in the Isles. While the Dunyveg chief was growing up, his uncles, Sorley and Alasdair, ably guided his affairs. Once he reached maturity, there appears to have been a division of labour, with Sorley preoccupied with Ireland, and Angus with the Isles. This is hardly surprising. The three-cornered contest between Clan Iain, the English and the Irish demanded all Sorley's attention, and created problems that would have broken all but the strongest of men. Although he kept an eye on Ireland, from the late 1570s most of Angus' attention was absorbed by his feud with the Macleans. But while Sorley was able to rise above his own problems, Angus was submerged in his. This created a critical imbalance in the affairs of Clan Iain Mor. It was thanks to Sorley that Clan Iain survived and prospered in Ireland; and thanks to Angus that it withered and died in the Isles. The greatest criticism that can be made of Sorley is that he appeared blind to this crisis.

Not many years after the death of Sorley, the Dunyveg and Antrim branches of the family drifted steadily apart. The separation was far from amicable. In 1596 Sorley's son, James, attacked Angus Macdonald's house in Kintyre, killing ten or twelve men, before riding off with a great deal of plunder.[34] James MacSorley was not only holding Angus' land in Ireland, but he had designs on his lands in Scotland. He wrote to James VI claiming, in effect, that his cousin Angus was a traitor as well as a bastard.[35] MacSorley came to Scotland and was well received by the king, although his claim to the Dunyveg lands was disallowed. We should not be too surprised at this treachery. It was clear to all by this time that Angus was leading the house of Dunyveg to ruin. Even his own son, also called James, in seeking to take control of the clan, attempted to burn his father to death. Oddly enough, King James, who hated Macdonalds in the Isles, appears to have taken a liking to Macdonnells in Ireland. James MacSorley was knighted and granted an estate on Kintyre, which must have been a sore provocation to Angus. Like his grandfather, James V, the king appreciated the importance of a Scots presence in Ulster, even if the Scots in question were Gaels.

As the Macdonalds of Dunyveg marched to destruction, the Macdonnells of Antrim continued to navigate the treacherous waters of Irish politics. Along with the O'Neils and O'Donnells they took part in the great Ulster rising against the English known as the Nine Years' War, but changed sides just in time.

Sir James MacSorley died in 1601 and was succeeded by his younger brother, Randal. When James VI of Scotland became James I of England and Ireland in 1603, he continued to favour the family. Soon after his succession, he granted Randal the entire region of the Route and the Glens, as well as additional grants of land. This incited the jealousy of the English government in Ireland, especially Sir Arthur Chichester, who saw in Randal and the other Celtic lords a barrier to his scheme to anglicise Ulster. He made strenuous efforts to poison the king's mind against the Macdonnells; but James, always willing to listen to slanders against the Macdonalds and other Gaelic people in Scotland, was not willing to abandon them in Antrim. They proved their use to the king by co-operating wholeheartedly in building up the Ulster Plantation, although Randal and his family continued to be good Catholics. Like the house of Argyll, they discovered the knack of standing between two worlds, a talent never developed by any other branch of the clan. James continued to show high favour towards Randal, creating him Viscount Dunluce in 1618 and Earl of Antrim in 1620, the first time a member of Clan Donald had held this elevated title since the forfeiture of the Earl of Ross in 1476.

Despite their growing good fortune in Ireland, the family never lost sight of their ancient Scottish patrimony, and made some attempt to reclaim it, as we shall see, before it finally passed into the hands of the Campbells. Antrim died at Dunluce in 1636. Randal, his son and namesake, succeeded as second earl. His father had seen to it that he had been brought up in the Highland manner of his family, and bequeathed to him the idea that he was not just an Irish aristocrat but a chief of Clan Donald. In pursuit of this, Randal conceived of a plan that was to bring the great Clan Campbell to the threshold of ruin.

8

THE FALL OF THE HOUSE OF DUNYVEG

Angus of Dunyveg took charge of his clan at a particularly dangerous time. James VI had grown to maturity, and was soon to see Clan Donald as one of the principal sources of disorder in the Isles. After the death of the fifth Earl of Argyll in 1573, the Macdonalds of Kintyre and Islay were never again to enjoy close relations with the Campbells, and so lost an important ally at court. But worst of all, by 1578 Lachlan Mor had become chief of the Macleans of Duart, and he was to prove himself one of the most formidable opponents ever faced by Clan Donald. The never-forgotten Maclean claim to the Rhinns of Islay was to revive in a ruinous way. Almost from the outset, Lachlan was to be a source of trouble. Soon after taking control, he claimed that Colin Campbell, the sixth Earl of Argyll, had stirred up Angus Macdonald against him. In a complaint to the Privy Council he alleged that his tenants on Islay had been attacked, and the fort on Loch Gorm seized. The quarrel was patched up, and Angus married Maclean's sister; this was but a temporary reprieve.[1]

With a volcano about to erupt in the Isles, Clan Donald was faced with serious problems elsewhere. Donald MacAngus, eighth chief of Glengarry, was under attack by the Mackenzies of Kintail, anxious to push his family out of Lochalsh, the last fragment of the earldom of Ross still remaining in Macdonald hands. The Mackenzies began their assault in early 1581, killing Glengarry's kin and seizing his livestock.[2] In April Glengarry himself was surprised and taken prisoner from his home on Lochcarron and held for over a month. Rory and Dougal Mackenzie, brother to Colin, the chief of Kintail, also captured a number of Donald's servants and kinsmen, including his uncle and three of his sons. Among other things, Donald alleged that a number of these men had their hands tied with their own shirts, and then, when defenceless, they were stabbed to death and left without burial. Donald was taken to Castle Strome, where the garrison was forced to surrender after their chief was threatened with death. The following June, the

Mackenzies captured Donald Makmorach Roy, a close kinsman of Glengarry, whom they allegedly put to death in a particularly brutal fashion: 'first cutt of his handis, nixt his feet and last his heid, and having cassin the same in a peitpott, exposit and laid out his carcage to a prey for doggis and revenus beistis.'[3]

To resolve the matter, the Council ordered that Castle Strome be placed in the temporary custody of the Earl of Argyll, completely overlooking the charges of torture and murder. Colin Mackenzie later received a royal pardon for the murder of Donald Roy, and Glengarry was confirmed in possession of his Lochalsh lands; but this was a matter not easily laid to rest.

In April 1585, just as Sorley Boy was close to bringing his long struggle in Ireland to an end, an odd entry appears in the records of the Scottish Privy Council. Angus of Dunyveg, who is described as an obedient subject, was being 'menaced and harassed', although by whom is not made clear.[4] Proclamation was to be made at the market crosses of Dumbarton, Inverness, Inveraray and other places, ordering the lieges to assist him in the defence of his lands and against the violent pursuit or invasion of any person. The same proclamation also ordered Donald Gorme of Sleat, Rory Macleod of Lewis, Tormod Macleod of Harris and Lachlan Maclean of Duart to appear before the Council to answer for 'gude reull and quieting of the Ilis and Hielands'. We can detect in these bald statements the beginnings of a great tidal wave that was to engulf the Western Isles in the years to come. It took the form of a new civil war among the leading families of the old Lordship of the Isles, far worse than that which led to the Battle of Bloody Bay. This struggle did much to prejudice the young James VI against Highlanders in general and Clan Donald in particular.

All Highland conflicts tend to be reducible to struggles over land, but the exact cause of these new disorders is not revealed in contemporary record. Only tradition provides us with any clues. It appears to begin with a family quarrel between Donald Gorme Mor, the chief of Sleat, and a kinsman by the name of Hugh MacGillespick Clerach.[5] Hugh, who had been outlawed in the early 1580s and had taken to piracy, appears to have conceived a violent hatred for the young chief of Sleat, possibly believing that he had a better claim to lead the clan.[6]

Soon after he came of age in 1585, Donald Gorme Mor sailed to Islay to visit Angus of Dunyveg. He was forced by bad weather to take shelter on Jura, on part of the island belonging to Lachlan Mor Maclean. Hugh MacGillespick had also landed on Jura, unbeknown to Donald, and seeing an opportunity to embarrass the chief, he stole some cattle belonging to Maclean and left the island. The following night Maclean's men, discovering both the loss and the presence of the Macdonalds, fell upon the intruders at a place called Inverknock-wrick, and killed sixty of them.[7] Donald, who was sleeping on board his ship, managed to escape. Inevitably, this incident was followed by a bloody feud, which threatened to envelop Angus. To try to stop matters going too far, he decided to mediate, sailing to Duart to talk to Lachlan Mor. The dispute over the Rhinns of Islay, although not settled, had been slumbering for some time, and Lachlan was Angus' brother-in-law, so he probably felt safe enough. It was a serious mistake: no sooner was Angus in Lachlan's power than he took him prisoner, refusing to release him until he renounced the Rhinns. Fearing for his life, Angus agreed. Before he was freed, he had to leave his eldest son, James, Maclean's own nephew, and his brother, Ranald, as hostages.

Soon after, Maclean came to Islay to claim his prize. He took possession of the old fort on Loch Gorm, where he received an invitation from Angus to visit him at Mullintrea, where he had a house. Maclean, clearly believing that no one could possibly be as ruthless as he, and trusting in Angus' assurances of safe conduct, agreed to come. Angus promptly ladled out the same broth he had been forced to taste in Duart Castle. Maclean and all his men were taken captive. The Maclean chief's life was only spared because of the special pleading of his nephew, James Macdonald, whom he brought with him from Mull. James Macdonald was Lachlan's saviour, on this occasion: but he was destined, by the ironic twists of fortune, to be the future author of his uncle's destruction.

Angus, believing that his brother, Ranald, Maclean's other hostage, had been killed at Duart, ordered the execution of all his captives, some eighty men in all. They were killed at the rate of two every day, until only Lachlan himself was left. However, this cold-blooded, serial murder receives no mention in contemporary record, and is almost certainly a gruesome fiction.[8]

Much of the above account exists only in tradition, and must therefore be treated with some caution. The essential facts, however, are real enough. By the summer of 1585, Francis Walsingham, one of Queen Elizabeth's chief ministers, had been informed that Lachlan and Angus were engaged in a deadly feud. Angus detained Lachlan until his clan produced hostages as a token for his good behaviour. But no sooner was he released, and regardless of the fate of the hostages, he went on the warpath, taking advantage of the absence of Angus in Ireland. Before long, the conflict sucked in all the principal families of the Isles.[9] Angus was aided by Donald Gorme Mor of Sleat, Macleod of Lewis, Clanranald, the Maciains of Ardnamurchan, the Macneils of Gigha, the Macallasters of Loup and the Macphees of Colonsay. Lachlan obtained the support of the Macleods of Harris, the Macneils of Barra, the Mackinnons of Strathordale and the Macquarries of Mull.

This bitter and murderous conflict came at a difficult time for the Scottish government. Colin Campbell, the sixth Earl of Argyll, died in 1584. Archibald, his son, was still a minor, and the affairs of the clan were placed in the hands of a group of guardians, drawn from the main Campbell gentry. One of the main reasons for the success of the Campbells, perhaps the chief reason, was that, unlike the Macdonalds, they had always managed to present a united front. But now serious disputes broke out within the family, embracing murder and conspiracy to murder. It was to be some years before they were able to act again as an effective force in Highland politics, robbing the government of its watchman in the west.

For the English, always concerned about Scots incursions in Ireland, this dispute offered a new opportunity to undermine Clan Iain Mor and, at the same time, keep King James preoccupied with domestic affairs. Maclean, desperate for allies, approached the English authorities in Ireland, offering his services:

> If the Queen's Majesty would take him under her protection and countenance, he would kindle such a coal of fire in Scotland, and at her Highness will and pleasure, so keep the King occupied with stir and troubles, as he should not have liesure to hearken after foreign practices, nor attempt anything with France or Spain, which might disturb her majesty or her dominions.[10]

Lachlan's search for allies did not stop with the English. A Spanish ship from the doomed Armada was forced to take refuge in Tobermory harbour. Always quick to seize an opportunity, Lachlan obtained the services of 100 soldiers and two cannon.[11] These men were then used, as previously discussed, to ravage the Small Isles, including Eigg. Mingary Castle, the stronghold of the Maciains, was unsuccessfully besieged. Angus responded by bringing a party of English mercenaries to the Isles, with which he ravaged Mull, Tiree and Coll. The struggle continued along its bitter course, one blow following hard upon another: 'thus for a whyle they did continuallie vex one another with slaughters and outrages, to the destruction almost of their cuntries and people.'[12]

For King James, the troubles in the Isles parallel Queen Elizabeth's troubles in Ireland, and the solution in both cases was to be much the same. England set out to complete the conquest of Gaelic Ireland, a goal that was achieved after the Battle of Kinsale in 1601 and victory over the Earls of Tyrone and Tyrconnell in the Nine Years' War. James set out to complete his own conquest of the west, an area that was only part of the realm of Scotland in the most imperfect sense. Even the English, trying to prevent further Scots migration to Ulster, realised how limited the king's authority was in the west. Edward Wotton, the English ambassador in Edinburgh, wrote to Walsingham in the summer of 1585, saying that 'The Highlanders care not much for the King, and obey him at their pleasure'.[13] If this was obvious to the English, it must have been even more obvious to James. Unlike most of his ancestors, however, he was given the time, the opportunity and, above all, the power to bring about important changes in the government of the Highlands and Islands. Before James, government interest in the Highlands had tended to be intermittent; this was now changing. It would no longer be possible, as Angus Macdonald was to discover, for the chiefs to hide away among their kin, in the way that John Moidertach had once done so successfully.

The first sign along the new road came in 1587, when parliament passed an act to be known as the General Bond or Band.[14] This made all chiefs or landlords responsible for the behaviour of their individual tenants or clansmen. Each had to provide the government with large amounts of money or sureties, in proportion to their wealth and the number of their followers. It was open to any individual to seek damages, payable from these sureties. Landlords would then have to make up the shortfall, as well as pay a heavy fine to the government.

Lachlan, perhaps sensing political change in the wind, agreed to submit to the authorities, but Angus remained obdurate, refusing to hand over his Maclean hostages. Grateful for any sign of obedience from the wild men of the west, the government received Lachlan into favour for a time, although he clearly found it difficult to bring his violent nature under control. John Maciain of Ardnamurchan, one of Angus of Dunyveg's allies, had, prior to the outbreak of the feud, expressed an interest in marrying Janet Campbell, the Duart chief's widowed mother. Taking advantage of a lull in the conflict, and sensing a fresh opportunity, Lachlan agreed to the match. Learning nothing from the experience of Angus Macdonald, Maciain came to Mull, where the marriage duly went ahead. During the night, after the wedding party from Ardnamurchan had gone to bed, Lachlan and his men fell upon them, killing eighteen, before entering the bedroom of his new stepfather. He too would have died but for the intervention of Lachlan's mother. Instead he was taken off to a dungeon and subjected to daily torture. This grim episode was ever after to be known as 'Maclean's Nuptials'. It is tempting to reject this as yet another traditional tale without basis in fact, but it is all soberly noted in the Privy Council records.[15]

The year prior to this outrage, parliament passed an act defining 'murder under trust' as statutory treason. This was prompted by events in the Western Isles, where such crime had become a regular occurrence. 'Maclean's Nuptials' was probably the first example of murder under trust committed after the passing of the legislation, but the crime was never punished.

Casual murder was one thing: the involvement of Spanish and English troops in the island wars quite another. In 1589, determined to end the disturbances, James and his Council invited Angus, Lachlan and Donald Gorme Mor to Edinburgh under safe conduct. As in the past the Islanders found that Stewart guarantees guaranteed nothing. As soon as they appeared in the capital, they were all arrested. Despite the recently granted remissions for crimes committed during the feud, all were to be brought to trial. Both Angus and Lachlan were charged with the murder of men, women and children; and rather than face a jury, they threw themselves on the mercy of the king.[16] It might be thought that James had a unique opportunity to put a sudden end to a messy, unpleasant quarrel. There was, after all, enough evidence against both men to hang them ten times over, and probably not too many people would have quibbled over the royal breach of trust. When given a similar opportunity in 1427, James I had acted decisively. But James VI simply fined the miscreants and, after a period of detention, let them all go back to the Isles, where trouble was not long in following.

The important thing to understand about James VI is that he was arguably the most down-at-heel monarch in Scottish history; always short of money, he was continually looking for ways of finding more. Above all, he was convinced that the Isles were a rich source of revenue, unjustly withheld from the empty royal treasury. It was this conviction that later led him to embrace a plan for settling industrious Lowlanders in the northern Isles, a scheme which called for the physical extermination of the local people. It was also to play a part in the final ejection of Clan Iain Mor from Islay. So Angus and Lachlan, like many other serious offenders, were pardoned for a cash payment, as Donald Gregory argues.[17] Yet, to be fair, there is another dimension, which Gregory does not consider. James I's arbitrary conduct at Inverness in 1427 had created more problems than it solved, leading directly to the defeat of the royal army at the Battle of Inverlochy. The sudden removal of Lachlan and Angus would have created a vacuum in the Isles, which the royal government was not in a position to fill, and into which even more trouble is likely to have been sucked. At least some guarantee for the future good conduct of the Island chiefs was provided by John Campbell of Cawdor, who bound himself as surety for Angus, and John Campbell of Ardkinglass who promised to answer for Maclean.

Before being allowed to leave Edinburgh in 1591, Angus had to provide hostages for his good behaviour, one of whom was his eldest son, James, previously held hostage by Lachlan Mor. James was destined to replay, in the minor key, the life of Donald Dubh, spending a good part of his life in captivity simply for who he was. He was also fated to be the impotent witness to the death of his branch of Clan Donald.

There is no way of knowing if the Campbell guarantees for the future good conduct of the Macdonalds and Macleans would have worked. Perhaps they might, at least in the short term: they were, however, never given a chance. For in February 1592 Campbell of Cawdor was murdered, a serious symptom of the crisis that had gripped his clan since the death of the sixth Earl of Argyll. This and the murder the same month of the Earl of Moray had a seriously unsettling effect throughout the north and west of Scotland. Soon after, the Earl of Huntly, Moray's murderer was in revolt, assisted by Alasdair nan Cleas – 'Alasdair of the Tricks' – the tenth chief of the Keppoch Macdonalds. In attempting to bring the rebellion under control, Archibald Campbell, the seventh Earl of Argyll, was defeated at the Battle of Glenlivit in 1594. With Huntly and Argyll at each other's throats, it is no surprise that neither Angus nor Lachlan paid much heed to their promises of good behaviour.

Two years after the encounter at Glenlivit, with matters now a little more settled, James Macdonald was allowed to return to the west in the hope that he might persuade Angus to submit. To back this up, King James was prepared to use military force if necessary. Maclean and Donald of Sleat were sensible to the danger they faced, and hurried to make their peace with the king, as did Donald MacAngus of Glengarry. Angus inexplicably declined to follow their example. James at once granted the Rhinns of Islay to Lachlan Maclean, even though his conduct had, at points, been no better, if not worse than that of the Dunyveg chief. James' grand expedition to the Isles was now scaled down to one against the Macdonalds of Islay and Kintyre. This was the most serious threat the family ever faced; for, following the breach with their Irish kin, the Glens of Antrim no longer offered the refuge it had in ages past. James MacSorley not only refused to give Angus military aid but he also told King James of this request. With the king, Argyll, the Macleans and even the Antrim Macdonnells ranged against him, Angus was forced to seek terms.

Angus' capitulation took an unusual form. Not wishing to face the king in person, he surrendered his lands to his son, James, who went to Edinburgh in October 1596 in his father's place. James, who had spent some time at court and had become something of a royal favourite, was clearly expected to obtain better terms. This manoeuvre, however, was threadbare and inept, for the simple reason that Angus' lands were already forfeit to the crown, and he had thus no right to grant them to a third party. James received a knighthood from the king, but no greater concession than that. The surrender terms were tough. Sir James had to remain at court as a hostage, Angus was instructed to quit his lands on Kintyre and Gigha and keep good order in his remaining territories. Dunyveg Castle was to be surrendered to a royal garrison, and Angus was ordered to appear in court in person before Christmas. Once all these steps had been taken, King James would decide on what terms Angus would be allowed to keep his land on Islay, Colonsay and Jura.[18]

This was a bitter blow. Kintyre was the richest part of Angus' domain, and where he usually resided. It would gravely weaken his position in the Gaelic world, between the hostile Macleans to the north, and the equally hostile Macdonnells to the south. With the Scottish branch of Clan Iain Mor in such danger, it was now that Randal MacSorley made his takeover bid. He wrote to the king, hinting that Angus had no right to his lands on the grounds of illegitimacy, '. . . and in so doing geve it would pleas the king to accept him as his vassal he sould also acknauledge the lands occupyit be him in Ireland to be haldin of the king and his successors agains all uthers, bot sould also procure sindrie great men of that cuntrie to do the lyk'.[19]

For James, always anxious about his rights to the English throne as the heir to the unmarried Elizabeth, this was an interesting offer, but it is doubtful if he took it seriously. The claim that Angus was a bastard was in clear conflict with the evidence. Besides, even if he was, the inheritance would, in theory, have gone to his cousin Coll MacGillespic, the grandson of Colla, the one-time Captain of the Route and the older brother of Sorley Boy. Moreover, MacSorley's promise to obtain the allegiance of the Irish chiefs was far too politically dangerous, bringing a clear risk of ruining James's delicate relationship with Elizabeth. But MacSorley most likely did not really intend that the proposal would be taken seriously. It was, rather, an astute piece of political flattery, for it was clear that James would soon be in the place of the ailing Elizabeth. From their own individual perspectives, both men made a useful contact, which, as discussed in the previous chapter, continued to develop.

There was one serious side effect to MacSorley's contention that Angus of Dunyveg was illegitimate: it was a slur on Lady Agnes

Campbell, Angus' mother, and through her the whole house of Argyll. When MacSorley appeared at Stirling to press his case, he was vigorously resisted by the seventh Earl of Argyll. There was, however, more than simple family honour in this. Archibald Campbell was one of the most complex men of his time. He had lost his father at an early age, and had been deeply affected by the strife within his family, which appears to have left him with a morose and suspicious frame of mind, something of which is captured in his Gaelic nickname Gilleasbuig Grumach – Archibald the Grim. During his time, Clan Campbell underwent a profound change: long gone was the third earl's aim of winning the affection of the Gaels by a peaceful process. Archibald the Grim was interested in land and power. There were two ways of achieving this: simple territorial expansion and the acquisition of additional feudal rights. Both were to be pursued with equal vigour, and were to become the defining feature of the Campbells throughout the following century. In many ways, the modern perception of Clan Campbell as the Mephistopheles of Highland history is largely the creation of Archibald the Grim.[20]

Archibald had little love for Angus of Dunyveg, or anyone else, for that matter. However, it made better sense to have the troubled and incompetent Angus as a neighbour, than the energetic Antrim branch of the family. All attempts to re-establish the unity of Clan Iain Mor could expect to meet with Campbell resistance.

With Angus continuing to ponder his dilemma, a new policy was taking shape in the mind of the king. James was later to define his feelings towards the Gaelic people in his book, *Basilikon Doron*. Although, as he put it, there was some show of civilisation among those who dwelt on the mainland, those who dwelt in the Isles were 'alluterly barbures'. The only way of dealing with them was to plant colonies of Lowlanders who would combine civilising the better sort with 'rooting out or transporting the barbures stubborne sort, and planting civilitie in their roomes'.[21] In 1597, giving flesh to this theory, parliament passed an act requiring all chiefs to produce their title deeds before the Lords of Exchequer before 15 May of the following year. Those failing to respond would be forfeited. Both the king and his chief advisers were well aware that many would be unable to produce valid deeds, and so land would be made available for the projected Lowland plantation. The principal victims of this were the Macleods of Lewis, and, to a lesser extent, the Macdonalds of Sleat, who were to lose the Totternish peninsula to a company of Lowland adventurers.[22]

The scheme only ever got off the ground in Lewis, where a plantation was established before the end of 1598. Here it remained for some years, against the bitter opposition of the Macleods and Macdonalds, encouraged by Kenneth Mackenzie of Kintail, who had his own designs on the island. The whole project was, in all respects, atrociously handled. Having declared its intention, the government could hardly expect Donald Gorme of Sleat to sit back and let a successful plantation scheme endanger his own position on Skye. His obvious anger perhaps does much to explain a curious proposal in the English records of the time. This is an anonymous offer of service to Queen Elizabeth on behalf of Donald, who is described as the 'Lord of the Isles and the chief of the whole Clandonnell Irish'. His followers are said to include Clanranald, Glengarry, Keppoch, Maciain of Ardnamurchan and the Macdonalds of Dunyveg, along with the Camerons and others. In return for the many favours shown by the queen and her predecessors to Donald's own predecessors, the Lords of the Isles, it is proposed to begin a new rebellion in the Isles.[23] It is impossible to say if this is a genuine proposal to revive the Lordship of the Isles, or a gesture, born of anger and frustration. No such overture is likely to have been made without Donald's knowledge, but we cannot say how far the other families knew of the proposal. The probability is that they did not; for while the Lordship of the Isles may have remained a fond memory, who had the right to lead it was still a contentious issue. In any case, the time for such schemes was long past.

To the frustration of both the king and Sir James Macdonald, Angus ignored the settlement of October 1596. Sir James was once again sent home, but this time with the apparent approval of the king to remove his father from the headship of the clan. He went about the task in the most exuberant manner.

It is impossible to say if he had any clear purpose in mind as he approached his paternal home at Askomull in Kintyre; and it is almost certainly not true that he had the king's permission to murder his parents. However, once on the ground, he made opportunistic use of a violent local dispute. His kinsman, Gorrie Macalister of Loup, who had recently come of age, killed his former guardian in a brawl. Fearing for their own lives, the guardian's sons took refuge with Angus. Sir James arrived at this time, and, with the support of two to three hundred Macalisters, surrounded his father's house. Although both James' father and mother were in residence, the building was set alight. Ignoring the pleas of his mother, the fire was allowed to rage, until the roof began to collapse. To prevent the occupants escaping, trees had been placed across the door. Angus, badly burned, managed to free himself, only to suffer the additional indignity of being dragged through the mud. Despite his injuries, he was put in irons and held captive for four months.[24] Given the treatment he received, it seems probable that Sir James hoped for his father's death. Here, once again, Macdonald history seemed to be repeating itself. This ugly episode mirrors something of the dispute between John, last Lord of the Isles, and his own son, Angus Og. It was to be part of the misfortune of Clan Donald that they, and not the Campbells, were often the authors of their own destruction.

James, with the vigour once shown by Angus Og, set about restoring the fortunes of his family, brought close to ruin by his father. His first task was to settle affairs with Lachlan Maclean of Duart. The two men arranged to meet at Loch Gruinart in Islay in the summer of 1598, to consider a final settlement over the Rhinns. Unable to reach agreement, the two sides came to blows, and Lachlan Mor was killed. These are the bare facts of the so-called Battle of Loch Gruinart. But the death of Lachlan Mor is shrouded in as much mystery and speculation as the death of Shane O'Neil at Cushendun in 1567. Most of the detail we possess is derived solely from tradition; much of it fairly far fetched. The English, who enjoyed good relations with Lachlan, were convinced that he had been treacherously murdered, as was David Calderwood, the historian of the Scottish Church.[25] Calderwood goes so far as to suggest that King James himself was implicated in the crime. He certainly was not displeased that Lachlan was out of the way, and refused to consider his death as an example of murder under trust. The Maclean chief was too closely associated with the Earl of Argyll, whom James disliked, both as a man and as a political opponent. A reconstruction of the events at Loch Gruinart from the English diplomatic records does in fact suggest that the episode was more complex than a simple act of treachery.

According to the report of George Nicholson to Sir Robert Cecil, Lachlan came to the meeting, at Sir James' request, with a relatively small entourage of 200 men. As befitting the occasion, he came dressed only in silk and armed with a rapier, a dress sword rather than a Highland weapon of war.[26] If this is truly the case, he behaved with remarkable naïveté. The history of the whole affair would suggest the need for caution. Having fallen into one Macdonald trap, Lachlan is unlikely to have been lured so easily into another. That Sir James could be as violent, unpredictable and impulsive as the Duart chief had clearly been demonstrated by the business at Askomull. In the fight at Loch Gruinart, again according to Nicholson, the Macleans gained a temporary advantage over the Macdonalds, suggesting that they were not so ill prepared. Lachlan, fighting in his silks, is said to have killed forty Macdonalds on his own, so he must have used something stronger than a rapier. Sir James may have come as he did to Askomull, prepared to contemplate murder; but the facts suggest that there was indeed some kind of battle, perhaps arising from the intransigence of both men. When Sir James was eventually arraigned on a variety of charges, including the attempted murder of his parents, no mention is made of the Loch Gruinart affair, and the king himself was always of the opinion that it was a fair fight.

James hoped to build on this success against a deadly rival by settling matters with the king. In return for evacuating Kintyre and leaving Dunyveg Castle at the disposal of the government, he asked for a grant of the remaining estates on Islay. Argyll and John Campbell of Cawdor are said to have thwarted this proposal, although this assertion rests on supposition, rather than evidence.[27] There is nothing to suggest that the Campbells had an active interest in acquiring either Kintyre or Islay at this time.[28] Indeed, even if they had, Argyll lacked the political leverage to bring it about. James disliked and distrusted Argyll, whom he said resembled the Earl of Gowrie, a man who had once tried to kidnap him. In appointing men to deal with affairs in the Isles, the king constantly overlooked Argyll. As late as 1602 he continued to hold him at a distance:[29] it was not until he needed someone to take action against Clan Gregor after the Glen Fruin Massacre, that he turned back to the Campbell chief. Sir James' proposal was rejected, it would seem because of the prospect of a civil war between his supporters and those of his father. Probably more to the point, the amount of rent he was prepared to offer was far less than the king believed the Islay estates to be worth. Sir James later blamed Argyll and Cawdor as the authors of his misfortune; but this is reading backwards from subsequent events.

Sir James remained in control of his father's lands until about 1603, although without formal title. During this time some of the other branches of Clan Donald were involved in serious disputes. Oblivious to the continuing threat of Lowland colonisation, the Macleods and Macdonalds of Sleat went to war once again over the Totternish peninsula. In the seesaw struggle that followed, the Macleods attacked Donald Gorme's North Uist estates. Here they were intercepted and defeated by a smaller force of Macdonalds, ably led by Donald MacIain MhicSheamus, a kinsman of Clanranald. The feud continued to have such a serious impact on the economic wellbeing of the Isles that the people were 'forced to eat horses, doggs, cats, and other filthie beasts'.[30] Another battle followed in 1601, when the two sides met near the Cullins on Skye at a place called Binquhillin. Once again, the Macleods got the worst of the encounter. Angus Macdonald of Dunyveg, unable to bring order to his own affairs, was later to play a part in reconciling the two sides. This was followed by three weeks of feasting, when, according to tradition, Donald Mor MacCrimmon, one of a great dynasty of Skye pipers, composed and played a salute to the Macdonalds.[31]

The feud between Glengarry and the Mackenzies, bubbling under the surface for some years, erupted again in 1601. Angus, son of Donald MacAngus, the eighth chief of Glengarry, carried out an extensive raid on the Mackenzie lands around Kintail and Lochalsh. Soon after, the Mackenzies captured Castle Strome, the last Glengarry stronghold in Wester Ross, which was promptly destroyed. Considerable doubt must remain over the true facts. Strome Castle appears still to have been intact in 1607, when it was surrendered to the Mackenzies, together with other Glengarry property in the area. It was demolished some time after this. Faced with inexorable pressure from the Mackenzies, it was simply no longer possible for Glengarry to maintain his foothold in the old earldom of Ross, separated by some distance from his main estates. However, the family received some compensation in 1611, when Donald MacAngus gained Knoydart from Cameron of Locheil. Occupation of the area was only taken in face of the resistance from the Macdonalds of Knoydart, an offshoot from Clanranald. Ranald Macdonald, the seventh and last chief of Knoydart, was killed by the Glengarry men at a place on the coast called Rudha Raonaill.[32]

Glengarry's war with the Mackenzies came to a climax with the Kilchrist Raid, an episode famous in Clan Donald history, although one draped in a considerable amount of myth. Under the leadership of Alan Macranald of Lundie, a party of Glengarry men penetrated Ross, as far to the east as the parish of Kilchrist, near Beauly. Here they are said to have locked men, women and children in the local church and burnt them all to death. If this was not bad enough, the Glengarry piper composed a pibroch, mocking the screams of the dying. This story was later reported to Samuel Johnson during his famous tour of the Hebrides, although some of the details were distorted. In noting it, Donald Gregory expresses surprise that it receives no mention in the records of the time, which appears not to have alerted his scholarly instincts.[33] The fact remains that while stories of church burnings are fairly common in tradition, they are rare in fact. Much later, when the landlord's request for compensation for stolen cattle was lodged with the Privy Council, no mention was made of the alleged atrocity. 'Cillie Chriosd', the Glengarry gathering tune, celebrates a successful raid, not a gruesome massacre.[34]

In 1603, soon after James became the first King of Great Britain, Angus managed to oust his son as chief of Dunyveg, with the help of the Campbells. The Earl of Argyll held Sir James for a time, before delivering him to the care of the Privy Council. He was immediately incarcerated in the bleak castle of Blackness on the shores of the Firth of Forth. Here he planned his escape, but the details were discovered, and he was transferred to a more secure prison in Edinburgh Castle. For several years afterwards, Angus Macdonald was left in possession of his estates on both Islay and Kintyre, but without a firm title this was a far from satisfactory position.

In the years following the Union of the Crowns, the political situation in both the Western Isles and Ulster underwent a profound change. This was to have a far greater impact on the Celtic peoples than the changes that came with the collapse of the Lordship of the Isles. The independence of the Gaelic sea world was finally coming to an end. It used to be fashionable to date this from the Statutes of Iona, imposed on the island chiefs in 1609, which forced them to accept fundamental changes in their way of life; but these new rules had little short-term significance. The real transformation came with James' accession to the thrones of England and Ireland, which immeasurably increased royal power, especially naval power. A few years later, the Earls of Tyrone and Tyrconnel, the most powerful Gaelic chieftains in Ulster, left Ireland forever under pressure from the English authorities. This episode is famous in Irish history as the Flight of the Earls. Their vacant lands were used to set up a plantation of Protestants, migrating from England and the Lowlands of Scotland. Plantation had been an expensive failure in the Western Isles; but it was a great success in Ulster, the consequences of which we are still living with today.

James, and many of his predecessors, had sometimes encouraged and at other times ignored Clan Donald's adventures in Ireland to embarrass the English. Now, as King of Great Britain, this was something he could no longer tolerate. Moreover, the Macdonalds and the other chiefs of the Highlands and Islands could no longer count on the support of the English, as they had in the past, in their struggles with the Scottish crown. More seriously, James' Ulster Plantation drove a Lowland, English-speaking stake into the heart of the Gaelic world. Ireland could no longer provide, as it had for many ages, an outlet for the surplus military potential of the Isles. With Lowland power advancing, the old warrior society of the Isles appeared a dangerous anachronism. James defined his own feelings towards the Islanders in *Basilikon Doron*. Now, safe on his English throne, his views were reinforced by the fashionable playwright, William

Shakespeare, whose play *Macbeth*, written in about 1606, contained the following lines:

> The merciless Macdonwald,
> Worthy to be a rebel, for to that
> The multiplying villanies of nature
> Do swarm upon him, from the Western Isles
> Of kerns and galloglasses is supplied.[35]

Bit by bit a Lowland noose was closing around a Gaelic world. Interestingly, however, the final crisis of Clan Iain Mor was precipitated by factors completely beyond its control.

In early 1603, just before the king set out for London, Clan Gregor advanced into the Lowlands, massacred the Colquhouns in Glen Fruin, and came within a hair's breadth of the town of Dumbarton. James was outraged. The offenders were to be hunted down and exterminated; even the very name Macgregor was outlawed. But the children of the mist were not so easy to pin down, for they lived in no defined territory of their own. Many lived in lands under the control of Argyll and his cousins, the Campbells of Glen Orchy. Argyll enjoyed reasonably good relations with the Macgregors, who acted as his hatchet men from time to time, most recently in his feud with the Ogilvies. His support in hunting them down had to be obtained at a price; that price was to be Kintyre.

In October 1604 James wrote to the Privy Council, advising them of his intention to use Argyll against the Macgregors, and mentioning some unspecified reward for his services.[36] Two years later Argyll met Lord Scone at Perth to discuss a grant of the crown lands in Kintyre. Of course, there had to be some pretext for this award against the existing Macdonald tenants. In this regard, the Council records contain an undated and anonymous memorandum, consigned by the editors to 1607, the year Argyll was given Kintyre, but possibly written much earlier. It takes the form of a comprehensive attack on Clan Donald, very much in the vein of *Basilikon Doron*.

> The Erle of Argyle will embark him in actioun agains the Clan Donald, being the strongest piller of all the broken hieland men, quha never in any aige wer civill, bot hes bein the scoolmaisteris and fosteraris of all barbaritie, savignes, and crueltye, – hes evir from the beginning bein addictit nocht only to rebellioun within this continent land [the mainland] and the iles, bot evir wer assisteris of the northern Irische people . . . in all thair rebellionis. Now, this nobleman in action of blude being enterit with the same Clan Donald, nocht only will procure thair ruitteing out and utter

suppressing, bot upoun that same respect will evir be ane feir to
those in the northe of Ireland to rebell, having ane enemye lyand
sa neir to thame . . . sa long as the said Clan Donald remaynes
unremovit furth of the saidis landis, his Majestie nor na otheris
sal half any proffeit, and the uncivilitie and barbaritie sall continew
nocht only thair [Ireland] bot in the Iles.[37]

The anonymous author most certainly knew the mind of James, with
his references to barbarism and profit. It is a document written in the
Campbell interest. This, and the references to Ireland, might provide
some clues to its authorship. Towards the end of the previous century,
Denis Campbell, the Protestant Dean of Limerick, wrote a report on
the conditions of the Isles for the English government.[38] In his support
for the Campbells and hostility towards the Macdonalds, he takes a
very similar approach to the writer of the above, suggesting a closer
connection than mere chance.

As well as Kintyre, Argyll was also given a grant of the Dunyveg
lands on Jura. Angus Macdonald was left with a tenuous control of
the estates on mid- and south Islay. Argyll was encouraged to establish
Lowland plantations on Kintyre on the same basis as those being set
up in Ulster. In the charter granting him the authority to establish a
burgh on the shores of Loch Kilkerran – the future Campeltown – it
was specifically stated that no leases or feus should be granted to any
bearing the name Macdonald, Maclean, Macleod, Macalister and
Macneil.[39] Clearly distressed by his family's declining fortunes, Sir James
made another unsuccessful attempt to escape. Thereafter, he was held
in irons. All his appeals for release were simply ignored. In desperation,
he made a third attempt to escape in December 1607, with no greater
success than his two prior efforts. After this he was put on trial for
treasonable breaking of ward and condemned to death, although the
sentence was never carried out.

When it looked as if Angus Macdonald might offer some resistance
to the new arrangements, the king authorised a naval expedition to
the Isles, under the command of Andrew Stewart, Lord Ochiltree and
Andrew Knox, Bishop of the Isles. James and later his son and successor,
Charles I, distrustful of the motives of the nobles, made increasing use
of churchmen as senior civil servants, often with disastrous results.
Ochiltree and Knox arrived in the Isles in August 1608. Angus was
realistic enough to accept the situation, and surrendered Dunyveg
Castle, together with the fort on Loch Gorm, formerly held by the
Macleans. Ochiltree summoned the other chiefs to meet him at Aros
in Mull. Macdonald of Sleat, the Captain of Clanranald, and other
leading chiefs joined Angus here. Having bowed to royal authority,

Angus was allowed to return home. The others were a little less willing to listen to proposals that included, among other things, the destruction of large numbers of birlinns, the ancient basis of west Highland sea power. Seemingly learning nothing from past breaches of faith, most of the chiefs agreed to board Ochiltree's ship, only to be arrested after dinner. All were taken to prisons in the Lowlands. Suitably cowed, they were only allowed back to the Isles after agreeing to meet Bishop Knox on Iona in the summer of 1609, and here the famous Statutes were agreed. The aim was to create good order in the Isles, but it was to be based upon an attack on the culture and racial pride of the Gaelic people. The clans were to lose much of their military power, their naval power and their poets. Future chiefs and clan gentry were to be educated in the Lowlands. There was no provision, of course, for any form of Gaelic education. If fully implemented, the Statutes would have brought the clan system to an end, a century and a half before Culloden.

The Statues of Iona have been responsible for much muddled thinking.[40] It used to be argued that they created a unique bond between the Stewarts and the Highland chiefs that was to last until 1746: this is not true. That bond was created under specific political circumstances that had nothing at all to do with the Statutes. However, something had changed, and the chiefs were intelligent enough to realise this. By the seventeenth century the old style of clan warfare, practised during the conflict between the Macdonalds and Macleans, was over. Now that Ulster was closed off, the chiefs could no longer maintain large armies of redshanks. For many years to come the clans could, of course, be put on a war footing; but this was increasingly in response to a political situation beyond the confines of the Highlands and Islands. We only have to consider the differences between the three '45s. In 1545 the clans rose to establish an independent Gaelic world; in 1645 they fought against the Campbells rather than for Charles I; and in 1745 they were drawn into a war which took them far from their homes.

In 1612 Angus of Dunyveg, old and debt-ridden, agreed to mortgage his estates on Islay to John Campbell of Cawdor, Sir James Macdonald's own brother-in-law. In a surprising move, the mortgage was redeemed by Sir Randal MacSorley before Cawdor had a chance to enjoy his new acquisition. Angus, little regarded among his kin, died soon after. Paradoxically, it was Randal's attempt to restore the lost unity of Clan Iain Mor that precipitated the final crisis of the Islay Macdonalds, rather than Campbell plots.[41] Randal made a serious miscalculation: although seemingly acceptable to the king, he was not acceptable to the people of Islay. Soon they were complaining bitterly to the Privy

Council about the introduction of Irish laws and customs to their island, an indication of how far the two wings of Clan Iain had drifted apart. Before the matter could be settled, Ranald Oge, allegedly a bastard son of Angus, seized Dunyveg Castle from the royal garrison in March 1614. This was the first act in a drama which was to last for just over a year.

The events following from Ranald's seizure of Dunyveg are Byzantine in their complexity. One is reminded of Russian dolls, the difference being it is not figures within figures but intrigues within intrigues. No sooner had Ranald and his laughably small party taken the old family stronghold than it was retaken, in the name of the king, by Angus Og, Sir James's younger brother, aided by his cousin, Coll Coitach. Angus at once claimed that Donald Gorme, an illegitimate son of Sir James, had put Ranald up to taking the old family stronghold. Before Ranald could be questioned about this, he conveniently escaped. Angus, who clearly had his own ambitions, appeared as the loyalist, casting further suspicion on his older brother. His opening move was reasonably well played; but he almost immediately spoiled it by asking for a pardon for any offences he might have committed in ousting Ranald. What offence, it is reasonable to ask, could he possibly have committed in taking prompt action against traitors? To the Privy Council it simply looked as if he was trying to prolong his hold on Dunyveg. Angus had been the last Macdonald governor of the castle prior to its surrender to Bishop Knox in 1608, and only left with reluctance. However, the government agreed to issue the desired remission. This was carried to Islay by Bishop Knox himself, who came with fifty soldiers, ready to take repossession of Dunyveg. Rather than receiving the castle back into his care, the hapless Bishop found himself surrounded by a large party of hostile Macdonalds. He later wrote in bitter complaint of 'how traitourouslie I have bein oft defaissit be that pestiferous clan'.[42]

Bishop Knox's boats were burnt both literally and metaphorically. Before being allowed to leave, he was forced to agree that he would attempt to obtain a seven-year lease of the crown lands on Islay in favour of Angus in place of Randal MacSorley. Coll Coitach was likewise to be confirmed in the possession of some church lands on the island. To ensure he would fulfil the terms of his release, Knox was forced to leave behind his son, Andrew, and his nephew, John, as hostages. Filled with deep resentment against Clan Donald, the Bishop had also come to believe that Argyll was behind the whole affair, or so Angus had led him to believe. But why should Angus, assuming he was not hopelessly naïve, dance to a Campbell tune? Besides, what had Argyll to play for? He was already heavily in debt, and spending much time outside Scotland in the company of his new English wife. It was his kinsman Campbell of Cawdor, rather than Argyll himself, who was to be the beneficiary of the decline and fall of Clan Donald on Islay. One thing at least is absolutely certain: Angus Og was far out of his depth.

Bishop Knox made no attempt to keep his promise. Instead, John Campbell stepped quickly into the breach, offering an absurdly high rent for the crown estates. He then undertook to remove Angus from Dunyveg at his own expense, provided the government supplied him with some artillery. Before he could carry out his commission, this already complex affair was made even more so by the sudden and surprising intervention of the Earl of Dunfermline, the Chancellor of Scotland. He sent one George Grahame, a Gaelic speaker, to Islay to negotiate the release of the hostages left by Bishop Knox. Later, at his trial, Angus claimed that Grahame had promised him that, in return for freeing the hostages, Dunfermline would do his best to secure a pardon for him and a grant of the Islay estates. Angus then handed over Knox's relatives and, according to him, was authorised to act as the constable of Dunyveg on behalf of the Chancellor. This gave him the authority, he was led to believe, to defy Cawdor.[43] Dunfermline, who denied this story, may have had his own designs on Islay. At the very least, he may have attempted to outmanoeuvre Cawdor. Or perhaps Grahame, anxious to fulfil his commission, made false promises to Angus. It is hard to believe that Angus would have surrendered the hostages, the only ace he possessed, without some kind of reassurance. Sadly for him, he was altogether too trusting.

Neither Grahame's assurances nor Angus' protests could stop Cawdor building up his forces before Dunyveg and elsewhere on Islay. Ranald MacJames, Angus' uncle, surrendered the fort on Loch Gorme on 21 January 1615. Once Cawdor's cannon were in place, it was clear that the fall of Dunyveg was only a matter of time. Coll Coitach, a great survivor, made his escape just in time, after which Angus, unable to obtain terms, surrendered unconditionally. He was taken to Edinburgh, put on trial and hanged that summer.

Coll, in contrast, evaded all attempts to capture him, taking to a life of piracy. His nickname 'coitach' is usually taken to mean left-handed or ambidextrous, but it can also mean cunning or crafty. As it appears relatively late in his career, it would seem that the latter is the correct translation.[44] He appears to have been a totally unscrupulous man, and in his brief summer as a pirate did not discriminate in whom he attacked. Even his kinsmen, the Macdonalds of Sleat, had to take defensive measures against him.

The truly tragic figure in this whole affair is Sir James Macdonald, still languishing in captivity, an impotent witness to the misfortunes of his race. Betrayed by both his brother and his brother-in-law, he spent much of his time sending written appeals from his cell. He sent a poignant appeal to the king at the beginning of July 1615: 'If his Maiestie be not willing that I sall be his heigness tennent in Ila, for Goddis cause let his Matie hauld it in his awin hand; for that is certane, I will die befoir I sie a Campbell posses it.'[45] He received no reply, and thereupon he made one last attempt to escape. This time he succeeded. Unlike the previous attempts, the ground had been well prepared. It would appear that Sir James had made prior contact with Alisdair nan Cleas, the Keppoch chief, who with the aid of his own kin and the son of Clanranald had prepared the escape route. As soon as the fugitive was out of Edinburgh, a boat was in place to carry him across the Forth. His party then made its way quickly back to the Highlands. Although closely pursued, they managed to evade capture. On Skye Sir James and Alasdair met Donald Gorme. He would not join them in person, but allowed some of his men to accompany the rebels to Eigg, where they met up with Coll Coitach. Now some 300 strong, they proceeded to Islay, where they were met by the Maciains of Ardnamurchan. In June 1615 Dunyveg fell. After this, Sir James proceeded to Jura to raise the old tenants of his family, while Coll went to Kintyre on a similar mission. All this was aided by the absence of Argyll, hiding in England from his many creditors.

The old patrimony of Clan Iain in Scotland had been restored by force of arms. Having achieved this much the rebels then sat back and waited, watching as the initiative passed from their hands. Desperate to secure his position, Sir James launched a correspondent offensive. His pleas for peace and land were coupled by continuing attacks on the Campbells, who 'crave ever to fish in drumlie [mucky] waters'. Nothing availed. At the request of the Privy Council, the king ordered Argyll to return to Scotland to deal with the emergency. He did so with some reluctance, apparently having mellowed under the influence of his Catholic wife. But return he did. Soon the rebels were in full retreat from both Kintyre and Islay. Coll Coitach, perceiving in good time that the cause was lost, opened up negotiations on his own behalf. In return for betraying some of his kinsmen, he was allowed to keep his own life.[46] He later settled as Argyll's tenant on Colonsay, where he behaved just as unscrupulously as any Campbell, driving off and murdering the Macphees, the long-established residents of the island.[47] Sir James managed to escape with Alasdair of Keppoch to Ireland and from there to the Continent. He never returned to the Isles.

Ruins of castle and chapel, Finlaggan (Photograph by David Caldwell)

A Highland chieftain, painted by Michael Wright around 1660 (National Galleries of Scotland)

Aros Castle, scene of the meeting of chieftains in 1609, and ruinous since the seventeenth century (William Daniell's *Voyage Round Great Britain*)

Seal of Angus Mor of Islay – 1292
(The British Library)

Seal of Alexander of Argyll – 12
(The British Library)

Detail from MacLeod wall-tomb, St Clement's, Rodel, Harris, (Crown copyright, Royal Commission o
the Ancient and Historical Monuments of Scotland)

There is an interesting postscript to the fall of Clan Iain Mor. In 1618 Argyll was given permission to go abroad, where he promptly converted to Catholicism and entered the service of Spain. He was denounced as a traitor, whose crimes included being seen in open friendship with James Macdonald and Alasdair of Keppoch.[48] There appears to have been no personal bitterness between the three men, who were eventually pardoned and allowed to settle in London. James left no legitimate successor, so with his death Clan Iain of Dunyveg passed into history. It was left to Argyll's own son to reap the bitterness left by its passing.

9

WAR AGAINST KING CAMPBELL

The fall of Clan Iain Mor left the Campbells in possession of most of the mainland and insular territories of the ancient Scots kingdom of Dalriada. They were also in control of the lands held by Somerled after his naval victory of Epiphany 1156. Archibald, the seventh Earl of Argyll, had converted to Catholicism and lived in exile, permanently alienated from his Protestant clan. If his neighbours expected any relief from this, they were to be disappointed. Perhaps because of his growing sympathy for the old faith, Archibald was, at the time of the Islay crisis, no longer quite as 'grim' as he had been in the past. However, his son and namesake, Archibald, Lord Lorne, was, if anything, to be even grimmer. Unlike his father, he had few soldierly skills. His particular talent lay in manipulating the feudal system, enabling him to extend his power far beyond the Campbell territories. Faced with the onward march of Campbell feudal superiorities, families like Clanranald looked as if they would eventually go the same way as Clan Iain Mor. But the more immediate threat to Clanranald came with the destruction of the Maciains of Ardnamurchan, which brought the Campbells to their southern frontier.

The fourth Earl of Argyll had acquired the superiority of Ardnamurchan and Sunart some years before, although the title was not enforced. Successive Maciains continued to hold their estates without troubling to acknowledge the authority of *Maccailein Mor*. However, towards the end of the sixteenth century, the Maciains were enveloped by a bloody succession crisis. To secure his position against internal opposition, John Maciain acknowledged Archibald the Grim as his feudal superior. John died in about 1611, leaving Alasdair, a minor, to succeed to the chieftainship. The following year Argyll appointed Duncan Campbell of Barbreck to act as a guardian, administering the estates from Mingary Castle.[1] Barbreck was capable enough, but he had an arrogant and cruel streak in his character, and ended by completely alienating the local people. John Macdonald Mhic Iain, one of the chief tenants, came to Edinburgh to complain to the Earl of Argyll in person. Finding that Argyll was not in town, he appealed to his agent, William Stirling of Auchyle. He duly wrote to Barbreck on Argyll's behalf, urging him to treat the Maciains with kindness. Barbreck simply ignored this reasonable request. With no option left to them, they appealed to Clanranald.

In 1618, under the command of a second John Moidertach, 200 men of Clanranald descended on Ardnamurchan and Sunart with 'gritte pypes blowing afore thame', driving out Barbreck and his supporters. But with the support of the law, he was soon back in place, as cruel and as vindictive as in the past. In the late summer of 1624, Barbreck was faced with a second rebellion, led by Alasdair Maciain, now grown to manhood. In desperation, the Maciains seized an English ship and took to piracy. Many other western clans sympathised with the plight of the Maciains, none more so than Clanranald, which was warned by the Privy Council to offer no assistance to the rebels.[2] Faced with a potential crisis, the Campbells reacted with speed. The principal gentry of the clan assembled at Inveraray to organise their defences.[3] Lord Lorne, acting head of the family, absent on business, was immediately summoned home, where he received from the government his first commission of fire and sword. Under close pursuit, many of the Maciains landed in the country of Clanranald, where they took to hiding. Lorne landed in Ardnamurchan in the late spring of 1625 and quickly stamped out the embers of the insurrection. Of the prisoners taken, ten were hanged on the spot and a further fourteen sent to Edinburgh for trial. Lorne was duly thanked for his services. From this point forward Clan Iain of Ardnamurchan ceased to exist, Clan Campbell's second Clan Donald victim in a decade. Most of the survivors found a permanent home among the people of Clanranald, and were presumably quick to take arms with them against the Campbells when the opportunity arose twenty years later.

Not many years after this, Lorne's northern offensive continued, with a slight change of emphasis. Bit by bit government policy had increased the burden of debt carried by many Highland landlords. The legal requirement for chiefs to find securities, to pay feu duties and crown rents and to make regular appearances before the Privy Council in Edinburgh, greatly increased their need for ready cash. As incomes, especially from the more marginal estates, were limited, this could only be obtained by borrowing, and all such borrowing had to be secured on land. By late 1633, Lord Lorne had taken over debts in excess of £21 000, a truly formidable sum for the time, which John Moidertach, the Captain of Clanranald, owed to Donald Macdonald of Sleat. Faced with this he had no choice but to grant Lorne wadsets of lands in Moidart and Arisaig on the mainland, as well as additional grants on South Uist. In addition, he had to agree that, even if the mortgage were redeemed, he would continue to acknowledge Lorne as his feudal superior. Within a period of five years all the Clanranald estates, both in the Isles and on the mainland, were incorporated within a Campbell feudal superiority.[4]

The early years of the seventeenth century had seen a steady weakening of the Gaelic people in a political, cultural and economic sense. However, under threat from the Campbells and Lowland hostility, many of the septs of Clan Donald were soon to undergo something of a spiritual renaissance, which gave them a new sense of purpose and direction. Beyond the land of the Campbells, the sixteenth-century Reformation had made little impact in the western Highlands. Many chiefs were deeply hostile to Calvinism, especially as it was associated with the House of Argyll, and remained loyal to the old faith. But with the absence of priests Catholicism atrophied and degenerated, soon mixed with a variety of pagan practices. This changed in 1623 when Pope Urban VIII authorised an Irish Franciscan mission to the Highlands and Islands. These Gaelic-speaking priests were greeted with widespread enthusiasm, making thousands of converts, particularly on the old lands of Clan Iain Mor, including Kintyre. Coll Coitach was particularly supportive of the mission. However, the most important convert by far was John Moidertach of Clanranald. Soon after he was received into the church in 1624 he wrote to the Pope, showing greater enthusiasm than political or strategic sense, that 'we shall with the help of our kinsfolk and friends subdue the greater part of Scotland, without the assistance of anyone else; though we cannot keep it long against the power of the King unless aided by your Holiness and the power of the Catholic kings'.[5] This renewed religious enthusiasm, when combined with deep hostility to the power of the Protestant Campbells, was a potentially explosive mixture. All that was needed was cause and opportunity to ignite the west.

The Antrim Macdonnells had never lost sight of their Scottish heritage, which the failure to acquire the Dunyveg lands on Islay in 1614 did nothing to deter. A second opportunity came a few years prior to the death of the first Earl of Antrim. From his London exile Archibald the Grim was keen to secure an inheritance for James Campbell, his eldest son by his second marriage. Against the opposition of Lord Lorne, James was given a grant of Kintyre in 1626. However, the estate was heavily burdened with debt, and so, under the nose of his half-brother, he sold it to the Earl of Antrim in January 1635, who acquired it on behalf of his son, Randal, Viscount Dunluce. Lord Lorne, with the support of some of his chief kin, was quick to react to this unwelcome development. He petitioned the Privy Council, warning them of 'the feareful prejudice that may arise thereby to the disturbance of the publict peasce if the Earle of Antrim and his sone or anie of the Clandonnald . . . sall recover the possessions of thair wounted inheritance from whiche by his Majesties royall force and auetoritie they wer worthilie expelled'.[6] Lorne also predicted another Macdonald rebellion and said they would import priests, which would 'mak the whole people turn papistes'. The sale duly fell through and, by grant of the king, Kintyre was acquired by Lorne. Dunluce, who succeeded his father as second Earl of Antrim a few years after, was left with a deep sense of resentment.

In the years after 1603 the Privy Council on behalf of the absentee monarch ruled Scotland. This worked reasonably well while James VI was alive, for he was known and understood by the chief men of the realm. Although he formulated the constitutional nonsense of absolute monarchy, he was a realist, taking proposals only so far as he thought politically advisable. This was particularly true of religious policy. With some skill he had managed to persuade most Scots of the virtues of a modified Episcopacy, against their Presbyterian inclinations, but when he met with resistance he stopped short of imposing the High Anglicanism of the English Church, with its fondness (shared by the king) for prayer books and ritual.

Things began to change with the succession of Charles I in 1625. Although he had been born in Scotland, Charles had grown up in England; he knew little and cared less for the ancient realm of the Stewarts. One of his first acts was to introduce a new revocation, the most sweeping in Scottish history. By this measure he reclaimed all land grants right back to the death of James V in 1542, wiping out at a stroke all the lucrative gains the Scottish nobility had made at the expense of the church during the Reformation. The intention was good: he simply aimed to establish the kirk on a more satisfactory financial basis – but Charles' good intentions usually had disastrous results. Lacking all his father's political acumen, he took absolutism too literally, failing to consult the nobility on this drastic measure. Past revocations had alienated Highland chiefs; this one alienated virtually the whole of the Scots aristocracy. In practice, the revocation of 1625 was never fully implemented, but Charles never entirely regained the trust of the people he depended on to rule Scotland.

Having made one serious mistake, Charles proceeded to make a second, with even more disastrous results. Failing to learn from his father's cautious example, he decided to push a reluctant Scotland further along the Anglican road. The centrepiece of this was a new Prayer Book, which the king ordered the people of Scotland to accept, sight unseen, in the summer of 1637. This resulted in a religious and political explosion, unseen since the Reformation. Nobles, churchmen and people united in a great wave of opposition, which finally took the form of the National Covenant of February 1638. This document, second only in Scottish history to the Declaration of Arbroath, contained a revolutionary proposition – that there should be no innovations in religious practice that had not first been tested by free parliaments and general assemblies of the church. Those who held to the National Covenant were soon to be known as Covenanters. With matters slipping out of his control, the king tried to take some of the heat out of this self-induced crisis by sending James, Marquis of Hamilton, to Scotland to negotiate with the Covenanters. He also came with the supplementary aim of testing the depth of opposition to the new cause.

It is difficult to know what to make of James Hamilton. Although not entirely without charm or ability, his political talents were of a limited nature. He indulged in elaborate conspiracies when only plain speaking would do. He found a bad situation, and then proceeded to make it worse.[7] If Charles already had too many enemies, Hamilton succeeded in giving him even more. By far the most serious of these was to be Archibald Campbell, Lord Lorne.

Although the National Covenant was well received in many parts of Scotland, it met with resistance in conservative Aberdeenshire, an area under the control of the Marquis of Huntly. Moreover, it made no impact at all in the western Highlands and Islands, especially in those areas under the control of Clan Donald. Hamilton would have been aware of the military potential of the Highlanders if it came to a trial of arms, an increasingly likely possibility. He was also closely acquainted with Randal Macdonnell, the second Earl of Antrim, and was clearly aware of his territorial ambitions in Scotland, as he made clear to the king in a letter written in June 1638: 'The Earle of Antrim may be of youse in this business, for he is beloved by divers of his name, and hath some pretentiounes to lands in Kintyre, Iyles, and Heaglands, and will no doubt repaire to Iryland and bring such forces with him as will put thoes countries in that disorder . . . as I hoope that part of the countrie will dou us bot lyttle hurt.'[8]

Hamilton was also in contact with Donald Gorme of Sleat, who promised him his own support as well as that of Glengarry and Clanranald 'with our haill name of Claine Donald'.[9] But Hamilton was realistic enough to know that this great western alliance he was building up was based not on affection for Charles but on hatred of the Campbells. He left the king in no doubt about this simple fact. In his political manoeuvres, conducted over the tense summer of 1638, Hamilton was laying the foundation for the war between Clan Campbell and Clan Donald that was to engulf the Highlands from 1644 to 1647.

The odd thing is that Hamilton, in stirring up these passions, had done his best to ensure that Lord Lorne would be an enemy of the king. Lorne was still a privy councillor and, although he was a staunch Protestant, he was not yet a Covenanter. It might be argued that Hamilton, in forcing him to watch his back, was ensuring his loyalty, or at least his neutrality. If so, it was hardly necessary. Archibald the Grim was still alive in London and it was always open to the king to use him to supplant Lorne. In bringing about the unity of Clan Donald Hamilton had ensured that, when the moment was right, Lorne would come out against the king. The details of the plot soon leaked out and Lorne was quick to write to Hamilton, saying he did not know why he deserved such treatment. If attacked by the Macdonalds, he continued, he would take steps to defend himself.[10] Knowing the chief threat he faced was from Antrim, Lorne did much to cultivate Thomas Wentworth, Charles' Lord Deputy in Ireland, whom he knew had little liking of the Gaels in general and the Macdonnells in particular. He wrote to Wentworth in late July, complaining about the race of Clan Donald, 'who hes evir takine thair adwantage of trowbelsome tymes to execute their re-bellions'.[11]

On the advice of Hamilton, Charles allowed a General Assembly, the first for many years, to meet in Glasgow in November 1638. If Hamilton, in the role of High Commissioner, hoped to control and direct this assembly, he was badly mistaken. Refusing to heed his calls to disband, the assembly declared not only the king's Prayer Book illegal, but went on to abolish episcopacy itself. War was now inevitable. While the Glasgow Assembly was still in session, the seventh Earl of Argyll died, and before long the new earl threw the full weight of his clan behind the Covenanters. That ancient unity between the Crown and the Campbells, which had done so much to weaken Clan Donald, was now broken.

The so-called Bishops' Wars of 1639 and 1640 saw little real fighting. Charles, who had ruled without an English parliament for some years, lacked the resources to mount a full-scale campaign against the Scots. Instead he was forced to rely on various plots and schemes hatched by Antrim, Huntly, Hamilton and others, which, while breathtaking in the scale of their ambition, had little real effect. In June 1639, while the royal army was poised on the Scottish border, the king met Antrim and Donald Gorme near Berwick. Both men were given commissions of lieutenancy over the Isles. In reward for their services, Charles promised Antrim Kintyre, while Donald was to have Ardnamurchan and a number of the islands.[12] But in the face of Wentworth's obstruction, Antrim was unable to mount his planned expedition to the Isles.

While Antrim seethed in frustration, Argyll set about closing the backdoor into Scotland in the spring and summer of 1639. Some 300 Macdonalds were forced to flee to Ireland to take refuge against the Campbell troops. Kintyre and Islay were fortified. Archibald Macdonald of Sanda and his son Archibald were arrested, together with two of Antrim's agents. Colin Campbell of Ardesier invaded Colonsay, the home of Coll Coitach. Coll himself was taken prisoner, although it is not absolutely certain if this took place on Colonsay itself.[13] His sons Archibald and Angus were also taken, although Ranald and Alasdair evaded capture, making their way to Ireland. Alasdair's escape was to be a source of particular regret to the Campbells. Alarmed by these developments, Antrim wrote to Wentworth: 'My Lord, I beseech you, consider of these courses, and, if your lordship will not send present relief, that my name will be cutt off: and sooner than they should all be cutt off, I shall advise them to shift for themselves. For the love of God, my Lord, let us not sleep any longer, and give us leave to revenge my friends.'[14]

No help was forthcoming. Antrim was perhaps beginning to regret his negotiations with Hamilton, and the effect this was having on his people. He had earlier expressed the gloomy view that 'until the end of the world no MacDonnell shall be allowed to enjoy a foot of land in Scotland'.[15]

Antrim's plots had raised animosity between the Campbells and Macdonalds to a fever pitch. Even after the conclusion of the first Bishops' War in June 1639, Argyll continued to hold Coll Coitach and his other prisoners and refused to demobilise. His soldiers prevented the return of the Macdonald refugees from Ireland. Colonsay and Oronsay, previously tenanted by Coll and his followers, were given to Campbell of Ardesier. All this was designed to ensure that if the war were renewed, as looked very likely, Antrim and his supporters would have no leverage in the south-west Highlands and Islands. Argyll prepared his defences well. When the second Bishops' War broke out in the summer of 1640, there was little stir among the Macdonalds in the west, apart from an unsuccessful raid by Alasdair MacColla on Islay.[16] Argyll was given a free hand to campaign against the royalists to the east of his domains, principally the Stewarts of Atholl and the

Ogilvies. But this also had an unsettling effect on the men of Glengarry and Keppoch, who continued in arms against the Campbells right into the following year.

In the 1640s the Campbells of Breadalbane and the Macdonalds of Keppoch, aided by Maciain of Glencoe, met in battle at a place called Sron a Chlachain above the village of Killin. This clash was more in the nature of a private encounter, rather than an episode in the civil war that was engulfing Scotland, and receives no mention in the official records of the time. We cannot even be certain about the date. In some accounts it took place in 1640, while others date it to 1646.[17] In itself this is of no great significance, but for one thing: although it was a Macdonald victory, their casualties included Angus Og, the son of the Keppoch chief, Maciain of Glencoe, and the father of Iain Lom, another of the Keppoch Macdonalds. Iain Lom – 'Barefaced John' – was to be one of the greatest, perhaps the greatest, of all the Gaelic poets. In his lament for the death of Angus Og at Sron a Chlachain he mentions the death of his own father in an offhand, almost casual way:

Although I left my father there it his not he that I mention
But the piercing which the sword made about your kidney.[18]

But his father's death would appear to have had a far greater impact than the poet admits, for it left him with an almost pathological hatred for the Campbells. This was far in excess of the rest of the Keppoch family, whose martial energies were more often directed against the Mackintoshes of Clan Chattan. As his most violent attacks on the Campbells are dated prior to 1646, this would suggest that the Battle of Sron a Chlachain took place at the earlier rather than the later date.

The war of 1640 left King Charles even worse off than before. Forced to buy a peace with the Scots, who had captured Newcastle, he could only raise the necessary funds by calling parliament. If Charles expected this would ease a difficult situation, he was to be sadly mistaken. The puritan gentry, many of them sympathetic to the Covenanters, dominated parliament. Under the leadership of John Pym, John Hampden and later Oliver Cromwell, they demanded major political and religious concessions. Little by little the political crisis in England became steadily worse. Looking for allies, Charles even turned to his former enemies, coming to Scotland in the summer of 1641. Argyll was created a marquis, although he was no more sympathetic to the king's plight than before. Charles had one small victory, though. James Graham, the fifth Earl of Montrose, was one of the original signatories of the National Covenant. Growing increasingly suspicious and jealous of the influence of Argyll, however, he began to move away from his former allies, heading down a road that was to have a remarkable outcome. This was to have some long-term benefit for Charles, but in the short term the political situation became even worse. In October 1641, before the king returned to London, the Catholic Irish rose in revolt.

Of all the king's subjects, the Irish had most reason to be discontent. The Ulster Plantation had robbed them of the best land, and made them a second-class race in their own country. Wentworth and the English authorities in Dublin had done nothing to disguise their view that the Irish were a conquered people. The growth of radical Protestantism in Scotland and England had both encouraged and alarmed them. They were encouraged because they saw it was possible to force the king to make religious concessions, and they were alarmed by the intense anti-Catholic rhetoric of the puritans and Covenanters. Beginning among the discontented communities of Ulster, the rebellion soon spread across the rest of Catholic Ireland.

The rising of 1641 put the Earl of Antrim in a difficult position. While himself a Catholic he remained loyal to the king, although many of his tenants were sympathetic to the rebels. Needless to say, Antrim, despite his protests, was suspected of complicity in the Irish rising, especially by Argyll, who soon saw an opportunity to turn the tables on his enemy by launching an invasion of Ulster.

Alasdair MacColla was also deeply involved in events in Ireland. Also a Catholic, he initially took Antrim's lead in remaining aloof. Instead he and his brother joined one of the Catholic companies in a mixed regiment raised to protect the Route. But this did not work well, and soon relations within the force began to break down. Alasdair and the Catholic companies then joined the rebels. Once this became known in Scotland it raised fears that it would mean a revival of Antrim's earlier plans to invade the west of Scotland. Argyll quickly seized the initiative. The fortifications in Kintyre were repaired and the Privy Council approved the continuing detention of Coll Coitach and his sons. In England parliament and king were in a political deadlock that was to end later that year in the outbreak of the Civil War. Unable themselves to respond to the crisis in Ireland, both king and parliament agreed that the Scots should send an army to Ulster, which was to include a Campbell regiment raised by Argyll.[19] Argyll was also given the power to appoint a governor for Rathlin Island. The occupation of Rathlin would do much to improve his security in the south-west Highlands.

In Ireland, Alasdair began to make a reputation for himself as a soldier. In early 1642 he won a victory against a party of Protestant settlers at the Battle of the Laney. This was a fairly small-scale encounter, and could have passed into history as of no more than local significance. It has, however, been persuasively argued that it marks the beginning of the Highland charge, a tactic which, in its most developed form, was to allow the Gaels to win battle after battle until Culloden in 1746.[20] In essence, this consists of an initial discharge of firearms, followed by close-quarter combat with sword and shield. Detailed discussion will be postponed until we consider the Battle of Tippermuir, fought in September 1644.

Alasdair and his brother Ranald continued to prove their military skills in the Irish wars, coming close to winning the Battle of Glenmaquin in the summer of 1642. Robert Stewart, who commanded the opposing side, paid tribute to their conduct: 'Coll Kittaghs sonnes cryed up for their valour as invincible champions, with their Highlanders and some others assaulted my brigade fiercely in so much that we were not far from comeing to to push of pike, but . . . our men . . . galled them with continuall shot . . .'[21]

In the spring of 1642 the main Scots army landed in Antrim, followed soon after by the Argyll regiment, commanded by Sir Duncan Campbell of Auchinbreck, which landed on Rathlin, before proceeding to the mainland. Worried by this, Randal Macdonnell, who had spent some time away from his estates, hurried back and took up residence at Dunluce Castle, from where he attempted to open negotiations with the Scottish commander, Robert Monro. His gambit failed. Monro took him prisoner, possibly for his own safety, before handing his lands and property, including Dunluce, over to the Campbells. Antrim was taken south to Carrickfergus, the headquarters of the main Scottish army. Fortune had not been kind to him. His great scheme to revive the power of Clan Donald in the Isles had come to nothing, and what was worse, he had not come to Argyll: Argyll had come to him. The Campbells were in the Glens, and showed every sign of remaining there. Clan Iain Mor had reached the lowest point in its history.

Before the end of the year Antrim escaped, turning up at York to confer with the king, now at war with parliament. The political and military situation was delicate. Despite the king's marginal success against parliament at the Battle of Edgehill, the two sides were still evenly matched. In their search for allies, both turned to the Covenanter government in Scotland, which refused to be drawn at this stage, preferring to act as an arbiter. But Charles' search for allies would not stop with Protestant Scots. Soon he began to move into more dangerous territory.

There were many in both England and Scotland profoundly suspicious of the king's contacts with Catholics, who, through his wife,

Henrietta Maria, had formed a strong party at court for some time. It was in his best interests that his individual problems in Scotland, England and Ireland were, as far as possible, kept separate. But now Antrim, serving his own interests and the king with equal enthusiasm, proposed another grand scheme, even greater than that of 1639. Peace would be made with the Catholic Irish, now organised in a confederacy based at Kilkenny. All the king's friends in all three kingdoms would unite in a mighty offensive against puritans, Covenanters and, of course, against Campbells. Neither he nor the king seem to have paused to consider that the union of all the king's friends would, at one and the same time, bring the union of all the king's enemies. Antrim returned to Ireland in May 1643 to lay the foundations of this scheme, only to promptly fall prisoner to the Scots for a second time with important papers in his possession, revealing all the details to his enemies. The second Antrim plot caused widespread outrage in Scotland, revealed in the correspondence of Robert Baillie, a leading minister.

> A commission was given to Antrim to treat with the Irish rebells, that the English and they might agree . . . the first service of the reconciled Ireland and England should be the disposal of the dissafected Scots; that they should goe by sea to Carlile, wher Nithsdale and other Southland lords should joyne; that Colekittoch's sones should waken our Isles; that McClaine and Gorrum, and the other clanes dissafected to the Campbells, should goe to armes; that Huntly and his son Aboyne, with Bamfe and Airlie, Montrose and the Marshall, should raise our North . . . that so in a trace we should become a field of blood . . .[22]

These details were enough to precipitate the Covenanters into a military alliance with the parliamentary party known as the Solemn League and Covenant. In pursuit of this a Scottish army entered England in 1644 and helped defeat the royal army at the Battle of Marston Moor, the most serious setback Charles had suffered to date. It was now imperative that a diversion be created in Scotland.

Amazingly, Antrim managed to escape a second time in October 1643, making his way to Oxford, the king's main base, where he met with Montrose. For some time prior to the signing of the Solemn League and Covenant, Montrose had been arguing for a pre-emptive strike against the Covenanters. Now he and Antrim devised a scheme for joint military action. On 28 January 1644 a bond was drawn up between them, in which Montrose was named as Lieutenant General of Scotland and Antrim as General of the Highlands and Islands. Montrose promised to raise the royalists on the Borders and the north and east of Scotland by 1 April, while Antrim promised to raise his supporters in Ireland and the Isles – 10 000 men, so he claimed – and attack Argyll by the same date. As a foretaste of this, Alasdair and Ranald MacColla had begun a naval attack on Campbell positions in the Isles the previous November. James Campbell of Ardkinglas eventually managed to chase the two brothers back to Ireland, but it took him six months to do it.

It was one of the features of Montrose's character that he constantly overestimated both his support and his own capacity. His offensive came to an abrupt halt at Dumfries, well short of his target. Antrim was also late in meeting the target date. By the summer of 1644 he had, however, assembled about 1600 men, recruited mostly from his own estates, Irish in the main, but also some Macdonald refugees.[23] These men, mostly musketeers, were soon to prove themselves to be superb soldiers, cool and controlled under fire. All – Irish and Scots – had particular reasons for hating the Campbells. Overall command was given to Alasdair MacColla, again indicating just how far this would be a war against the Campbells rather than for the king. Antrim's expeditionary force was intended as a spur to urge the rest of Clan Donald and the other anti-Campbell forces into action; it would not be enough in itself to bring down Argyll and the Covenanters. Everything depended on the willingness of the Highlanders to take up arms.

In early July 1644, about the time of Marston Moor, Alasdair's little army landed on Ardnamurchan, carried there from Ireland in three ships, wives and children accompanying many of the fighters. In taking this less direct route, Alasdair had once again proved his military capacity, outflanking Argyll by avoiding a direct attack on Islay and Kintyre. Commenting on his arrival, Patrick Gordon of Ruthven was later to write that he now began a war that 'opened all the waines of the king-dome, and drew furth oceanes of blood'.[24]

Alasdair enjoyed some early success by taking the castles of Lochaline and Mingary – the old Maciain stronghold – from the Campbells, allowing him to establish a defensible base. But, and this is hardly surprising, the expected support from the western clans failed to materialise. Although they had lost none of their fighting spirit, the clans were demoralised by successive failures, most recently seen in Alasdair's own abortive attack on the Isles. It had been his intention to pass command to Donald Gorme of Sleat, who had received the king's commission in 1639. But Donald had recently died and his son, Sir James Macdonald, was far less enthusiastic about such a risky enterprise. It has sometimes been suggested that Alasdair lacked sufficient intelligence or confidence to assume command himself. This assumption is based on a simple misunderstanding about the conservative nature of Gaelic society. Despite his soldierly skills and his proud antecedents, Alasdair was in a land-based society, no more than a son of a fairly minor figure, Argyll's one-time tenant on Colonsay. He would not, therefore, have expected great men like Clanranald and Sleat to take his lead: some more substantial figure was needed. Perhaps it would have been different if Antrim had appeared in person. Antrim, however, was a politician rather than a soldier, and, unlike Argyll, he had the good sense to realise this.

Macdonald of Keppoch was the first important chief to join Alasdair in his recruiting march, but this was still not enough. He took the dangerous step of moving away from the west Highlands into Atholl, where many of the people, although generally royalist in sympathy, had few cultural or social connections with their wilder neighbours to the west, and none at all with the Irish. Tragically it looked as if the whole venture was about to end in an armed clash between men whose political outlook was the same. It was at this point that Montrose, now a marquis, made his dramatic entry onto the scene. Riding through southern Scotland in disguise and almost alone, he arrived just in time to prevent a battle between Alasdair and the men of Atholl. His appearance was widely welcomed; Alasdair willingly surrendered command and the combined force marched on to Perth, where an army had been hastily assembled to meet them. On 1 September 1644 Montrose and Alasdair swept this army aside when they won their first great success at the Battle of Tippermuir.

The honour of Tippermuir probably belongs more to Alasdair than Montrose, his first opportunity to practise, on a larger scale, the technique he had developed at the Battle of the Laney in 1642. The Highland charge, in other words, had finally come to the Highlands. It took the classic form, soon to become familiar to many Lowland armies: an initial discharge of muskets followed by close-quarter engagement with blade weapons. But Tippermuir, apart from the innovation of guns, was in many ways little different from Highland battles of ages past, which began with a discharge of missile weapons followed by an onward surge, like Kinloch-Lochy in 1544. The other side of the equation tends to be overlooked: the changing nature of Lowland armies.

It is important to realise that Tippermuir was the first time that Highlanders and Lowlanders had met in full-scale battle since Inverlochy in 1431. At Inverlochy, and the earlier battle at Harlaw, both Highlanders and Lowlanders would have fought with similar weapons and techniques, usually wearing chain-mail or some other form of body armour. By 1644 Highlanders had not lost their skill in the use of blade weapons: Lowlanders, in contrast, had. At Marston Moor the Scots had faced soldiers armed and organised very much like themselves, musketeers whose secondary defence while undergoing the dangerous operation of reloading was provided by pikemen. But neither pike nor unloaded musket were much use against shield and broadsword. More than this Lowland amateur soldiers, quickly raised and badly trained, were little use against men educated all their lives in a warrior tradition. The Highland charge was not a great innovation, but a technique with ancient roots. It would take a century of intermittent experience for Lowlanders to learn that it could be defeated, using defence in depth by well-trained, professional soldiers.

Tippermuir marks the beginning of a year of victories. Although many of the recently recruited clansmen returned home loaded with booty, Alasdair's Irish infantry did much to secure a second victory less than a fortnight later at the Battle of Aberdeen. Argyll, in attempting to pin the enemy down, exhausted himself in a fruitless pursuit, resigning his command before the onset of winter, retiring to spend the season at Inveraray, his Highland capital. Fate was to allow him no peace.

The twin victories of Tippermuir and Aberdeen electrified the Gaelic people, lifting their earlier demoralisation by a new realisation that the Covenanters could be beaten in the field.[25] Before the onset of winter Clan Donald, like some sleeping giant, was beginning to stir. In October Alasdair left Montrose to attend to his bases in Ardnamurchan, under attack by the Campbells, and to carry out another recruiting drive in the west Highlands. But the news of the recent royalist successes had already done its work. No sooner had Alasdair arrived than he was met by John Moidertach, the Captain of Clanranald, described by Patrick Gordon as one of the greatest men among the Clan Donald.[26] Soon after they were joined by the men of Glengarry under the leadership of Donald Gorme Macdonald of Scotus, the uncle of the acting chief. On the way through Lochaber Alasdair met the Macdonalds of Keppoch. From Glencoe, came the men of Clan Iain Abrach. Stewarts of Appin and some of the Camerons added to the growing strength of the army. With the exception for the moment of the House of Sleat, virtually the whole of Clan Donald was now in arms.

Alasdair rejoined Montrose in Atholl sometime in November. It was at this time that the first major difference in the war aims of Montrose and the Gaels began to appear. Montrose wanted to make for the Lowlands; Alasdair and the men of Clan Donald refused to turn from the Campbells. Montrose was faced with an ultimatum: go to Argyll or lose your army. According to Patrick Gordon it was John Moidertach who made the point that his people: 'With all the clane Donald, have such a mind to revenge the injurie and tyranous oppression wherewith Ardgyll, more than any of his predecessoures, had insulted over them, resolves that, unlesse the generall make his first worke to enter wpon the Cambelles and the whole countrie of Ardgyll, they would goe no forder on, but would againe retre unto there countrie.'[27] A council of war was called. Alasdair supported John's argument, although Montrose continued to argue in favour of a move to the south. Against this there was little the marquis could do but agree, although Alasdair helped make a virtue from necessity by saying that 'if McAllanmore could be brought lowe, the whole highlandes with one consent woud take armes for the king'.

That December, for the first time since the Macdougalls defeated them in the thirteenth century, the Campbells faced a challenge in their own dominions. It found them totally unprepared. As the army advanced down Glen Shirra, Argyll managed to escape in his galley down Loch Fyne, but his country was at the mercy of Clan Donald. All those capable of bearing arms were killed, houses destroyed and livestock driven off.[28] John Moidertach split off from the main party to lead a separate raid on the lands of some of the main Campbell gentry, including those of Auchinbreck, Barbreck and Lochnell. At this time Alasdair earned the title of *fear thollaidh nan tighean* – 'the destroyer of houses'. Clan Donald's raid on Argyll was certainly destructive of property and livestock. However, it was perhaps not such a holocaust of human life, as Patrick Gordon suggests, because the Campbells were able to make a remarkably quick recovery. Nevertheless, it sent a tidal wave across Scotland. In the 1570s when the fifth Earl of Argyll was in dispute with the government, he was considered unassailable in his heartland. Now this view had been shaken to the foundation. 'The World', Robert Baillie wrote, 'believed that Argyll could be maintained against the greatest armie, as a country inaccessible, but we see there is no strength or refuge on earth against the Lord.'[29] In his own report on the campaign, Father James MacBreck highlighted the crusading element:

The Catholic regiments, however, and their leader, Alexander MacDonald, longed earnestly to fight it out with the Campbells, who had long been the fiercest persecutors and, whenever they could, the murderers and assassins of Catholics, in the north of Ireland and the whole of Scotland. The entire conduct of the war, and the whole hazard of their cause, turned upon this simple point, and they considered that they would effect nothing worthy of their efforts unless they crushed the Campbells, devastated Argyll with fire and sword, and administered a terrible and telling chastisement to this hideous receptacle of bandits, plunderers, incendiaries and cut-throats.[30]

Early in 1645 the royal army left Argyllshire, marching past Inverlochy Castle and onwards up the Great Glen towards Inverness, finally making a halt at Kilcumin at the foot of Loch Ness. It was here that Angus Macdonald, the Glengarry chief, finally joined the men he had sent out earlier. It was also here that, according to tradition, Alasdair and Montrose were joined by the poet, Iain Lom, who came with an important message: a Campbell army had advanced to Inverlochy. Montrose was faced with a simple choice. He also knew that there was a Covenanter army at Inverness, commanded by the Earl of Seaforth, the chief of the Mackenzies. Of the two, this was likely to be the easier target; for Seaforth was, at best, a lukewarm supporter of the Covenant. But he knew, from recent experience, that his army, largely composed of Macdonnells and Macdonalds, would fight at its best against the old enemy. Besides, neither Alasdair MacColla, nor John Moidertach nor any other Macdonald would march away, leaving their homes at the mercy of the Campbells. He would therefore return to Lochaber, but not by the direct route.

As soon as the royalists had gone the Campbells regrouped. Argyll reappeared at Inveraray, bringing some Lowland troops. Campbell soldiers came out of the castles and strongholds untaken by the enemy; Sir Duncan Campbell of Auchinbreck had brought the Argyll regiment back from Ireland, presumably to the delight of the Earl of Antrim. Now about 3000 strong – 1000 Lowlanders and 2000 Campbells – the army marched through Appin and on to Inverlochy. Once there command was given to the experienced Auchinbreck. Argyll, who had been injured in a fall from his horse, retired to his galley on Loch Linnhe on the urging of his friends.[31] This was later to lead to accusations of cowardice, but he must have been aware by now that, whatever his skills as a politician, his talents as a soldier were limited. In the heart of Lochaber the Campbell army was well placed either to pursue the enemy up the Great Glen or to threaten their lands. We have no information, but it would seem reasonable to suggest that Auchinbreck reckoned on drawing Montrose and Alasdair back to meet them in the open ground around Inverlochy, rather than face a possible ambush in the Great Glen, as the Frasers had in 1544. The enemy did return; not, however, by the expected route.

Montrose knew that the direct route to the Campbell camp at Inverlochy past Loch Lochy would be under close observation by enemy scouts. Instead he decided on a march worthy of Alexander the Great, taking a route difficult enough in summer and considered impossible in winter. His army entered Glen Tarff, turning south-west and marching parallel to the Great Glen, their movements concealed by the ridge of Meall a'Cholumain. They crossed the pass of Allt na Larach, 2000 feet into the mountains, struggling, at points, through deep drifts of snow. From there it was down to Glen Roy and on to Keppoch, where the rivers Roy and Spean meet. The Spean was crossed at Dalnabea: from there they continued on to Inverlochy, arriving on the enemy flank on 1 February as night closed in, after a 36-hour march. Tired, hungry and cold they stood to arms through the night. There was some skirmishing with the enemy, who, not expecting a full-scale attack from this direction, assumed they faced no more than a raiding party. When dawn broke on Sunday 2 February they found the whole royal army poised to attack. There is no way of knowing the mind of the ordinary soldiers of Clan Donald as they made ready for battle, but all would have been well aware, through poetry and tradition, that it was here at Inverlochy, 200 years earlier, that Donald Balloch and Alasdair Carrach won a great victory over the Earl of Mar.

Montrose, with about 1500 men, had half the Campbell strength; but he had the advantage of surprise, which he now exploited to the full. He placed two of his Irish regiments on the flanks, one commanded by Alasdair and the other by Magnus O'Cahan, while another under James Macdonnell was held in reserve. The Highlanders were placed in the centre, under Montrose's own command. He also had a few horsemen led by Thomas Ogilvie. Auchinbreck responded quickly. He placed most of his clansmen in the centre with a few companies to stiffen the Lowland levies on either wing. A small party also held Inverlochy Castle.

Montrose, it seems, was quick to spot the weakness in Auchinbreck's disposition. He was now well aware how vulnerable Lowlanders were to the Highland charge. The Campbells, in contrast, were also Highlanders, and could be expected to have retained skills in the use of blade weapons. He ordered his Irish regiments to advance against Auchinbreck's flanks. Alasdair and O'Cahan held their fire until within short range, when they released a single volley. No sooner had this happened than they emerged out of the dense cloud of gunsmoke and fell on the shaken Lowlanders with broadsword and the light Highland shield known as a targe. Despite the presence of the Campbell soldiers among them, the raw levies were unable to withstand the shock, and quickly scattered across the field. Soon, the main body of the Campbell troops, now exposed on both flanks, was under attack from the front by their fellow Highlanders. For a time they fought back with great bravery; but under intense pressure, the front ranks fell back, creating confusion in the lines behind. The whole army collapsed in disorder under the despairing eyes of Maccailein Mor. Hundreds were killed, cut down fleeing the battlefield or drowned in Loch Linnhe. Some tried to escape to the safety of the nearby castle, only to be intercepted by Ogilvie and his cavalry. Perhaps as many as 1500 men were killed in all, including Campbell of Auchinbreck.

Inverlochy was the Flodden of Clan Campbell, the greatest defeat it ever suffered. Observing the carnage from nearby hillside, Iain Lom composed *The Battle of Inverlochy* in celebration of the triumph. In his poem the Lowlanders who fought with the Campbells, the Irish, the other Highland clans and even Montrose himself are all irrelevant. This was the victory of Alasdair MacColla and Clan Donald over the hated Campbells:

> Early on Sunday morning I climbed the brae above the
> castle of Inverlochy. I saw the army arraigning for battle,
> and victory in the field was with Clan Donald . . .
>
> The most pleasing news every time it was announced
> about the wry-mouthed Campbells, was that every company
> of them as they came along had their heads battered with
> sword blows.
>
> Were you familiar with the Goirtean Odhar? Well was
> it manured, not with the dung of sheep or goats, but by the
> blood of Campbells after it congealed.
>
> Perdition take you if I feel pity for your plight, as I
> listen to the distress of your children, lamenting the company
> which was in the battlefield, the wailing of the women
> of Argyll.[32]

Some of the Campbell women confined their wails to poetry, like the widow of Campbell of Glenfeochan, whose losses were truly tragic, including her husband, her father, her three sons, four brothers and nine foster brothers. The sister of Sir Duncan Campbell of Auchinbreck, despite her marriage to John Maclean of Coll, made her own feelings plain:

> Were I at Inverlochy, with a two edged sword in my
> hand, and all the strength and skill I could desire, I
> would draw blood there, and I would tear asunder the
> Macleans and Macdonalds. The Irish would be without
> life, and I would bring the Campbells back alive.[33]

These were bitter passions, not easily laid to rest; and for Clan Campbell the agony was far from over.

10

HONOUR IS MY CAUSE

News of Inverochy spread quickly across Scotland, causing further amazement to Robert Baillie and his colleagues, forever searching for some godly purpose in these successive disasters.[1] At Inverness the Earl of Seaforth's army simply disintegrated. The palpable sense of panic caused is captured in the *Wardlaw Manuscript*: 'There is nothing heard now up and down the kingdom but alarms and rumores, randevouzes of clans, every chieftain mustering his men, called weaponshowes. Montrose and Mackoll in every manes mouth . . . and if a few goates be seen uppon the topps of hills in the twilight its concluded to be Coll Coll Mackoll.'[2] Yet because Montrose's army was composed of irregular troops, Highland infantry and Gordon cavalry, it tended to come and go at will, so he was never quite able to risk a descent on the Lowlands. Only Alasdair and the Irish infantry provided a solid nucleus, around which the men of Clan Donald would form from time to time. This was one of the chief weaknesses of the whole campaign. Although Montrose was successful in reducing the strength of the Scots armies in both Ireland and England, it was never quite enough to make any difference to the cause of the king, soon to face Oliver Cromwell and the formidable New Model Army. Moreover, if Montrose believed that Alasdair and his Macdonald kin would be content that their war against the Campbells had ended at Inverlochy, before the end of the summer he would come to see that this had been a mistake.

Before discussing the Battle of Auldearn, we have to raise some questions about the leadership of the Highland war, particularly in relation to Alasdair MacColla's qualities as a commander. There is a long tradition, derived from George Wishart, Montrose's pastor and biographer, that sees Alasdair as the lesser man, persisting to the present day. But Montrose had never seen how Highland troops could be used to best effect until he met Alasdair MacColla. All the serious mistakes made during the campaign were made by Montrose. In particular, his neglect of military intelligence was notorious. Often he did not know where his enemy was and made no attempt to find out. This took him close to the threshold of disaster at Fyfie in the autumn of 1644, where, in the absence of Alasdair, he was almost trapped by Argyll. Similarly he was nearly caught totally unprepared by General Baillie at Dundee in April 1645. And it was Alasdair, as we shall see, who turned Auldearn, so nearly a disaster, into a triumph.

Even the editor of Iain Lom's poetry, that celebrates the Highland warrior and not the Lowland marquis, says that he showed no capacity for independent command.[3] This is simply untrue, as his continuing successes against the Campbells in 1646 were to shown. Even at Knock-nanuss in Ireland where he eventually lost his life in 1647, he was victorious in his own section of the battlefield. It was Montrose, rather, who never again enjoyed military success after separating from the Highlander. His tactical errors, fatal for a commander, led to defeat at Philiphaugh and then at Carbisdale several years later. The myth that Alasdair was brave but incompetent – perpetuated first by Wishart and then by Sir James Turner – derives from a simple misconception: he was assumed to be fighting Montrose's war and sharing his aims. This, he never did.

After his near success in pinning Montrose down at Dundee, General William Baillie, the Covenanter commander-in-chief, made the mistake of dividing his army, sending one part north under Sir John Hurry. With Hurry poised to attack the country of the Gordons, a family who provided the royalists with much-needed cavalry, Montrose was drawn after him. Hurry acted with some skill, drawing Montrose into the hostile country around Nairn, where he could not rely on the local people for information on enemy movements. Close to Inverness, Hurry received reinforcements, including the regiment of Sir Mungo Campbell of Lawers, recently recalled from Ireland. Meanwhile, Montrose camped at the little village of Auldearn, east of Nairn, on the miserable, wet night of 8 May. True to form, Montrose, taking comfort from the night and rain, did not gather adequate intelligence.

Hurry clearly intended to take the enemy unawares, marching through the night to do this. His musketeers, worried about their wet guns, were given permission for a test fire, turning their weapons to-wards the sea to prevent the noise being carried to the enemy. This was a serious error. Alasdair had sent out some scouts who picked up the report of the muskets and hurried back to tell him the news. With considerable coolness, Alasdair set up a defensive screen in front of the camp. He did this just in time, for the leading enemy regiments were now emerging out of the dark. In his eagerness to destroy the enemy, Hurry seems not to have formed a proper line of battle, throwing in his regiments in a piecemeal fashion. The first to engage Alasdair was that of Campbell of Lawers. In his struggle with Lawers, Alasdair attacked, was driven back and counter-attacked. His courage and tenacity were legendary:

> He was ever in the front, and his strenth, his curage, and dexterittie let his enemies sie, even with terror, wonderful feats of armes for his fellowes to imitate, his strong arme cutting whatsoever and whosoever did him resist. He brak two swords; and when they had fstened a number of pikes in his targe, wherewith they could have born thre or four ordinarie men to the ground, they could not make him to shrink, or bow so much as an kne to the ground; but with a blow of his sword the strength of his vallarous arme cute all the pikes asunder that stuck in his target, whill non durst approach within the lenth of his weappon.[4]

This gave Montrose time to organise the rest of the army, and soon the Gordon cavalry were attacking Hurry on both flanks. His rear ranks began to run away, while the foremost regiments, including Campbell of Lawers', were destroyed. Iain Lom has absolutely no doubt to whom the laurels of victory belong:

> Health and joy to the valiant Alasdair who won the battle of Auldearn with his army;
> You were not a feeble poltroon engaging in crossing of swords
> When you were in the enclosure alone.
> Helmeted men with pikes in their hands were attacking you with all Their might until until you were relieved by Montrose.[5]

With another victory under his belt, Alasdair would also have been gratified to meet his father, Coll Coitach, and his other brothers, released in a prisoner exchange about this time.

Not long after the Battle of Auldearn, Alasdair left Montrose for another recruiting drive to the west, and took no part in the events leading to the royal victory at Alford in July, where the infantry in Montrose's centre was commanded by Angus Macdonald of Glengarry. He finally rejoined the army in the Mearns with a fine force of Highland infantry. Donald Moidertach came with 500 men of Clanranald in place of his father, John, now too old to engage in active campaigning. There were also more Glengarry Macdonalds, as well as Macleans, Stewarts, Macnabs and Macgregors, some 1500 men in all. To obtain fresh supplies, Donald set off with the men of Clanranald, sweeping widely over the area. He is said to have met one old man who said the Mearns had not been plundered since the time of Donald of Harlaw.[6]

With his Highland infantry and Gordon cavalry, Montrose had about 5000 men in all – the strongest he had ever been – and enough to attempt a probe beyond the Highland line. He finally caught up with General Baillie just outside the village of Kilsyth on 15 August. In terms of the numbers engaged, Kilsyth was the greatest battle of the whole campaign; it was also, in the truest sense, a soldier's battle, for the generals on both sides appear to have lost control. The day was hot, so the Irish and Highlanders threw off their plaids, fighting with their shirts tied between their legs: therefore Kilsyth, rather than Kinloch-Lochy, deserves to be remembered as *Blar na Leine*. The Battle of Kilsyth seems to have begun in a contest between the Macleans and Clanranald, both in the centre under Alasdair's command, as to who would have the honour of leading the charge. As the whole line surged forward, for once charging uphill, it was to be the Clanranalds who were the first to break into the enemy ranks. Baillie's army, already badly disorganised by the rough country over which they marched, began to panic. The raw levies to the rear, although not yet engaged, simply dropped their weapons and ran away.

An anonymous Highland poet celebrated the victory of Clan Donald at Kilsyth in an ancient war song that echoes the *brosnachadh* recited before Harlaw:

The men of Alba melt before them after every conflict,
waged on behalf of right and justice and not by way of
boasting

Not by boasting but of firmness of heart in waging conflict
came the better part of their heritage, a stake worth
contesting, that noble race of Domhnall.

The young warriors of Colla's tribe, who can match them?
The men of Alba, unrenowned as they are, are not fit to
share with them.[7]

Having disposed of the last enemy army Montrose and Alasdair, avoiding the plague-ridden capital, marched into Glasgow. For a brief moment, Scotland was at their feet. But the trouble started almost at once. Montrose was eager to cross the Border to aid the king, beaten two months before by Cromwell at the Battle of Naseby. Alasdair and the Gaels, already frustrated by Montrose's refusal to allow the whole-sale plunder of the hated Gall, had no intention of advancing any further into the Lowlands, and they most certainly never had any intention of crossing into England. It was harvest time and many of the Highlanders were already heading home. There were also worrying rumours that the Campbells were stirring once again. Most important of all, from Alasdair's point of view, the Earl of Antrim, his chief and still the king's lieutenant in the Highlands and Islands, was planning to reclaim the old lands of Clan Iain Mor. Alasdair told Montrose of his intention to return to Argyllshire. Making a virtue of necessity, he assembled the army at Bothwell, where Alasdair was knighted and given a furlough with the rest of the Highlanders, promising to return within forty days. Wishart records the scene: 'Macdonald, in a formal speech, returned thanks in the name of all to the Lord Governor for his great condescension, and ... solemnly promised their speedy return. Yet he resolved not to return; and he never again set eyes on Montrose.'[8]

Needless to say, neither Wishart nor anyone else knows what Alasdair had resolved to do at this time. But this has done nothing to stop the wholesale condemnation of his conduct. John Buchan, whose understanding of Scottish history is shallower than most, says that the Highlanders who left with him knew no better (a view that seems to encapsulate centuries of Lowland prejudice) and that Alasdair alone deserves censure.[9] It is certain Alasdair did not return: but what was he to return to? It may also be of some interest that he never responded to Montrose's repeated communications, suggesting, perhaps, some lingering bad feeling rather than bad faith?

Before returning north, Alasdair left Montrose with the bulk of the crack troops he had brought from Ireland in the summer of 1644. If we accept Wishart's view then we have to assume that he simply abandoned these men, some of his closest comrades. But Montrose, not waiting for Alasdair's promised return, and well within the forty-day limit, led these men to disaster. David Leslie had returned with the cavalry from the Scottish army in England, totally surprising him at Philiphaugh, just outside Selkirk. Montrose escaped with a few of the cavalry, but the Irish infantry who survived the battle were massacred in cold blood, along with the women and children who accompanied them. We have no evidence, but it is possible that Alasdair never forgave him for this.

After leaving Glasgow Alasdair returned to Argyll. His people gathered round him like a magnet. The Macdonalds of Largie, Clanranald, Glengarry, Glencoe and others supported him in a new war against the Campbells. He was also aided by the Lamonts, formerly loyal to their Campbell overlords, who were to pay dearly for their treachery. In December 1645 Alasdair and his allies signed a band at Kilmore, agreeing to root out the name of Campbell.[10] This plan gives all the appearance of using the same kind of terror previously employed against Clan Gregor.

Unfortunately, we have little hard information about Alasdair's second raid on Argyllshire, even though he remained for well over a year. As well as preventing the Campbells from regrouping, his other aim was the recreation of Clan Iain Mor. A base was established at Dunaverty Castle, the old Clan Donald fortress on Kintyre. Donald and John of Clanranald cleared the Campbells from Islay.[11] After this Coll Coitach was resettled in Dunyveg Castle after a gap of over thirty years. Alasdair seems to have spent most of his time attempting to reduce the remaining Campbell castles, many of whose garrisons were close to starvation. Only once did the Campbells make an attempt to engage the Macdonalds in the field. Under the leadership of Donald Campbell of Lochnell and John Campbell of Bragleen, they assembled in Glen Euchar and attacked Alasdair at Lagganmore. Once more they were beaten. Bragleen and the other prisoners were locked in a nearby barn, together with all the women and children who could be rounded up. All were burned to death. Ever after the site of this grim atrocity was known as Sabhal Nan Cnamh – 'the barn of bones'.[12] This story exists only in tradition and must, like so many others of the same kind, be treated with caution. It must not be assumed, though, that Alasdair was incapable of this kind of atrocity, and it is certainly in keeping with the Kilmore Band.

Alasdair's second campaign in Argyll is a little like Hannibal's in Italy: he could beat the enemy in battle but he lacked the means to take their main strongholds. This would have been a serious worry.[13] Although he was able to count on the occasional support of his Clan Donald kin, the regiments he brought from Ireland had never been reinforced and were now seriously under strength. Some 500 had been lost at Philiphaugh. If we add to this the many who would have died of sickness and battle wounds in the course of the campaign, Alasdair may have had only a few hundred professional soldiers by the summer of 1646. The news that Antrim was coming in person with more men would have been very welcome.

Antrim landed in Kintyre in the early summer of 1646 with much-needed reinforcements. His presence had an electrifying effect on all of Clan Donald, as an anonymous poet testifies:

Welcome to Scotland to the Marquis and his army,
as they march with martial strains to the land of his
ancestors, the regal people that were lordly.
Macdonalds of Isla were they, and kings of the Isles
of heroes. May sovereignty over land and sea be to
the royal company of the banners . . .

Every deceiver will get what he deserves, and
every traitor will be laid low. We will not have
a yoke to bear, and offenders will not have their
will. The people of the wrymouths [Campbells] will be trampled
under our heels, and Clan Donald will be on top, as was
usual for that people.[14]

For a brief season Clan Iain Mor sprung back to life, and Alasdair had
achieved a lifetime's ambition. But by now the royal cause was lost
beyond recall. Beaten by Cromwell, Charles surrendered to the Scots
army in England, hoping to obtain terms from the less implacable of
his enemies. Before entering into discussions, the Covenanters insisted
that he order all royal forces in Scotland to disband. Antrim, elated by
his welcome, initially refused to obey.[15] Clan Donald in arms, once
welcomed, was now however a serious embarrassment to the king. To
persuade Antrim to leave Scotland, Charles sent a secret message, promising him that he would receive all the old Macdonald lands once
Argyll was forfeited. It was this kind of duplicity that had brought the
king to ruin, but it had the desired effect, and Antrim returned to
Ireland after ordering his army to disband. Some of his recent reinforcements left with him. Alasdair remained. No more trustworthy
than the king, it is virtually certain that Antrim authorised this defiance,
wishing to retain a bridgehead in Scotland. But this partial peace had
left Alasdair even worse off than before. Before the end of the year he
had lost some of his most important allies, including Glengarry and
the Macdonalds of Sleat, who made their peace with the government.
Although he continued to hope for support from Antrim, Alasdair
was intelligent enough to realise how dangerous his position was, especially when the main body of the Scots army returned in early 1647,
after surrendering the king to the English. He was now little better
placed, if not worse, than Sir James of Dunyveg prior to Argyll's
offensive in 1615. Some effort was made to negotiate with the enemy,
and he even offered to leave Scotland, provided he could take his people
with him.[16] But no concessions would be made to a man who, like
Montrose, would not be pardoned on any terms.

Alasdair did his best to defend himself. As David Leslie moved west,
the lands to the north of Kintyre were devastated to deny him supplies.
Angus Macdonald of Largie burnt Inveraray. Alasdair came to Tarbert
sending out messages to all potential allies, including Sleat, Clanranald
and Glencoe. But his real hopes lay in Ireland, where the confederate
government agreed in the summer of 1647 to raise 5000 men jointly
with Antrim to aid the resistance.[17] Before these men could come Leslie
entered Kintyre. Accompanying him was James Turner, whose later

Memoirs have done so much to blacken Alasdair's reputation as a soldier.

According to Turner, the northern passes into Kintyre were the key to the whole campaign. If Alasdair had not been so befuddled with drink he would have blocked these passes and so 'he might have routed us, at least we sould not have entered Kintire bot by a miracle'.[18] A simple glance at a map demonstrates what nonsense this is. The long tongue of Kintyre is far more vulnerable to attack from the sea than by land. Alasdair, with his forces badly under strength, had to place himself in a position to react to any eventuality. Pushing his cavalry well ahead of his infantry, Leslie may have arrived earlier than Alasdair anticipated, but although the Highlanders had no cavalry, Leslie only just managed to push his way into Kintyre before the enemy was upon him. That the fight at Rhunahaorinie was not quite the pushover Turner suggests is attested in both contemporary account and tradition. Gordon of Ruthven says that Leslie lost many of his best men, and a number of young men of the Macdonalds of Largie were also killed.[19] However, once the battle was lost there was little more that could be done. Alasdair left for Ireland, taking many of his men with him.

Some of those left behind took refuge in waterless Dunaverty. There is, however, some doubt that Alasdair ordered this. It is much more likely that, realising how implacable their enemy was, and mindful of the massacre of Philiphaugh, all those unable to find boats sought whatever refuge they could find. Unable to withstand a siege, they were forced to surrender and promptly massacred. It is, however, true that Alasdair left a garrison in Dunyveg, under the command of his elderly father, perhaps hoping that by the time Leslie was able to land on Islay he would have returned with Irish reinforcements. This was not to be. Coll Coitach was taken prisoner and the castle surrendered. The old chief was later hanged, allegedly from the mast of his own galley placed across a cleft of a rock.[20]

With the situation in Scotland lost beyond recall, Alasdair threw himself into the continuing wars in Ireland. Donald of Clanranald and Angus of Glengarry, taking refuge from the Covenanters, joined him there. Seemingly unaware of Turner's opinions of Alasdair as a soldier, the Irish authorities appointed him as lieutenant general of the Munster army and governor of Clonmel. In November 1647 he was killed at the Battle of Knocknanus after leading his men in one last Highland charge. Iain Lom greeted the news with despair:

> I got the news from Dungannon that has dimmed my sight, my utter woe that Alasdair was dead;
> And the truth from the harper when he landed at Port Patrick my

mind made no glad response to his music.
Sad to me is the dispersing of the men of Islay and the noblemen of
Kintyre . . .[21]

There is an interesting postscript to the life of Alasdair MacColla. He
left two sons, Colla and Gilleasbuig, who settled in Antrim. During
the reign of Charles II the Colonsay Macdonalds were posthumously
restored by act of parliament, although their patrimony was still under
the control of the Campbells. In 1686, following the rebellion and
execution of the ninth Earl of Argyll, Sara Macdonald, the sole surviving
heir of Gilleasbuig MacAlasdair, was granted a charter for Oronsay
and adjacent lands on Colonsay by James VII, 'in consideration of the
singular bravery and constant fidelity of the late . . . Coll McDonnell
alias McGillespick Vc Donell of Colonsay and Archibald McDonnell
his son, in the cause of the King's father . . .'[22] This reward, long overdue,
was enjoyed for a limited time. After the restoration of the Campbells
in the Revolution of 1688, no more is heard of Sara Macdonald, perhaps
the last of Clan Iain of Dunyveg.

Like most of the Gaels, Clan Donald had little influence over the
events that followed. Charles I was beheaded in 1649, against the wishes
of even the most radical Covenanters. Scotland broke with England
and was beaten by Cromwell at the Battle of Dunbar in 1650. Charles
II, with some Highland support, invaded England, only to be beaten at
the Battle of Worcester, whereupon he fled to the Continent as Scotland
passed under English military rule. The only resistance to this came
from the Highlands, where Angus Macdonald of Glengarry was to be
particularly active.

In December 1652 Charles II issued a commission giving Glengarry
and other leading chiefs willing to resist the Cromwellian regime the powers
to act as a council of war, including the power to appoint a commander-
in-chief. Here we can detect the first rumblings of the rebellion, which
broke out the following year. Glengarry was tireless in his efforts to forge
a new Highland alliance, taking on the mantle of Alasdair MacColla.
Sadly for him, he never found his Montrose. Under the uninspiring
leadership of the Earl of Glencairn, a Lowlander, the chiefs finally raised
their standard in the summer of 1653. Charles clearly recognised the
importance of Glengarry to the whole enterprise. He appears to have held
out the promise of the earldom of Ross, thus conferring upon him the
leadership of the whole of Clan Donald, although he later denied this.[23]

The so-called Glencairn Rising was beset with too many internal
divisions ever to be a serious threat to the Cromwellian authorities in
Scotland. Among those who broke ranks was Sir James Macdonald of
Sleat. Not only did he refuse to assist Glencairn, but also he told the

English governor of Inverness that a rising was in preparation.[24] He was later to show himself deeply resentful of Glengarry's pretence at the leadership of Clan Donald, so it is possible that this may have coloured his attitude at this early stage. Matters became worse when Lord Lorne, the eldest son of the Marquis of Argyll, joined the rebels. Glengarry had fought at Inverlochy and was no friend of the Campbells, either as Covenanters or royalists. A furious quarrel broke out and Glengarry had to be restrained from attacking Lorne and his party. Matters did not improve when John Middleton was sent by Charles to take over from Glencairn. Unable to make a decisive impact, the rebels were gradually worn down by the English, who built a number of new forts in the Highlands, including one at Inverlochy, command of which was eventually to pass to one John Hill. By 1654 the Glencairn Rising was effectively over, although Glengarry continued to hold out, not surrendering until May 1655.

Although Cromwell's government behaved well in its rule of the Highlands, ending some of the abuses arising from the feudal system, its demise was welcomed, as Highlanders and almost everyone else greeted the Restoration of Charles II in 1660. The king was keen to reward his loyal supporters. He had no money or land to offer; but he could at least be generous with titles. Glengarry was not given the earldom of Ross, as he had expected, but he was raised to the peerage as Lord MacDonnell and Aros in December 1660; his clan thereafter adopted this spelling of their name. Glengarry's advance caused alarm to Sir James Macdonald of Sleat, as it threatened his own claim to be the head of Clan Donald, now that the links with the house of Antrim were fading. He himself could expect no additional honours from the king, for he had collaborated with the Cromwellian regime, but he took to gathering signatures confirming his own rights. This appears to have had little impact, for by the summer of 1672 even the Privy Council was recognising Lord Macdonnell as chief of the whole clan.[25] However, when he was given an opportunity to demonstrate his new authority he failed to act, unlike the chief of Sleat.

Considering Glengarry's services, Charles was not over-generous. There is no way of knowing for certain if he ever promised to make him Earl of Ross. However, there were too many in Scotland who would not welcome the resurrection of the ancient Macdonald power and, for once, the Campbells cannot be blamed. Soon after the Restoration the Marquis of Argyll was arrested and executed, more as a symbol of past disorders than for the long list of crimes laid at his door. Despite his proven loyalty during the Cromwell period, Archibald, Lord Lorne, was not allowed to succeed to his father's title and estates.

No real attempt was made to fill the vacuum the eclipse of the Campbells had created in the west Highland power structure. Soon disorders became steadily worse, and as Restoration government was essentially government on the cheap, the least expensive solution seemed to be the most traditional. Lorne became ninth Earl of Argyll in 1663, although the title of marquis was never restored to the family. He was, however, not allowed to keep the lands previously awarded to his father by the forfeiture of the Gordons of Huntly in the 1640s, although he continued to be burdened by the debts they had incurred. Pursued by his many creditors, he in turn pursued his debtors, the chief of whom were the Macleans of Mull. The ensuing struggle, the most serious Highland disturbance of the Restoration, was soon to draw Clan Donald to the side of the beleaguered Macleans. It had first to deal with an internal crisis, one of the worst ever to grip the family. It is also one of the most puzzling.

In September 1663 Alexander, the thirteenth chief of Keppoch and his brother, Ranald, were murdered at home by some of their own kinsmen. The motive for this crime is still unclear, although it appears to have involved both a change of leadership and a change of direction.

Alexander had been a minor at the time of his father's death in 1649. He and his brother had grown up among the Macdonalds of Sleat. During this time, Alasdair Buidhe, their uncle, had headed the clan as Tutor of Keppoch. Alexander finally took over from Alasdair in 1661, a development that was probably less than welcome to the older man. Within a very short space of time Alexander seems to have made himself highly unpopular with almost everyone in the clan. The details are uncertain, but it would appear that he was trying to bring some of the wilder elements under control by restricting casual raiding, which many clansmen had come to regard as a right;[26] however, the methods he used were none too gentle. Alasdair Macdonald of Inverlair, one of the leading clan gentry, had caused the chief particular offence. In December 1661, with a band of sixty men, Alexander arrived at Inverlair and proceeded to devastate the place. Houses were pulled down, stock driven off and Macdonald of Inverlair and his people generally bullied.[27] Alexander is reputed to have said to Inverlair that 'one of them tuo must dye'. Inverlair complained to the Privy Council, but when this proved ineffective he decided that he would be the arm of the law: he would not be the one to die.

Close to the house of Alasdair Buidhe, Inverlair met a group of fellow conspirators: Buidhe was careful to keep himself out of this, but he obviously knew what was going on. Allan Dearg and Donald Gorme, his own sons, took part in the meeting which was held on the Tutor's own lands. Inverlair and the rest swore on their dirks, holier than a

Bible oath for Highlanders, to murder their chief and his brother, at a spot know as Torran nam Mionn – 'the mound of the oaths'. On Friday 25 September, probably only a day or two later, the murderers broke into Keppoch's house and stabbed the two brothers repeatedly. No sooner was this done than Alasdair Buidhe calmly assumed the chieftainship once more, while the murderers returned to their homes unmolested. There matters would have rested but for the efforts of one man – Iain Lom, the bard of Keppoch.

Iain Lom was a singular individual, combining qualities usually associated with Biblical prophets and Greek furies. His well-known hatred of the Campbells was, on occasions, a source of embarrassment even to his own people. Towards the end of the Middle Ages a body of Campbells, said to have come from Glassey, settled in Brae Lochaber and, as the MacGlasserichs, formed the hereditary bodyguard of the Keppoch chiefs. Perhaps their negligence in September 1663 added to Lom's fury. He appears to have been one of the first to discover the mangled bodies of the chief and his brother, as he testifies in *'Murt na Ceapaich'* – *'The Keppoch Murder'*.

> Early on Saturday, a short time ago calamity struck as
> a blow, as I stood over the white bodies that were losing
> blood beneath their cloaks; my hands were streaming with
> blood after I had been staunching your wounds, and placing
> you in the coffin is an office which has most weakened my
> strength . . .

> Many have been the murders committed in the world
> since Abel was killed by his brother, but this act was as
> though Adam had been killed by him – when those impious
> ones murdered the head of their household – but vengeance
> will not be forgotten by the Holy Father or His Son . . .

> It is a matter of great reproach and dishonour to the
> entire MacDonald clan if they delay to arouse themselves to
> exact immediate vengeance. Honour and law demands
> Unconditional annihilation of one who murders a
> superior, a king, the head of a household or clan.[28]

Alasdair Buidhe was not to be the instrument of that revenge. Soon Iain's relentless search for justice had alienated all in his own clan, forcing him to seek refuge in Kintail, perhaps in fear of his life.

> I am banished from Clachaig, I am without land
> Or biggin, and the reason is not that I am behind with
> The rent.

I am banished from my native soil, and my land has
Been seized by Soil Dunghill, who think they can establish
Their claim to it.

My property and my furniture are scattered to the
Hillside, and I am like a hare between dogs, without
Chance of escape into cornfield or hay.

Because I am not a murderer, who would stab with
His dirk, as did the friends in the Big House.[29]

Unable to obtain justice from his own people, Iain came to Glengarry
to appeal to Lord Macdonnell, who was widely known to consider
himself as the head of all Clan Donald. But he refused to take any
action which might anger Alasdair Buidhe, who had served alongside
him during the Glencairn Rising. The bard then turned to Sir James
Macdonald of Sleat, the foster father of the murdered men. If Glengarry
proved negligent, surely Sleat would act? But Sir James was no keener
than Lord Macdonnell to interfere in the affairs of his Clan Donald
kin, perhaps causing the kind of civil war that led to the ruin of Clan
Iain Mor. Justice, however, had to be served in some way, especially as
Iain Lom refused to shut up. This was a delicate matter, requiring great
care. Alasdair Buidhe, it was clear to all, was the main beneficiary of
the crime, both in the outcome and in his refusal to punish the
murderers. However, an attack on him would be treated as an attack
on all Clan Donald of Keppoch. The matter, moreover, could never be
brought to trial, as this might reveal some embarrassing facts. Iain
Lom would have vengeance, not justice.

In July 1665 Sir James obtained the approval of the Privy Council to
proceed against Alasdair Macdonald of Inverlair as well as the two
sons of the Tutor and their accomplices. Under Archibald Macdonald,
brother of the chief, Iain Lom guided a party of fifty Sleat Macdonalds
to Lochaber. Inverlair was ready for them, having previously been
denounced as a rebel by the Privy Council. Fighting from the cover of
a log house, Alasdair and his kin put up a desperate defence, before
being forced into the open after their hideout was set on fire. Alasdair
and another six men were killed. Iain Lom promptly cut off their heads
and carried his gruesome trophies away. This whole pantomime was
clearly conducted with the approval of Alasdair Buidhe, prepared to
sacrifice Inverlair as a scapegoat. His two sons, just as guilty, were
never apprehended. In tradition Iain Lom is said to have taken his
heads to Glengarry, where, as a deliberate reproach to Lord Macdonnell,
he washed them by the shores of Loch Oich close to Invergarry Castle.
This spot was ever after known as Tobar nan Ceann – 'the Well of the

Heads'. In 1812 Alasdair Ranaldson, then chief of Glengarry, erected a monument to this famous incident, which manages to be wrong in both detail and date.[30] The heads were then sent on to Edinburgh, to be displayed on poles erected on the Gallows Hill of Leith, although only five appear to have completed the journey.

This bizarre tale has an interesting postscript. In the middle of the nineteenth century one Dr Smith of Fort William, doubting the truth of the story, excavated the mound where Inverlair and his people were reputedly buried. He reported the discovery of seven headless skeletons. A further excavation was carried out in 1914: this time all the skeletons were missing.[31]

During the time of Alasdair Buidhe and after, the Keppoch Macdonalds continued to be one of the most lawless of the Highland clans, largely owing to their uncertain status. With no title to the lands they occupied in Lochaber, there was little the government could do to restrain them. One of the most notorious of the Keppoch raiders was Donald Macdonald, also known as the Halked Stirk. In 1670 he attacked the property of Sir Alexander Menzies of Weem, in an apparent attempt to stop evictions. Menzies appealed to the Privy Council, which decided to hold Macdonald of Sleat responsible for the activities of the Halked Stirk, and interestingly not Lord Macdonnell. Sleat had been of some service in the Keppoch murders, although this time he appears to have done little. In general, the Restoration government's approach to Highland affairs was disastrous.

Clan Campbell's disgrace in the early 1660s brought their neighbours only a temporary respite. Lord Macdonnell, as part of his drive to have himself recognised as chief of Clan Donald, made some attempt to buy Islay from the bankrupt house of Cawdor. This annoyed Argyll, who, despite the fact that he had insufficient funds to acquire Islay himself, demanded first refusal. As part of his counter-attack against Lord Macdonnell, he set about buying up his debts in concert with the Earl of Seaforth.[32] Pursuing a chief for debt was one of the most effective ways of pulling the carpet from under him. Glengarry was now in this position. This was of great concern, because it looked likely that he would share the fate of the Macleans of Mull, being edged from their lands by the Campbells. Iain Lom, in happier form, turned his biting pen in defence of the house of Duart:

> It would be of a piece with the changing fortune of your
> course, if it is the boar that presses on you as a
> threat, that the infection of leprosy should enter into his
> vitals.[33]

The plight of the Macleans was ignored by the government, despite the fact that they had given much for the royal cause during the Civil Wars. Instead they sought allies among those families also threatened by resurgent Campbell imperialism. Lord Macdonnell was to be their most important friend, bringing them the support of his own family as well as the Macdonalds of Keppoch and Glencoe. The intermittent war on Mull was reforging the anti-Campbell coalition, which had proved so devastating earlier in the century. Despite Macdonald aid, Argyll prevailed against the Macleans by 1679, but he was walking on very dangerous ground. Surrounded by enemies both in the Highlands and Lowlands, he depended on the support of the Duke of Lauderdale, the Secretary of State who dominated Scottish politics during the reign of Charles II. Once Lauderdale fell from power in 1680, Argyll found himself sinking in political quicksand. In Lauderdale's place came James, Duke of York, a far less friendly figure. He was well aware of the problems caused for his family by the heavy concentration of Campbell power in the west. James, a convert to Catholicism, was facing considerable opposition in England as the heir to Charles. He needed all the support he could get, and who better than the loyal clans, many of them also Catholic. Soon in direct collision with James, Argyll fell from power in the most spectacular way, taking refuge in Holland, where he began to plot against the Stewarts. In his absence, the Marquis of Atholl harried his lands. Atholl was joined in this by virtually all of Clan Donald, delighted by the prospect of plunder and by this second fall of the Campbells in a generation.

As soon as James succeeded Charles in early 1685, Argyll made his move. But his invasion of western Scotland was ill conceived and badly executed. James had not had time to alienate Protestant opinion and Argyll was far from inspiring as a leader: he was quickly captured and just as quickly executed. Although his son, Lord Lorne, had remained loyal to the king, he was not allowed to succeed to the forfeited Campbell estates, even after he claimed to be a Catholic, a move that usually worked with James. Before long, all pretence of Catholicism forgotten, he left for Holland, where he watched and waited in the company of William of Orange.

In the wake of the rebellion, virtually all the clans that had joined Alasdair MacColla and Montrose in the 1640s were back in arms, ravaging the prostrate Argyllshire. Once again the cause of the Stewarts was bound up with hatred of the Campbells. Although during his brief period of power James did little to reduce the feudal burdens on the Macdonalds or any other clan, his treatment of the Campbells gave shape to the Jacobitism that was to dominate Highland politics for over sixty years. There seems to have been some kind of cruel irony at work here. Stewart policy had so often brought disaster to the Highlands. Many of the Gaelic people, including all of Clan Donald, were now set to embrace a cause soon to be abandoned by virtually everyone else in the United Kingdom. This was to bring even greater disaster, and the final journey along a road once highlighted by the Statutes of Iona.

11

THE SORROW OF GLENCOE

The Campbells of Argyll may have fallen from power, but the reign of James VII brought very little peace to the Highlands. Indeed in 1688, as the final crisis of his reign was being played out far to the south, an ancient land dispute had erupted back into life with bloody consequences.

For centuries the Macdonalds of Keppoch had maintained themselves in Lochaber, despite the best efforts of their nominal overlords, the Mackintoshes of Clan Chattan. For much of the time an uneasy stalemate prevailed. This ended in the 1670s when Lachlan Mackintosh of Torcastle decided to make vigorous efforts to press his claim. In 1681 he obtained a commission of fire and sword against Archibald Macdonald, but the issue was still unsettled when Archibald died in late 1682, to be succeeded by his son, Coll, the sixteenth chief of Keppoch.

Coll had been a student at St Andrews University at the time of his father's death. He came home with the intention of settling the dispute with Mackintosh by peaceful means. On the advice of Huntly, he came with some of his leading gentry to Inverness to meet Lachlan with an offer to pay an increased rent in return for a charter. With incredible lack of sensitivity, the Mackintosh chief had him thrown into prison, a mistake for which he paid a high price. Coll did not spend long in captivity, but his pride had been badly wounded, leaving him with a deep sense of resentment both against Mackintosh and the town of Inverness.

Lachlan continued with his campaign to have the awkward squatters removed from Lochaber. In the summer of 1684 he petitioned the Privy Council saying that 'by mere force and bangistry, the Macdonnels had possessed part of his country this 100 years and more, tho he hes interrupted them alwayes and gotten all that the laws could give him; yet they still despised all'.[1] With Argyll threatening to invade, however, matters were too delicate for the crown to risk assisting Mackintosh at this stage. In the past the chief had been able to call on the Clan Chattan confederation to support him in his personal quarrels, although this was becoming increasingly difficult. While 1500 men responded to the call of the captain in his quarrel with the Camerons in 1665, only 300 came out in 1679 against Keppoch.[2] Mackintosh had to wait until such time as the government was prepared to supplement his rather meagre forces. Early in 1688 his commission of fire and sword was renewed, but this time there was a greater chance of success, because he was to be aided by Captain Kenneth Mackenzie of Suddie, commanding a company of regular troops based at Inverness. With probably as many government soldiers as clansmen, Mackintosh marched unopposed into Lochaber in late July. Coll had only 200 fighting men, not nearly enough to oppose the invasion. Instead he withdrew into the hills and called on the aid of his neighbours and kin. In response, the men of Glencoe and Glengarry, as well as the Macmartins, a sept of Clan Cameron, came to join him on 4 August. With 800 men he was still half as strong as his enemy. He made up for this by placing his army on Moal Ruadh, the hill overlooking Keppoch to the north-east. Mackintosh and Suddie made the mistake of advancing up to meet him, setting the scene for one of the great Highland charges, in almost all respects a prototype for Dundee's victory at Killiekrankie the following year. Serving in Mackenzie of Suddie's company was one Donald McBane, formerly a tobacco spinner in Inverness. Years later he wrote of his experiences as a soldier in a vivid and unintentionally humourous manner. This is what he records of the Battle of Mulroy.

> The two clans was both on Foot and our Companie was still with McIntosh, who Marched towards McDonald and his Clan, until we came in sight of them, (which made me wish I had been spinning tobacco) McIntosh sent one of his friends to McDonald to treat with him, and see if he would come to reasonable terms, McDonald directly denyed, but would fight it be the event as it would: Then both parties ordered their men to march up the hill, a company being in the front, we drew up in a line of battle as we could, our company being on the right: we were no sooner in order, but there appears double our number of the Mcdonalds, which made us then fear the worst, at least for my part, I repeated my former wish, (I never having seen the like). The Mcdonalds came down the hill upon us without either shoe, stocking, or bonnet on their head, they gave a shout, and then the fire began on both sides, and continued a hot dispute for an hour; then they broke in upon us with sword and target, and Lochaber axes, which obliged us to give way, seeing my captain sore wounded, and a great many

more with heads lying cloven on every side, I was sadly affrighted, never having seen the like before, a Highlander attacked me with sword and targe, and cut my wooden handled bayonet out of the muzel of my gun; I then clubbed my gun and gave him a stroke with it, which made the butt-end to fly off; seeing the Highlandmen to come fast upon me, I took my heels and run thirty miles before I looked behind me, every person I saw or met, I took for my enemy . . .[3]

Suddie was mortally wounded, dying later at Inverness. Many more were killed, and many taken captive, Lachlan Mackintosh among them. He was forced to sign an agreement with Coll. He was later said to have been rescued by his friends, although it seems just as likely that Coll, embarrassed by his presence in Lochaber, allowed him to be rescued. Coll was later to express some regret over his encounter with Mackintosh, describing it as an unhappy accident, but at the time it greatly enhanced his prestige among his kin. The pibroch 'Blar na Maoile Ruaidh' was composed in celebration. Duncan Stewart, Coll's standard bearer, wrote a poem in his praise:

I would tell of some of your virtues, and that was to be courageous in pursuit. The effect was obvious on Clan Chattan, that Clan Donald, after having fired their volley, were wont to go forward courageously with sword in hand, and for both old and young to be at their throats with their dirks.[4]

Angus Macdonald, the bard of Glencoe, sang his own song of praise, reminding his listeners of the cause of the quarrel.

Lachlan tried to ruin you, when you were very young: he cast you in prison in the hope of depriving you of your right; but God ordained that you be freed from his net, and in spite of his treacherous artfulness, you presented to him a tenacious front, till you lowered his pride.[5]

Mulroy is usually described as the last private clan battle. It was, however, no more a private matter than the clash between the Campbells and Camerons in the dying stages of the Battle of Culloden. Much of the Captain of Clan Chattan's force was made up of royal troops, and he himself had an official commission. If it had been a private affair the government is unlikely to have acted with such anger. As far as the Privy Council was concerned, government soldiers had come under attack, and their commander had been killed. Before the end of the month dragoons and infantry were ordered into Lochaber, reputedly with orders to 'destroy man, woman and child pertaining to the laird of Cappagh, and burn houses and corn'.[6] Coll sensibly released his remaining prisoners and took to the hills, not willing to risk the further displeasure another fight with the royal army would bring on his house. Under the command of Captain John Crichton, the soldiers remained in the area until 10 September burning crops and houses. They were then called back south as a great political crisis was beginning to overtake James VII.

There is no evidence that Crichton and his men murdered women and children, but the suggestion that they might provides an interesting light on Lowland thinking towards Highland communities. A few years before, during the Argyll rebellion, the government, in a state of panic, ordered that all who joined the Campbell chief should be killed or disabled, so they would never be able to fight again. Women and children were to be transported to the remote Isles. Earlier still, James V had ordered the destruction of Clan Chattan, and James VI had given permission for the wholesale extermination of the Macleods of Lewis. During the Restoration unrepentant Covenanters had caused repeated problems for the authorities in the south-west of Scotland, but there was never any suggestion that whole communities should be wiped out. Highlanders, even Campbells, could be perceived as savages, and thus treated in a savage way. This was the shadow that was soon to fall on the people of Glencoe.

To be the Catholic king of a Protestant country in the late seventeenth century demanded caution, good sense and intelligence. While an admirable man in many ways, James was notoriously deficient in these qualities. By 1688, he had alienated virtually all the English political establishment. It is likely, though, that most would continue to tolerate his rule for as long as his heirs were Mary and Anne, his Protestant daughters by his first marriage. This changed in June 1688 when his second wife, the Catholic Mary of Modena, gave birth to a son, also called James. Faced with the prospect of a long line of Catholic kings, James' enemies acted. An appeal was made to William of Orange, himself half-Stewart and the husband of Mary, James' eldest daughter. William came and James left, in a kind of family quarrel later dignified as the Glorious Revolution. For the Highland clans the most worrying thing about the whole affair was that William came from Holland accompanied by Archibald Campbell, soon to be the tenth Earl of Argyll. This was a restoration altogether less welcome than that of 1660. The Revolution not only restored Argyll but it brought to power a new Whig establishment, hostile to Catholicism and Gaeldom in equal measure. Many of the clans had cause to rise against William, but they needed a lead. John Graham of Claverhouse, Viscount Dundee, came to them, the first of the Jacobites.

In April 1689, the Constitutional Convention in Edinburgh decided to replace James with William and Mary; Argyll took the crown south, while Dundee rode north. Support from the northern Lowlands was disappointing, but he had received assurances from Ewan Cameron of Locheil that the Lochaber clans were ready to rise in arms for James. This included Coll of Keppoch, still at war with the Mackintoshes. Coll was soon to have the unique distinction of being in rebellion against two kings at the same time. He was engaged in terrorising the hated town of Inverness when Dundee arrived in the Highlands, and never quite abandoned his private war, even after he became a Jacobite, to the obvious disgust of Dundee.

Dundee arranged a rendezvous of all the loyal clans at Dalcomera in Lochaber on 18 May. James Philip, Dundee's standard bearer, witnessed the spectacle, later consigning his impressions to pseudo-Homeric verse. The first to arrive was Alasdair Dubh, son of the Glengarry chief, with 300 Macdonnells.[7] He was followed by Alasdair, twelfth Maciain of Glencoe, and the most famous and tragic of his race. Philip describes his arrival in a suitably melodramatic style:

> Next came Glencoe terrible in unwonted arms, covered as to his breast with raw hide, and towering far above his whole line by head and shoulders. A hundred men, all of gigantic mould, all of mighty strength, accompanying him as he goes to war. He himself, turning his shield in his hand, flourishing terribly his sword, fierce in aspect, rolling his wild eyes, the horns of his twisted beard curled backwards, seems to breathe forth wrath wherever he moves.[8]

Glengarry and Glencoe were joined by others of their kin. Donald Macdonald, the Tutor of Benbecula, came with his charge, the sixteen-year-old Allan, Captain of Clanranald, and 500 men. Coll came with 200 of his Keppoch men. From Skye and the Isles came the Macdonalds of Sleat, led by the son of the chief, who in time was to be called by his kin Domhnull a Chogaidh – 'Donald of the Wars'. Coll of Keppoch was soon to acquire his own immortal title. Proving himself particularly proficient in obtaining supplies for the army he became widely known as Colla nam Bo – 'Coll of the Cows'.[9] James Philip says of Coll and his comrades: 'These all being chiefs sprung from the blood of Donald they among themselves form twenty companies, and unite the clansmen in one battalion. They all bear similar arms, and carry into battle, as an emblem of their race, a band of wild heather hung from the point of a spear.'[10]

Including the Camerons, Appin Stewarts, Macleans and others, Dundee gathered about 2000 men in all. By the summer he was faced with a Williamite army commanded by Hugh Mackay of Scourie, at least twice as strong as his own. The two forces finally met up on Saturday 27 July 1689 at the mouth of the Pass of Killiecrankie close to Blair Atholl in Perthshire. Dundee's hour had come.

We have to remember one thing about Dundee: he had never before commanded a Highland army. Indeed, up to this point, his career as a soldier had not been particularly distinguished. Ten years before, when he had been a captain of dragoons, his troop was badly cut up by poorly armed Covenanters after they became ensnared in a bog at Drumclog in Ayrshire. He would, of course, have been aware how Montrose, a distant kinsman, had made use of irregular armies. But all of Montrose's battles, with the exception of Kilsyth, where the Highlanders had charged uphill, had been fought on fairly level ground. Dundee, in contrast, had stationed his army on the slope of Creag Eallach, north of the River Garry and high above Mackay. Inferior in strength to the enemy, a downhill charge would add weight and momentum to his army. This, in essence, was the same position adopted by Coll of Keppoch at the Battle of Mulroy. Intelligent enough to take advice on how best to use his army, Dundee must have discussed with Coll the tactics used on that occasion.

There is no evidence that Coll himself was at Killiecrankie; at any rate, he receives no mention in any of the accounts of the battle. He may have been absent on another foraging mission, although as Dundee would be concentrating his forces in the face of the enemy, this does not seem likely. Still in pursuit of his vendetta against the Mackintoshes, he had been severely reprimanded sometime before by Dundee in front of the whole army. A proud man, he had accepted this with as good a grace as he could muster, although it must have rankled. It is possible, therefore, that he absented himself deliberately, although he rejoined the army after Dundee's death.

On a hot summer afternoon, Dundee made his final battle dispositions. On the extreme right he placed the Macleans; next came a small party of troops sent from Ireland by King James, now campaigning there. Then came the men of Clanranald, with Glengarry and Glencoe on their left together with the Grants of Glenmoriston. There was a fairly wide gap in the centre, covered by a small body of cavalry. After this came the Camerons, another party of Macleans, Macneils and others. The Macdonalds of Sleat took up position on the extreme left. From below, on the plain just above the house of Raon Ruairidh, with their backs to the River Garry, Mackay and his men waited throughout the long afternoon. Finally, at seven o' clock in the evening, with the sinking sun shining in the eyes of the Lowland army, Dundee ordered a charge.

In a remarkably short space of time the Battle of Killiecrankie was over. Mackay's army let off a devastating volley into the Highland ranks; but before they could reload the enemy was in their midst, cutting and thrusting with sword and dirk. Unable to withstand this many of the Lowland infantry broke, running for the bottleneck of Killiecrankie Pass, where hundreds were cut down. Donald McBane had a second lucky escape: to save himself from a pursuing Highlander he made a remarkable eighteen-foot leap across the Garry.[11] Mackay and some of the army managed to retreat in good order across the rear of the advancing Highland army, but he left behind many dead and wounded. Highland losses had also been heavy, as the Lowland musketeers had proved themselves far more effective than during the wars of Montrose. Donald Macdonald of Sleat lost five cousins and some sixteen of the Glengarry gentry were cut down. Iain Lom conveys something of the effect of Mackay's murderous fire:

> At Killiecrankie, where blows were struck and the day
> Was yours, you lost your nobles and your skilled fighters.
>
> On the parched hard ground, where a young hare could
> Not hide its ear, you met the discharge of grey lead.[12]

In all the Jacobites lost up to thirty per cent of their army, an horrific loss by any standard; by far the most serious casualty was Dundee himself, shot from his horse at the height of the battle. He could never be replaced.

Under the uninspiring leadership of General Alexander Cannon the rebellion continued for a time. Attempting to break into the Lowlands, the Highland army was checked in a savage street battle with the Cameronian regiment at Dunkeld the month after Killiecrankie. Thereafter the army was disbanded for the season. That October, on their way through Glenlyon, the Macdonalds of Keppoch and Glencoe carried out an extensive raid on the orders of General Cannon. Robert Campbell, the main landholder in the area, was virtually ruined, losing £7500 Scots in cattle and goods.[13] Cannon also ordered the destruction of Achallader Castle, a tower house at the south end of Rannoch Moor belonging to Glenlyon's kinsman and chief, John Campbell of Glenorchy, Earl of Breadalbane.[14] Glenlyon, already seriously indebted, was eventually forced, at the age of sixty, to take a captain's commission in the Earl of Argyll's Regiment of Foot, newly raised to help deal with the political crisis in the Highlands. There is absolutely no evidence, however, that he held Glencoe responsible for his personal misfortune.[15]

The Jacobite army reassembled in the spring of 1690. The equally pedestrian Thomas Buchan replaced Cannon as leader. Against the advice of his officers, Buchan made his army camp in the valley of the River Spey at an area known as Haughs of Cromdale, ignoring the danger of a sudden cavalry attack. Coll of Keppoch was sensible enough to ensure the safety of his own men by allowing them to settle on the nearby height of Tom an Uird. The inevitable followed. On 1 May Buchan was surprised by a cavalry force under Thomas Livingston and scattered in a comic opera route rather than a serious battle. Keppoch retreated to safety over Tom an Uird. After Cromdale the Highland war settled into a lengthy stalemate.

The Massacre of Glencoe continues to be one of the most talked about and least understood episodes in Scottish history. For many, it is wrongly perceived as just one more savage episode in an age-old blood feud between the Campbells and Macdonalds. This, it has to be stressed, is not just popular prejudice. The authors of one of the standard works on the reign of William and Mary claim that the crime was the work of the Campbells of Glenlyon, the most bitter enemies of the people of Glencoe, and that hardly any Macdonalds escaped from the carnage.[16] If serious historians can get away with this kind of ill-informed nonsense, what hope do ordinary mortals have? In a sense, it is the one event in Highland history that continues to be viewed through a fog of Lowland prejudice, perhaps conveniently so. The true horror of Glencoe is, however, obscured by stories of clan rivalry. Here, on British soil, a small community was selected for extermination, by order of a British king acting on the advice of a Secretary of State for Scotland and implemented by a Scottish commander-in-chief, both Lowlanders. The task was then delegated to a regiment in the British army. As we have already said, there is nothing new in the murderous intent behind this. There is, however, one crucial difference: at Glencoe theory became practice. The task of the remainder of this chapter is to understand how this came about.

To begin with, we have to understand the motives of William of Orange. He was a single-minded man with one chief objective: the defence of his beloved Holland against the imperial ambitions of King Louis XIV of France. For this task he always needed soldiers, and the United Kingdom was ideally placed to supply these. If he knew little of England, he knew almost nothing of Scotland, and even less of the Highlands. Scottish affairs bored him and, after Killiekrankie, the Jacobites were little more than an inconvenient obstacle in the way of his continental ambitions. A cold and distant figure, he looked for quick solutions to complex problems. Men could only expect to enjoy power under him insofar as they served this simple aim. He selected and dropped ministers as the occasion suited him. This atmosphere created a kind of Darwinian contest over the survival of the fittest; and by the summer of 1691 the fittest was Sir John Dalrymple, the Master of Stair and Secretary of State for Scotland, busy winning his own battle against George, Earl of Melville, the joint Secretary.

Dalrymple was one of those amoral figures of whom the modern world is only too well aware. Cynical, self-assured and ambitious, and a man of no great conviction himself, he was impatient of it in others. He had a cold, rational mind, intolerant of all political and religious enthusiasm, serving James and then William with equal ease, and without any trouble of conscience. Above all, he served himself. If William was unwilling to commit the resources and time to winning the peace in the Highlands, then the obvious solution was to buy one from the impecunious and debt-ridden chiefs. This proposal would have to be put to them by one who understood both their language and their mentality. Stair chose for this delicate task John Campbell, first Earl of Breadalbane, fated to be one of the most maligned and misunderstood men in Scottish history.

Breadalbane, sometimes known as Iain Glas – 'Grey John' – was a survivor. He had lived through some very dangerous times, witnessing the destruction of his cousins, the Marquis and the ninth Earl of Argyll. This created a lasting impression on his mind. Both men had made the mistake of openly embracing religious and political principles. Breadalbane, in contrast, would always take a pragmatic view, not committing himself too far one way or the other. Above all, he would do or say nothing that would endanger his own interests. He was said to be untrustworthy because of his self seeking: but who at that time was not? He had his own ambitions to head Clan Campbell and, as time would show, he was not really committed to the Revolution Settlement. He toyed with the idea of joining Dundee, in the end remaining safely on the fence. By the summer of 1691 it was perfectly clear that the Jacobite cause was lost. Breadalbane then set out to avoid further bloodshed and, by happy coincidence, advance his own career. He was, like Stair, a schemer, a man often too clever for his own good. Unlike Stair, he was not noticeably cruel or vindictive. It was his misfortune that the peace he achieved was systematically and deliberately undermined, thus setting the scene for the tragedy of 1692.

It was not, of course, only great men who were motivated by self-interest. The summer of 1690 had seen the arrival back in Lochaber of John Hill, the old Cromwellian commander of the fort at Inverlochy, brought there by General Hugh Mackay, who had been given the task of constructing a new stronghold at the foot of the Great Glen. Using the foundations of Inverlochy, the new Fort William rose in less than a fortnight. Hill was the obvious choice as governor, for he knew the local clans and had worked reasonably well with them in the past. But he was a man now advanced in years, short of money and with grown-up dependants. His posting to Fort William offered his only chance of advancement. Although not lacking in scruples, like so many of his contemporaries, he ultimately danced to the tune of others. Hill has been better handled by posterity than he deserves, for it was his ambition and lack of real moral courage that was to be one of the factors in the destruction of Glencoe.

The idea that the clans might be bribed out of rebellion was not new. George Mackenzie, Viscount Tarbat, had put it to General Mackay that the clans were fighting less out of love for James and more from fear of the return of Argyll, 'whose predecessors, during their greatness, had always quarrels with almost all the families of the Macdonalds, to the extirpation and ruin of a great many of them'.[17] It made sense, therefore, to buy out Argyll's feudal superiorities, which would be a far less expensive solution to the Highland problem than a full-scale military campaign. Killiekrankie had got in the way, but by early 1690 some of the clan chiefs, including Keppoch and Glengarry, were indicating that they might be receptive to the idea.[18] Towards the end of the year Tarbat reported to Melville that Coll of Keppoch was not only willing to live at peace, but was even offering to bring the rest of Clan Donald into service with William. The exception to this was Alasdair Dubh of Glengarry, who had changed his mind, embarking on a course that made him one of the most obdurate of the Jacobite leaders.[19] In this he was to act as a beacon for others, including Alasdair Maciain of Glencoe.

Tarbat's proposal was bound to cause resentment and jealousy. Great magnates like Argyll and Atholl were threatened with the loss of their traditional superiorities and the influence this brought. This was nothing when set against the ambitions of Stair, who knew the political rewards that would fall to the man who brought William domestic peace. Tarbat was quickly brushed aside and, on the suggestion of Stair, William authorised Breadalbane to open negotiations with the chiefs in the summer of 1691. He was told that he might offer up to £12 000 in total to buy up feudal jurisdictions or pay off pressing debts. Like Tarbat, Breadalbane knew the Highlands; unlike Tarbat, he was power-ful and senior enough to cope with the likely opposition from his cousin Argyll, amongst others. He was not, however, Stair's dupe. He expected senior political office as the price of his success. Above all, he hoped the government would look favourably on his scheme for forming a Highland militia, with himself (of course) in command.

In June 1691 many of the rebel chiefs, including Glengarry, met Breadalbane at the ruined castle of Achallader. Glengarry's presence is something of a surprise. Earlier in the year he had been greatly encouraged when the fortress of Mons in the Low Countries had fallen to Louis XIV, breathing new life into the flagging Jacobite cause. He promptly set about strengthening his own castle of Invergarry, fully intending to carry on the war. His presence at Achallader was, it would seem, to stiffen the resolve of his less committed colleagues. He was certainly determined to undermine any proposal that Breadalbane had to make, using all means necessary, not excluding deliberate deception.

The Achallader negotiations turned not on principle but on money. Leading the discussion, Locheil asked for £20 000 on behalf of himself and his fellow chiefs, but Breadalbane beat him down to the authorised figure. In discussing the individual amounts, Breadalbane abruptly told Maciain that his share would be set against some cows he had stolen the previous December. The two men quarrelled and Maciain departed, later telling his sons that he feared mischief from no man as much as Breadalbane.[20] In the light of later developments, this incident has been given far too much weight. Maciain was not important enough to affect the outcome of the negotiations. Far from bearing a grudge, Breadalbane not only obtained £150 for him to buy out Argyll's superiority over Glencoe, but also had him pardoned for a murder.[21]

Set against the continuing hostility of Glengarry, Breadalbane enjoyed some success in persuading Keppoch to sign his own separate truce agreement. In the end even Glengarry agreed, on the last day of June, to a truce lasting to 1 October. During this time messengers were to be sent to consult with James in France. The Treaty of Achallader was little more than a breathing space, allowing more time to reach a final settlement. It was almost certainly far less than most, including Stair and the king, had hoped for; but this does not detract from the simple fact that William now had a peace, however temporary, throughout the whole kingdom for the first time since he appeared in 1688 to challenge James. Patience, care and diplomacy might achieve even more. But no sooner was the treaty signed than it was sabotaged.

Breadalbane, pleased with his success, left the Highlands heading for Flanders to meet the king. No sooner had he left than an unholy alliance began to form among his enemies. Too many people had too much to lose: Colonel Hill, whose own attempts to secure a peace had come to nothing; Glengarry, for whom Achallader was a political failure; and Atholl, faced with a serious loss of influence and resentful of both

Breadalbane and Stair. It was rumoured that Achallader had been supplemented by a number of secret articles, including one to the effect that if any of the terms were denied Breadalbane would come out and support the Jacobites with a thousand men. Copies of these articles were soon circulated, although the original was never found. For those with the intelligence to see it was obvious, even at the time, that the secret agreement was a clumsy forgery. Why would an astute political operator have placed this loaded gun in the hands of men many of whom he knew to be his enemies? Why, moreover, if he was prepared to commit himself to the Jacobite cause, with all the dangers this would bring for him, would he do so with only part of his available forces? Even Glengarry, who used the articles against Breadalbane, had the sense to see through this obvious weakness and changed his own copy of the articles to read 'all his men'.[22]

The attitude of Glengarry was something of a puzzle: his own role has led some to conclude that he was the author of the forgery, while others have questioned his motives in revealing them. After all, the support of Breadalbane would have been of considerable help to the cause of King James, as John Drummond, the writer of the *Memoirs of Locheil* recognised. Drummond accepts the truth of the secret article: 'yet Glengarry cannot be justifyed in makeing use of them in the manner he afterwards did, seeing he was of the party in whose favour they were made; and that being allways present, they were spoke in confidence and secrecy, which ought to have putt a seale upon his lips, and not used as tools to bring ruine upon the speaker.'[23]

In this affair Glengarry was simply acting as a useful conduit for others. In September the Marquis of Atholl met him and falsely alleged that Breadalbane was plotting to cheat him out of part of the money promised at Achallader. Seemingly asking for no proof, he promptly changed sides and agreed to confirm that the secret clauses were genuine. In his anger, he also did his best to break the truce. All of this suggests that if Atholl did not write the secret articles himself, they were certainly written on his behalf.

Hill, always worried by his own petty prestige, was quick to convey news of the articles to the Council, without pausing to inquire too far into their provenance. Although William refused to accept their authenticity, there is little doubt that Breadalbane's influence was weakening. Dalrymple had looked for quick results; faced with the intrigues of his enemies and the obduracy of the Highland chiefs, this became a more remote prospect. Rather than sacrifice his own political career he was quite prepared to sacrifice human lives. Before waiting for the conclusion of the Achallader truce, William issued a Proclamation of

Indemnity on 27 August, pardoning all rebels who submitted by 1 January 1692. Those who did not would be 'answerable at their highest peril'.[24]

From this point forward Dalrymple became increasingly impatient in his view of the Highlanders, especially as Breadalbane's continuing attempts at negotiation were coming to nothing. Before the end of the year, in a more vengeful frame of mind, he was beginning to look for a target. By October he remarked that providence might intend the destruction of Clan Donald for being Papists, and rebuked Breadalbane for interceding on behalf of Macdonalds when, as a Campbell, he ought to hate them.[25] But Grey John held to his scheme for peace, and in late November argued that the rebels should be pardoned, even if they came in at the last minute. Dalrymple, however, was now preparing to make use of far less scrupulous people.

In the autumn of 1691 James Hamilton was appointed as Hill's depute at Fort William and lieutenant colonel in his regiment. Considering that Hamilton was set to be one of the minor architects of the Glencoe Massacre, and most likely the author of some its most despicable features, very little is known about him. He was certainly a man whom Dalrymple, distrustful of Hill, could make use of. To the obvious alarm of the governor, Dalrymple took to corresponding with Hamilton directly. The Master also found an ally in Sir Thomas Livingston, the victor of Cromdale and now the Scottish commander-in-chief, who was himself contemptuous of the Gaelic people.

In December, Melville was dismissed from the post of Joint Secretary, the whole burden of the office now falling on the Master's shoulders. He had certainly worked for this; but now there was no guard against failure. Things had to happen quickly. That same December he wrote to Hamilton, revealing the new and murderous direction of his thoughts: 'It may be shortly wee may have use of your garrison, for the winter time is the only season in which wee are sure the Highlanders cannot escape us, nor carry their wives, bairnes, and cattle to the mountaines. The Clan Donald is generally popish . . . And I well know that neither he [Glengarry], Keppoch, Appine, Locheil nor some other Chieftanes can well sleep, being within a good nights march of your garrison.'[26]

He wrote again a few days later confirming that an attack on the Macdonalds would be popular because they were Catholics. Stair, as we have said, was largely indifferent over religious affiliation, and was most certainly not a bigot; he was thinking here as a politician. At this time attacks on Catholics were always popular among Protestants; if these Catholics were also Highland savages, so much the better.[27]

As 1 January approached many chiefs at last began to awaken to the danger they were in. There had been fresh hopes of French intervention almost up to the last minute. This came to nothing. When James' dispensation finally arrived, allowing the chiefs to look to their own safety, some took prompt action. Coll of Keppoch travelled all the way up the Great Glen to take the oath at Inverness. Glengarry, too, made some overtures to Hill at Fort William. Clearly feeling responsible for Alasdair of Glencoe, who had tended to follow his lead, he hoped to have him included within a blanket submission. Clanranald and Sleat, far from Fort William, allowed the January deadline to come and pass.

The story of Maciain's anxious, last-minute trip to Fort William and then Inveraray is too well known to require repetition. In the end he was allowed to pledge his loyalty to King William, although he exceeded the deadline by several days. He returned to Glencoe in apparent safety, while his fate was decided far from the Highlands at William's camp in Flanders.

Dalrymple was looking to make an example. Troops had already been concentrated at Inverness as well as Fort William, with orders to proceed against Keppoch, Glengarry, Locheil, Appin and Glencoe. The Master expressed the hope that the soldiers 'would not trouble the government with prisoners'. However, given the scale of the task and the forces available, punitive action is likely to have been no more devastating than previous commissions of fire and sword. Frightfulness demanded a much smaller, more vulnerable target. By early January, Dalrymple was aware than some of the rebels had submitted, and expressed his sorrow that Keppoch and Maciain, whom he seems to have singled out as his particular targets, were now safe. As he sat at his desk writing to Sir Thomas Livingston on the evening of 11 January, Argyll came into his presence with some news that caused a rapid change of gear. 'Just now, my Lord Argyle tells that Glenco hath not taken the oathes, at which I rejoice. It's a great work of charity to be exact in rooting out that damnable sept, the worst in all the Highlands.'[28] The Master had his prey. It was to be the Macdonalds of Glencoe, not because they were the most culpable, but because they were the most vulnerable. Not only were they the smallest sept of Clan Donald, but the narrow valley in which they made their home was a trap rather than a fortress.

Over what remained of January 1692 the scheme for a wholesale massacre took shape and direction. One of the oddest features is a letter Dalrymple wrote to Hill on 16 January, saying that Argyll and Breadalbane had promised that the Glencoe people would have no retreat into their bounds. But we know from Breadalbane's letters after the massacre that he had no inside knowledge of what was intended, and neither man gave any instructions that the passes into their lands should be blocked. At most Breadalbane appears to have suggested a general campaign against the rebels. However, this false lead has been slavishly pursued by generations of historians. John Buchan says that Iain Glas was poised and waiting to strike, even though he was not in Scotland at the time of the massacre.[29] Dalrymple was careful enough to have the order for the massacre subscribed and superscribed by the king. It has been suggested that William was the unconscious instrument in a cunningly devised plot; that he signed orders, in other words, for the destruction of a whole community of people without any clear idea of what he was doing.[30] This is one occasion, it has to be said, in which the defence appears to amplify the crime.

It was Dalrymple who chose Argyll's Regiment of Foot for the task. This might in itself be enough to suggest that the Campbell chief, who was the regiment's senior officer, had some prior knowledge of what was intended. At this time, however, the post of colonel was often an honorary one, and Argyll, although he raised the regiment from among his own tenants, never exercised actual command or took part in any field operations. One of the most interesting aspects of the whole affair is that it managed to combine malevolence and incompetence in roughly equal measures. In his correspondence with Breadalbane, Dalrymple had himself highlighted the traditional rivalries between the Campbells and Macdonalds. Now, it seems, he was attempting to make use of this, perhaps as part of a deliberate plan to explain away the outcome. But the regiment failed to live up to his expectations. It is almost certain that if Highland-hating Lowlanders like the Cameronians had been used, the result would have been much more dreadful. The ordinary soldiers of the Argyll Regiment were Gaels and, as events came to show, they had little enthusiasm for their murderous orders.

By far the worst feature of the whole sordid business was, of course, that two companies of the Argyll regiment were billeted with the people of Glencoe thirteen days prior to the massacre. We have no way of proving who was responsible for this particular feature of the plan, but it may have been Lieutenant Colonel Hamilton, Hill's deputy. If so, it is likely to have been in consultation with Major Robert Duncanson of Argyll's, who brought the regiment from Inveraray to Fort William. The man selected to lead the advance party to Glencoe was Robert Campbell of Glenlyon, related by marriage, as Duncanson would have known, to Alasdair Macdonald, Maciain's younger son. This alone would help to lull the suspicions of the people of Glencoe. Above all, Dalrymple had said the whole business should be secret and sudden. Here is the key to the mode of operation: a direct attack would only alert all the surrounding clans. Best, then, if murder came dressed as a friend.

It is difficult to feel any sympathy for Robert Campbell. Although he was not in himself cruel or murderous, he was to be capable of a cruel and murderous act. What is worse – it seems fairly certain from observations of him after the massacre – is that his conscience was not salved by the fact that he was acting under orders, the bankrupt retreat for all moral cowards. The misfortune that followed him all his life was largely of his own making. Even before the raid of October 1689 his drinking and gambling had brought him close to ruin. It is clear that, lugubrious and impecunious as he was, he was not entirely without charm. His kinsman, Breadalbane, for whom he was a constant source of worry and embarrassment, saw him as an object of compassion when he was in his company. No sooner was he out of sight, however, than he wished he had never been born. Breadalbane had opposed Glenlyon's enrolment in the Argyll regiment, and when he later found out that he had been involved in the massacre he observed that an ill fate had followed the man all of his life. Glenlyon was never more an instrument in the hands of others.

On 1 February 1692 he took two companies of the Argyll regiment to Glencoe. Once there they were given quarters in the little communities scattered along the valley. That Glenlyon had no prior knowledge of the task expected of him is revealed by the threatening tone of the orders he received from Duncanson, camped a few miles away with the rest of the regiment at Ballachulish, late on Friday 12 February.

> You are hereby ordered to fall upon the rebels the Macdonalds of Glenco, and put all to the sword under 70. You are to have especial care, that the old fox and his sons do upon no account escape your hands; you are to secure all the avenues, that no man escape. This you are to put in execution at five a clock in the morning precisely, and by that time or very shortly after it, I'lle strive to be with you with a stronger party; if I do not come to you at five, you are not to tarry for me, but to fall on. This is by the King's SPECIAL COMMAND for the good and safety of the country, that these miscreants may be cutt off, root and branch. See that this be put in execution without feud or favour, else you may be expected to be treated as not true to the King or government, nor a man fit to carry commission in the King's service. Expecting that you will not fail in fulfilling hereby, as you love yourself.[31]

These instructions appear to have been brought to Glenlyon by Captain Thomas Drummond. His company was one of the two already stationed in Glencoe, and he was senior to Robert Campbell. Interestingly, he did not take command, and was presumably sent simply to stiffen Glenlyon's resolve. Considerable care was taken to see that he carried the whole burden. Duncanson did not appear at five or even shortly after. It was not until seven o' clock, two hours later, that he marched along the shores of Loch Leven to the mouth of Glencoe, by which time the whole ghastly business was largely over, as he knew it would be. Even Hamilton, advancing from Fort William with Hill's regiment to block off the eastern exit from Glencoe, did not appear until late in the day, although this was perhaps owing less to design than delays caused by bad weather.

Glenlyon acted on cue; but from beginning to end he botched the whole affair. The southern passes were not blocked, allowing most of the people to escape. Similarly the killings began with gunfire, alerting people up and down the glen. Maciain was one of the first to die, butchered by the party led by two Lowland officers, Lieutenant Lindsay and Ensign Lundie. Lady Glencoe was stripped and had the rings forced from her fingers, dying later as a result of the treatment she received. In all some thirty-eight people were murdered, men mostly, but also some women and children. Most fled across the snowbound passes, including John and Alasdair, the fox's cubs. Strong Macdonald tradition suggests that the Campbell soldiers warned many in good time. Again, according to tradition, the family of Campbell of Airds at Castle Stalker helped many of the fugitives.[32] Glenlyon was moved to mercy on two occasions: but both young men were promptly murdered by Drummond. The stock was rounded up and driven off, after which a terrible silence descended on Glencoe. Robert Campbell left, pursued by his own personal demons. In Edinburgh he was seen drunkenly defending his actions. Later, after the regiment moved to England on its way to Flanders, it was reported that Maciain of Glencoe hung about him night and day, and could be seen in his face.[33]

True to form, Hill immediately claimed credit for the massacre, saying that he had ruined Glencoe. However, after the search for scapegoats began, he quickly distanced himself, making the usual defence that he was only obeying orders. Dalrymple was only ever to express regret that the matter had been so badly handled. William cared little for the growing sense of outrage. He is likely to have judged the effects of the massacre not by the impact it had on Scottish public opinion, which mattered little to him, but how effective it had been in ending Highland resistance to his rule. And, as a piece of political terrorism, it enjoyed quick success. Before long, Clanranald, Sleat and other chiefs were hastening to submit. The only senior figure to express any real sense of outrage was Breadalbane who described the crime as 'barbarous, illegal, imprudent'. He wrote to his legal agent in Edinburgh in March saying, 'I have in great mens company expresst my publict dissent and disaproving of it as neither legal nor honourable as I heard it and I told E. A. [Earl of Argyll] this day that it will entail anew the old quarrell to his familie which he seemed to neglect.'[34] Later that month he was to write that what had happened had undermined all his attempts to secure peace in the Highlands. Yet after the king had been forced to agree that a Commission of Inquiry be set up a few years later, Breadalbane was to find himself singled out as one of the chief targets.

Guided by James Johnston, the new joint Secretary of State, the 1695 Commission was never a serious attempt to discover the truth. Its aim, rather, was to exonerate the king. In the search for scapegoats, Dalrymple was the obvious choice, and stood condemned by his plentiful and public correspondence. He lost office, one of Johnston's aims, but suffered no other penalty. Breadalbane, too, was singled out, although there was absolutely no evidence against him. He was, however, arrested and imprisoned for a time because of the uncertainty surrounding the Achallader negotiations in 1691. The first suggestion that the crime was a clan massacre instigated by the Earl of Breadalbane was made in a letter from Johnstone to William, although both men were very well aware of the true facts.[35] Following in the tracks of Bishop Gilbert Burnet and Lord Macaulay, this line has been taken by William's apologists for generations.[36] Parliament agreed that it had been 'murder under trust' and asked the king to send home Robert Campbell and the Lowland officers for trial. But no trials were ever held. The people of Glencoe were allowed to resettle in their valley, but were denied compensation for the lost stock. More important, they were also denied justice.

12

ONE EFFORT MORE

The Massacre of Glencoe was the last act of the first Jacobite War. Although the Highlanders remained wary of the Whig establishment, matters began to settle down into the old pattern after a time. Colla nam Bo was glad to have avoided the fate of Maciain, but the Mackintoshes were still a threat. Mulroy had done nothing to weaken the Captain of Clan Chattan's claim to the Macdonald lands in Lochaber. Although he enjoyed a measure of protection from Argyll and Breadalbane, Keppoch was once again threatened by a commission of fire and sword. These commissions may have been perceived with greater anxiety than they had in the past, for the verb 'to Glencoe' had now entered the language. After a gap of some years, Mackintosh finally made his move in 1699, advancing deep into the Braes of Lochaber in an attempt to arrest Coll, who proved just as elusive as he had been ten years before. Under the cover of a mist, the Keppoch cattle were rounded up; but when this cleared, the Mackintoshes came under threat from the local people aided by their Glengarry kinsmen. Rather than face the prospect of a second Mulroy, the men of Clan Chattan retreated to the east. It is doubtful if Coll himself would have pressed the issue, for the times were simply too dangerous. Obviously recognising that it was a hopeless task to force the Macdonalds from Lochaber, the Mackintosh chief finally agreed to a formal lease the following year.

By the beginning of the eighteenth century ancient Highland land disputes, occasionally erupting into violence, were largely a thing of the past. For years to come the Highlands and Islands remained separate from the rest of the United Kingdom in a geographical and cultural sense, but much less so politically and economically. Highlanders were now acutely aware of how they were affected by developments elsewhere. Because of this they were to emerge on to the national stage in a dramatic fashion as the new century progressed. Clan Donald emerged from the shadows and reached for new heights, only to fall to even greater depths.

William died in 1702, several years after his wife, Mary. In their place came Queen Anne, James VII's younger daughter. James had died in exile the year before William, and his son, James Francis Edward Stewart, now became the focus of Jacobite hopes. Anne had had many children, but none survived infancy. In looking for a Protestant heir, England turned to George of Hanover, a descendant of James VI and I. For years the English establishment had rejected a political union with Scotland, but there was now a danger that the two countries would go their separate ways on the death of Anne. If Scotland chose James Stewart, England's strategic interests would be severely threatened, much as they had been in 1650 when Charles II came to Scotland. To prevent this moves were made towards a Union of the Parliaments, which finally came about in 1707. This was a widely unpopular move, both in the Highlands and the Lowlands. In one of his last poems, Iain Lom, whose long and remarkable life was drawing to a close, attacked the Union, finding himself, for once, on the same side as many of the hated Gall. Jacobitism began to move beyond the Highland line as a general expression of Scottish national discontent. Once harnessed, it was likely to have an explosive effect. Much would depend, of course, on who would take the lead.

With the death of Anne in 1714 the ancient Stewart dynasty finally came to an end. In its place came the house of Hanover; not much loved, even in England, it was to take two generations before it set root. But the Hanoverian succession passed off peacefully enough throughout the United Kingdom, to the clear disappointment of James Stewart. From his exile in Lorraine he denounced the arrival of 'German Geordie' in a manifesto combining patriotism and frustration in equal measure: 'We have beheld a foreign family, aliens to our country, distant in blood and strangers even to our language ascend the throne.'[1]

There were many in Scotland who shared this frustration, although nothing happened until after George I deliberately snubbed the ambitious John Erskine, Earl of Mar. A man of no great principle, much like John Dalrymple, he was quite capable of changing his political coat to suit his interests, becoming Whig or Jacobite with equal ease, a talent that earned him the unflattering nickname 'Bobbing John'. Despite this he was a man of considerable political talent, and became Secretary of State for Scotland in the run-up to the Union of the Parliaments. His support for the Union earned the gratitude of Queen Anne, but made him very unpopular at home. When George came in September 1714 Mar hoped to graft himself on to the new regime. But he was distrusted by the king and dismissed from office. Angry and frustrated, he came back to Scotland ready to wave the rebel flag. In terms of the numbers involved, Mar was set to lead the greatest of all the Jacobite rebellions. Sadly, he was the worst man for the job.

Back on his estates, in late August 1715 Mar summoned his neighbours and friends to a *timchioll*, a great hunt. This was a convenient cover for what became a kind of Jacobite party rally. Among those attending was Alasdair Dubh, now the eleventh chief of Glengarry, who had fought with Dundee at Killiecrankie. He and the other chiefs witnessed the raising of the standard on the Braes of Mar on 6 September 1715 and the proclamation of James VIII. Glengarry and the other chiefs then returned home to raise their clans. Soon all of Clan Donald was in arms, although with varying degrees of enthusiasm. Glengarry was quick, Coll of Keppoch slow and Alan of Clanranald fatalistic. When General Alexander Gordon of Achintoul, selected by Mar to command the western clans, arrived at Glenorchy on 20 September, only the Macdonnells of Glengarry came to meet him. Coll of Keppoch, seemingly older and wiser, took some time to raise his own men, and played no part in any of the major campaigns. Alan, present at Killiecrankie as a sixteen-year-old, eventually joined Glengarry and Gordon with the men of Clanranald. Before leaving Moidart he is said to have given orders for the destruction of Castle Tioram, because he believed he would never return.[2]

Mar's rising found the government totally unprepared. Soon virtually all of Scotland from Perth northwards was in the hands of the Jacobites. To deal with the crisis, George appointed John Campbell, second Duke of Argyll, as the commander-in-chief in Scotland. To prevent Mar advancing south of the Forth, Argyll concentrated his own army at Stirling, although he was dangerously under strength. Gordon's task was to prevent Argyll's brother, Archibald, Earl of Islay, from sending reinforcements from the west. Yet the whole campaign proceeded with a remarkable lack of urgency. There would appear to have been two reasons for this. First, Fort William was now a permanent feature in Lochaber and, remembering the fate of Glencoe, many clans were understandably reluctant to leave their homes unprotected. This explains in large measure why the Macdonalds of Keppoch took so long to join Mar. Second, by 1715 much of the fire appears to have gone out of the old feud between the Campbells and the Macdonalds. When the campaign in Argyllshire finally got underway it was a pale reflection of those lead by MacColla and Montrose. The issue, of course, was no longer as clearcut as it had been in the past, for Clan Campbell was split right down the middle. Breadalbane had come down from a lifetime on the fence, and committed his own people to the Jacobite cause. Even Duncan Campbell of Lochnell and Sir James Campbell of Auchinbreck, two of Argyll's chief lairds, wavered for a time. Gordon and Islay eventually had a stand-off at Inveraray, but the attack was not pressed. In late October the clans disengaged, marching off to join Mar at Perth.

About this time Coll Macdonald finally raised the men of Keppoch. Instead of heading for Perth, he made his way north-east towards Inverness, perhaps unable to resist one last attempt to terrorise the hated town. But the unscrupulous Simon Fraser, Lord Lovat, had raised his own tenants for the government, and made ready to intercept the Macdonalds. Coll, sensibly deciding to avoid giving the Frasers long overdue revenge for the Battle of Kinloch-Lochy, turned south for Perth. Before he arrived, the cause had been lost.

Mar had qualities admirable in a politician, but disastrous in a soldier. He talked when he needed to act; he hesitated when he needed to strike. Time is the enemy of rebellion, but Mar treated it as an ally. He had enough strength to sweep Argyll aside and advance into southern Scotland, even before Gordon came with the western clans. It was not until November that he finally decided to move, making for Dunblane. Here, on the thirteenth of the month, he found that Argyll had moved forward to meet him on the open ground of Sheriffmuir.

As the two armies prepared for battle the men of Clan Donald found themselves brigaded on the right with the Breadalbane Campbells, commanded by John Campbell of Glenlyon, the son of the man who had carried out the Glencoe Massacre, hardly a comfortable arrangement. Glengarry is said to have turned to him and said, 'Your father has deprived us of the use of an arm,' alluding to the massacre. Glenlyon replied, 'Of that I am sackless; and the only rivalry I shall have with a McDonald is, which of us will best wreak on yon ranks today the injuries of our King.'[3] Glengarry, so the story goes, smiled and took Glenlyon by the hand, asking to be allowed to call himself his brother. Campbells and Macdonalds made ready to fight, for once on the same side.

Sheriffmuir was a confused encounter, because in the rush to prepare for battle neither army was entirely ready. Argyll's left wing was not properly formed and seemingly unaware that the Jacobite right wing extended well beyond their flank.[4] Quick to seize an opportunity, General Gordon ordered his men to attack, which they did in a classic fashion. The Highlanders moved forward and fired some dropping shots, which, as expected, drew a general salvo from the enemy. All fell to the ground; but Alan of Clanranald, the only man to advance on horseback, was hit and killed. At this crucial moment his regiment wavered. Glengarry, equal to the occasion, shouted, 'Revenge! Revenge today, and mourning tomorrow.' Hesitating no longer Clanranald charged with their comrades into the ranks of the English regiments to their front. These men had no experience of the Highland charge and it had a terrifying impact, as a contemporary writer noted: 'It is impossible to express the horror which some of the gentlemen of the English regiments say their men were possessed with at that unusual savage way of fighting.'[5]

Within a short space of time Argyll's left wing had been swept from the field. But matters were otherwise on the right: Mar's cavalry regiments had not moved far enough to cover the infantry on the left. Taking advantage of this and using his infantry and cavalry in a skilful combination, Argyll outflanked and defeated the Camerons and Appin Stewarts. A young English cavalry officer, one Henry Hawley, witnessed this spectacle, which left him with the lifelong illusion that the Highlanders were afraid of horsemen. Clan Donald were destined to rob him of this misconception on a wet January day in 1746.

Paradoxically, Argyll's success left him in an even more dangerous position than he had been at the outset of the battle. He was now aware that his left wing had gone, and as the victorious clansmen returned to the field he was outnumbered by a factor of at least four to one. Making ready for another attack, he placed his men behind some mud and turf enclosures at the foot of the hill of Kippendavie. But Mar disengaged, to the surprise of his army, one of whom, remembering Killiecrankie, exclaimed, 'Oh, for an hour of Dundee.'

Sileas na Ceapaich, the sister of Colla nam Bo, celebrated the Battle of Sheriffmuir in verse:

Clan Donald and the Macleans of great bravado then
got into order, the Breadalbane troop with their
speckled yellow banner – that was a renowned band
that Mar had. When they unsheathed their dark
blades blood gushed all over the field: many a Spanish
sword at that time was being thrust into a scarlet
coat.[6]

These brave words, composed to inspire a flagging cause, did little to change a stark reality: Mar had failed to advance beyond the Forth. The Battle of Sheriffmuir is usually described as a draw: while it cannot be said that Argyll won, however, Mar most definitely lost. He needed one great victory to inspire the Jacobites; Argyll simply needed more time. After Sheriffmuir Argyll grew stronger, while Mar grew weaker. Even the belated arrival of James in Scotland in late December could do nothing to revive a dying cause. He returned to his long and melancholy exile a few weeks later, while the clans drifted back to the west. Clan Donald was left to mourn the death of Alan of Clanranald, of whom it was written:

> The light of Clan Colla has been lowered
> Which matched the course of their exploits;
> 'Tis a cause of melancholy to the people,
> the death of the heirs of the lords of Clanranald.[7]

There were no major reprisals after the collapse of the rising, especially as many of the clans, in contrast to the 1690s, were quick to lay down their weapons. Coll of Keppoch, who had played a fairly minor part, was among the first to submit, surrendering at Fort William in April 1716. Even Glengarry, so obstinate in 1691, made an early peace. Ranald Macdonald, the new chief of Clanranald, left for the Continent and his lands were temporarily forfeit, but this had little long-term effect on his family, which remained defiantly Jacobite. The heaviest penalty fell on the Macdonalds of Sleat, whose lands were forfeited for a lengthy period. They were eventually returned to Sir Alexander Macdonald in 1727. Although Sir Alexander's own political sympathies were Jacobite, he was a cautious individual. He was one of the first to accept that the Stewart cause would never prosper without substantial foreign aid. True to this conviction, he refused to be seduced when Prince Charles appeared in Scotland in 1745, virtually empty handed.

Apart from passing a few measures like the Disarming Act, which only the loyal clans obeyed, the government was content to let matters rest. Jacobitism, it was felt, was too widespread to risk taking more serious reprisals. There were some, however, prepared to express a contrary view, most notably the Earl of Islay, who wrote during the rising:

> Nothing is a greater obstruction to us that all the Highlands have a notion (and I hope a just one) that when the Rebellion is over the Government will put an end to Highland troubles. They are the only source of any real danger that can attend the disaffection of the Enemies to the Protestant Succession. Several thousand men armed and ready to use arms, ready on a few weeks call, is what might disturb any government. The Captain of Clanranald ... has not £500 a year and yet has 600 men with him.[8]

The London government, however, had very little interest in Scotland, and virtually none in the Highlands. As the separate Scottish Privy Council had foolishly been abolished in 1708 following the Act of Union, there was no one to keep an eye on affairs in the north. If the

Highlands remained quiet, that was the best that could be expected. Even the recently raised Independent Companies were disbanded in 1717. The abortive Jacobite rising of 1719 did nothing to reverse this neglect.

After the failure of the '15 the affairs of Clan Donald settled in to a prolonged period of calm. There was no open support for the '19, although some Glengarry Macdonalds took part in the Battle of Glenshiel. One by one the old warrior chiefs passed into history. Alasdair Dubh of Glengarry died in October 1721 followed a few years later by Coll of the Cows. Ranald of Clanranald died childless in France in 1725, bringing the direct line of the first John Moidertach to an end. In his place came Donald of Benbecula, who had taken young Allan to Killiecrankie all those years before. Donald, well advanced in years, died in 1730, when his son, Ranald, became captain of the clan. As a sign of things to come, Ranald was a new kind of chief, more interested in balance sheets than arms.[9]

There is a well-established tendency to view the 1745 Rebellion as the great watershed in Highland history, after which the clan system went into terminal decline. The reality, as always, is far more complex. Following the Union of the Crowns in 1603 the Highlands had experienced change, slow and patchy at first, but increasingly rapid and widespread with the onset of the eighteenth century. Coll of the Cows was very much the last of a kind, and by 1740 it is doubtful if Angus and James Macdonald, the last of the chiefs of Dunyveg, would have recognised anything of their own world in contemporary Highland society. For many chiefs the burden of debt was quite crippling, passing down from one generation to another. The old tradition of collecting rents in kind and consuming produce in heroic clan feasts was clearly a thing of the past, as more chiefs, including the chiefs of Clan Donald, had an increasing need of ready cash. Food rents were now largely marketed in the Lowlands. In general, the old independent Highland economy was giving way to dependence on Lowland markets, a sign of which was the increasing export of black cattle, to be sold at Crieff and elsewhere.[10] Profit was placed before loyalty, with the house of Argyll leading the way. Looking for ways of increasing his income, the second Duke of Argyll, acting on the advice of Duncan Forbes of Culloden, his business manager, signalled the end of the clan system by insisting that farms be leased to the highest bidder rather than to men of his own name. Few others were as yet prepared to take this dramatic step, which alarmed the Highland gentry perhaps as much as the Lewis Plantation of 1597, and did much to revive anti-Campbell feeling. However, the quest for profit was not a Campbell prerogative, as an infamous incident in the late 1730s amply demonstrates.

Sir Alexander Macdonald of Sleat, in collaboration with his brother-in-law, Norman Macleod of Dunvegan, had over a hundred men, women and children kidnapped from their homes on Skye to be sold as indentured labour in the Americas. After the ship carrying them docked in the north of Ireland a few managed to escape, alerting the local magistrates. All were freed unconditionally. News of this incident quickly spread, especially after the Skye Presbytery denounced Sir Alexander for transporting innocent people. The two chiefs immediately defended themselves by saying the transported were convicted thieves, but subsequent investigation found that only four or five of them had ever been accused of sheep stealing and none convicted. Clearly alarmed that the matter would be brought to trial, Macleod of Dunvegan wrote to Duncan Forbes, Lord President of the Court of Session, as well as Argyll's business manager, in December 1739.

> I've felt too many convincing proofs of your friendship for the knight [Sir Alexander Macdonald] and me to doubt that the information come from Ireland anent us has given you a deal of concern on our account. All I would say (and I hope this is enough to you) is, that we are intyrly innocent of the crimes laid to our charge; inadvertency and headlessness we possibly may not be intyrly exempt from but if that can be charged on us, I'm sure its all that in justice can. You know better than I that were we never so innocent, a prosecution would be attended wt a multitude of inconveniences and ought in my weak judgement to be shunned if possible; you not only know best if it can be shunned but likewise the proper means how to shun it and are the only person in earth we would mostly nay intyrly rely on, do therefor in God's name what you think best for us.[11]

The matter was never brought to trial. Later Duncan Forbes was to do much to ensure that both men gave no support to Prince Charles Edward during the last Jacobite Rebellion. In the past, both Macdonald and Macleod had been known for their Jacobite sympathies. It has been suggested that Forbes had acquired some hold over them as a result of the above incident, although by 1745 the government would have cared very little about the fate of a few miserable clansmen, and there were more pressing reasons why neither chief supported the Prince.[12]

After the failure of the 1719 Rebellion the Jacobite caused seemed lost forever. Never an inspiring figure, James sank deeper into melancholy and resignation. The one hope lay in his eldest son, Prince Charles Edward Stewart, born in December 1720. Charles grew into a charming young man, with all the dynamism and charisma so lacking in his father. But until such time as he could rely on substantial foreign help, as he was clearly told by his Highland allies, he had little prospect of removing the house of Hanover from the throne of Britain. Finally, after many years of peace, France and Britain drifted towards war in 1743. The following year Louis XV equipped a major expeditionary force to carry Charles to southern England. Stewart luck, always bad, did not improve for the Prince, and the fleet was largely destroyed in a major storm. In these circumstances, James would have accepted the verdict of fate and retired; Charles, in contrast, did not. The following year he set out on a free enterprise venture, landing on the island of Eriskay, part of the territory of Clanranald, on 23 July 1745. His presence was less than welcome.

Charles always promised he would come with men, money and arms. In the event, he had seven men, little cash and few weapons. When news of this spread, Clan Donald, despite its long support for the Stewarts, was seriously split. While he was still on Eriskay, Charles received a letter from Alexander Macdonald of Boisdale, the brother of the Captain of Clanranald, objecting to the whole hopeless undertaking and advising him to return to France.[13] Taking his lead, the chief likewise refused to commit himself. Sir Alexander Macdonald of Sleat, now the most powerful chief of Clan Donald, simply ignored Charles' summons. He had previously promised the Prince his support when he saw a 'well-conceived scheme'.[14] But this was nothing more than an adventure, whose consequences were likely to be disastrous for the Highlands. In the end, apart from Alasdair MacColla, the seventeenth of Keppoch, none of the leading Clan Donald chiefs gave the rising their open support. But more romantic spirits saved Charles' ill-conceived scheme.

Judging by the evidence of poetry, Charles' presence electrified the ordinary people of Clan Donald. Alasdair MacMhaighstir Alasdair, perhaps the greatest of the Clanranald bards, celebrated his coming:

> Came the tidings of gladness,
> In the morn on my waking,
> That the Prince to Clanranald
> His advent was making.
>
> That the Prince to Clanranald
> His advent was making;
> Noblest scion of kingship,
> Safe and sound be thy coming . . .
>
> With Clan Donald the dauntless

Who in strife have gained glory
These would fight with the red-coats
On the battle-field gory.[15]

In the end, Clanranald did not disappoint Charles. His first break-
through came when Ranald, son of the chief, offered his support. To
distinguish him from his father he was known as Young Clanranald, a
title which has transfixed him forever in both history and romance.
Assured of his help, Charles came to the mainland and summoned his
supporters to meet him at Glenfinnan at the head of Loch Shiel, also
Clanranald territory, on 19 August. Despite the adherence of Young
Clanranald joined at Glenfinnan by Macdonald of Morar with another
150 men, Clan Donald's support was still too weak to give the rising
any prospect of success. Not until Locheil arrived with 600 Camerons
did things start to get underway. Alasdair of Keppoch with 300 'cliver
fellowes' joined later the same day. All witnessed the raising of the
Stewart standard. Alasdair MacMhaighster, who accepted a commission
in the army, commemorated the occasion in verse.

There came with banners streaming
Clan Donald's guileless band,
Next place in honour gaining,
As close as the shirt remaining,
As dogs on leashes straining,
The hunting field demand,
Woe to the foe they heather show,
Ship, lion, tree, red-hand.[16]

The poet also imagined the arrival of Argyll and the Campbells, clearly
more than a spirit of hope than any real expectation that the greatest
of the Whig clans would break ranks. His disappointment was later
expressed in *Aoir do na Caimbeulaich* – 'Satire on the Campbells' –
quite as savage as anything ever written by Iain Lom.

Sir Alexander Macdonald, soon to raise his own clan against the
Prince, kept Duncan Forbes of Culloden abreast of developments.

Young Clanranald is deluded, notwithstanding his assurances to
me lately; and, what is more astonishing, Locheil's prudence has
quite forsaken him. You know too much of Glengarry not to
know that he'll easily be led to be of the Party; but as far as I can
learn he has not yet been taken with them . . . That we will have
no connection with these madmen is certain, but we are bewildered
in every other respect till we hear from you. Whenever these rash
men meet with a check, 'tis more than probable they'll endeavor

to retire to their islands: how we ought to behave in that event we expect to know from your lordship.[17]

John, twelfth chief of Glengarry, never joined Charles, and appears to have made overtures to Forbes as early as September 1745.[18] But this was quite clearly little more than an insurance policy, for the Macdonnells were heavily behind the rising, eventually providing the strongest of the Clan Donald regiments. Alasdair Ruadh, John's older son, was arrested on his way back from military service in France. In his absence, the clan was led by his younger brother, Angus. On his way south the Prince was also joined by Alasdair, the fourteenth Maciain of Glencoe, who had been carried from the 1692 massacre in the arms of his nurse. As the army marched into the Lowlands, it is said to have passed the house of the Dalrymples of Stair. Fearing it would be destroyed in an act of revenge, Charles ordered a guard to be mounted. When they heard of this the men of Clan Iain Abrach, resenting the slur on their honour, insisted on mounting their own guard. However, this story is a late creation, first appearing in 1810, and is almost certainly a romantic fiction.[19]

The story of the '45 is too well known to require detailed repetition here. I propose, rather, to concentrate on the military performance of Clan Donald, particularly in the light of what happened at the Battle of Culloden in April 1746.

At the beginning the '45 was of little more significance than the '19, except that the government allowed matters to get completely out of hand. There were simply not enough troops in Scotland to cope with the emergency. Even the famous Black Watch, raised to deal with this kind of crisis, had been taken to fight on the Continent. The Highland garrisons were all under strength, and the roads built earlier by General Wade to move troops to the area, simply facilitated a rapid Jacobite march into the Lowlands. Sir John Cope, the military commander in Scotland, far from being the coward of legend, was a brave if not very imaginative soldier. However, his field army was made up of many raw recruits. He suffered an early blow to morale when Donald Macdonald of Tiendrish, using skilful guerilla tactics, surprised a larger government force at High Bridge on the River Spean. Finally, on 21 September, Cope was routed in a matter of minutes at the Battle of Prestonpans to the east of Edinburgh, with Clan Donald forming the right of the Prince's army.

Charles Edward managed to combine the virtues of Dundee with the vices of Mar. As a leader of men his talents were unsurpassed, giving him control of virtually all of Scotland less than two months after landing with his tiny party. But inspiration was no longer enough.

In trying to prod his reluctant army into England he made promises broad in scope but weak in detail: the French were coming, the English would rise. Without looking too far into these promises, the army crossed the western Border in November.

Despite what successive generations of armchair Jacobites have claimed, the invasion of England was never more than a reconnaissance in strength, much like that of Charles II, who came the same way in 1651. The main difference was that Prince Charles, with about 5000 men, had a third of the strength of his great-uncle, whose campaign crashed to disaster at the Battle of Worcester. Largely owing to the efforts of Lord George Murray, the Prince's most talented soldier by far, the army made the march as far as Derby unscathed; but by then the illusion was gone. The English did not rise and the French did not come. A war council was held on 6 December and all, barring the Prince, agreed to return to Scotland and wait there for the much-promised French aid. Beyond Charles, neither Lord George Murray nor any of the Highland chiefs believed that the Stewarts could be imposed on a hostile people. The Jacobite cause died at Derby, not Culloden.

Back in Scotland, Lieutenant General Henry Hawley, who had fought with Argyll at Sheriffmuir, made ready to meet the clans. A brutal man and a military ignoramus, his contempt for the Highlanders did much to explain his defeat at Falkirk. He failed to take proper precautions, allowing the Jacobite army to occupy the high ground above the town on 17 January 1746, emerging to meet them only just in time. He had seen Argyll defeat the Jacobite left at Sheriffmuir using cavalry, so he opened the Battle of Falkirk by sending his own dragoons charging against the Jacobite right, once again held by the men of Clan Donald, now some 1700 strong.[20] As the horsemen thundered down the clansmen waited until they were close enough before opening fire, killing at least eighty. Some scattered, but others came on, right into the Macdonald ranks. James, Chevalier de Johnstone, described the scene:

> The cavalry closing their ranks, which were opened by our discharge, put spurs to their horses and rushed upon the Highlanders at a hard trot, breaking their ranks, throwing down everybody before them and trampling the Highlanders under the feet of their horses. The most singular extraordinary combat followed. The Highlander, stretched on the ground, thrust their dirks into the bellies of the horses. Some seized the riders by their clothes, dragged them down and stabbed them with their dirks, several again used pistols, but few of them had sufficient space to handle their swords.[21]

In the fighting, Young Clanranald was trapped under a dead horse and could only be extracted with some difficulty. As the enemy cavalry retreated in confusion into their own ranks, Lord George, commanding the right, tried to hold the Macdonalds back preparatory to a general counter-attack; but this proved impossible. Soon the Jacobites were as disorganised in victory as the enemy was in defeat.[22] Duncan Ban MacIntyre, a poet serving with the Campbell Militia at Falkirk, although his political sympathies were clearly on the other side, witnessed the surge of Clan Donald:

> I together with MacPatrick
>   Traveled over moss and moorside,
> If we had not then gone fleeing
>   Our lives for certain had been taken;
> All the English men retreated
>   At the onslaught of Clan Donald
> 'Twould indeed their lives have shortened
>   To have faced the mighty heroes.[23]

Hawley got a bloody nose, deservedly so, for his incompetence and arrogance; but Falkirk was not the total Jacobite victory commonly assumed. The prince's army was in no condition to mount a pursuit, and, in a small-scale repetition of Sheriffmuir, the regiments on the government right fought better than those on the left. In the confusion Donald Macdonald of Tiendrish, the hero of High Bridge, was taken prisoner by Barrel's Regiment. He was later executed at Carlisle. Although we have no exact figures, Jacobite losses appear to have been much heavier than those at Prestonpans;[24] but the most serious loss came a few days after the battle.

Cleaning a gun, one of the Clanranald men mortally wounded Angus Macdonnell of Glengarry. His kin were enraged and demanded the life of the innocent offender. Young Clanranald initially tried to protect him, but rather than risk a feud or the possible desertion of the Glengarry regiment, the strongest of all the Clan Donald formations, he was forced to agree that his clansman should be shot. Angus of Glengarry, like a Scottish hero, was buried beside Sir John Graham, who had died fighting with the great Wallace at the first Battle of Falkirk, over 400 years before. Charles did not attend the funeral, claiming he had a cold. Stung by this insult, many of the Glengarry men began to drift away. Many in the demoralised Clanranald regiment also deserted. With no real sense of purpose, what remained of the rebel army eventually drifted north, soon followed by another government army, now under the command of William Augustus, Duke of Cumberland, the younger son of George II.

There was another, more pressing reason why many Macdonalds deserted after Falkirk: the Campbells were attacking their homes. Under the command of General John Campbell, the Argyll Militia ravaged Keppoch, Glencoe and other parts of Lochaber. This so angered the Jacobite chiefs, who perceived an attack on women and children as a breach of the rules of war, that Keppoch and Locheil took the extraordinary step of writing a letter of complaint to the Duke of Argyll in London. In response Argyll, himself upset by the burnings, protested to General Campbell about the use of the Argyll Militia in reprisal attacks against civilians. But, acting under orders, the General had no choice but to ignore Maccailean Mor.

The final confrontation came on Wednesday 16 April 1746 on Culloden Moor near Inverness and close to the house of Lord President Forbes. Tired, hungry and cold, the clan army was almost half as strong as their opponents. Charles, for the first time in the campaign, assumed direct command, ignoring the advice of Lord George Murray and others that the open moorland on which he chose to make a stand was totally unsuitable for a Highland army. It was true that they had charged across level fields at Prestonpans, but that was against frightened novices. Now faced with the cream of the British army, withdrawn from the war in Flanders, the clansmen needed the advantage of high ground.

Angry and frustrated by the Prince's obduracy, Lord George made ready to command his own Atholl Brigade, demanding the position of honour on the right of the field. Clan Donald was placed on the left, under the command of the Duke of Perth. In time this gave rise to a myth that the Macdonalds were so frustrated by being denied their traditional position that, in a huff, they refused to fight. This ill-informed nonsense has been dismissed many times, but is still trotted out with depressing frequency.[25] Some variations are quite perverse. In one account they are held to have thrown away the battle, with the intention of gaining their proper place – and victory – on the next encounter.[26] One thing should be made absolutely clear: this legend is not supported by contemporary evidence. We do, however, have a few ambiguous lines by John Roy Stewart, soldier and poet, who commanded the Edinburgh Regiment, placed just the right of the Macdonalds, who lamented from exile:

> Clan Donald, my beloved,
> Woe is me what befell,
> Ye charged not with the rest to the conflict.[27]

So where does this leave us? We know that some of the Macdonald officers were unhappy that they had been deprived of the position on the right, although the tradition that they had always done so is no more than an eighteenth-century invention. Sixty years before, the Macdonalds of Sleat had fought with great bravery at Killiecrankie, despite being ranked on the left of the field. The present discontent is likely to be no more than a general sense of malaise by men who had just completed an exhausting night march. There is no suggestion in those who mention this at the time of a general refusal to fight.[28] The conduct of the Macdonald regiments was certainly affected by their position, but in a far more straightforward way.

It made better sense to place the Atholl Brigade on the right, for it was now the strongest of the Jacobite formations. The enemy also occupied Atholl itself, so there was less incentive to desert. The three Macdonald regiments (the Glencoe men came under the command of Keppoch), in contrast, had less than half the strength they had at Falkirk, although their numbers were far from insignificant, as one of the standard histories of the Jacobite Rebellion suggests.[29] Understrength, tired and demoralised, the Macdonalds were also further away from the enemy. The Jacobite front line was not straight, but skewed away to the north-west, with the Camerons and the Atholl men closest to Cumberland's own front line, and the Macdonalds furthest removed. The ground on which they stood was deplorable, the worst terrain possible for a Highland charge. The Chevalier de Johnstone, who chose to fight alongside his friend Macdonald of Scotus, reports that it was so marshy that the water came halfway up the leg. Cumberland, keeping an eye on the movements of the Macdonalds to prevent himself being outflanked, moved Pulteney's Regiment from the reserve alongside the Royal Scots on his right. The position was also protected by some of his cavalry. Wading through water and mud, once clear of an enclosure wall, it was the Clan Donald regiments who were outflanked.

John Roy Stewart is right in one sense: Clan Donald did not charge with the rest. This was not out of a sense of slighted honour, but because a general order to charge was never given. Suffering under a sustained enemy artillery barrage, the regiments to the right broke ranks and made for the enemy. In doing so they skewed even further to the right, opening up a gap on the left, leaving the Macdonalds vulnerable on both flanks. But still they came on. Probing attacks were made to tempt the enemy to fire from a distance; but Pulteney's and the Royals were experienced soldiers, far too disciplined to fall for the feint. A report drawn up after the battle on the orders of Cumberland describes what happened.

They came running on in their wild manner; and upon the right, where his Royal Highness had placed himself, imagining the greatest push would be made there, they came down three several times within an hundred yards of our men, firing their pistols and brandishing their swords; but the Royal's and Pulteney's hardly took their firelocks from their shoulders each time, before the enemy retreated, abashed by the havock made among them by the firearms of the English.[30]

In describing the battle in a letter to his wife, Alexander Taylor, a Lowland Scot serving in the Royals, says the clansmen came on like hungry wolves.[31] According to Johnstone, the Macdonalds were within striking distance of a final charge, when the regiments on the right began to stream back in disorder through great clouds of gunsmoke. With his own rear ranks beginning to fall back, it was at this point that Alasdair of Keppoch shouted 'Mo Dhia, an do threig Clann mo chinnidhmi?' – 'My God, have the children of my clan deserted me?' This famous statement is sometimes taken out of context to mean that Alasdair charged alone. But he came forward in the company of the gentry of Clanranald, Glengarry and Glencoe as well as the men of Keppoch. Young Clanranald was severely wounded in the head, and Macdonald of Scotus was killed. William Macdonald, a younger son of the Glengarry chief was also killed. Mortally wounded, Alasdair of Keppoch was carried from the field by Angus Ban, one of his sons, and some fellow clansmen, dying in the company of other wounded clansmen in a nearby bothy. Led by nineteen-year-old Angus Ban, the Keppoch men retreated in good order, covered by the Irish Picquets and Royal Scots to their rear. Maciain of Glencoe was later to report that in the whole campaign he lost 52 men killed and 36 wounded out of no more than 150 in all. Most of these men must be presumed to have fallen at Culloden.[32]

Charles fled to the west, his dream in ruins. Hunted as a fugitive, he was aided on the mainland and the Isles by the people of Clan Donald, including many of those who had opposed his adventure. Sir Alexander of Sleat outwardly promised to hunt the fugitive, but his wife, Lady Margaret Macdonald, and his principal tacksmen aided Charles in his flight through the Isles. By September 1746, even Sir Alexander, who enjoyed good relations with Cumberland, was coming under suspicion. None of this did anything to mollify Jacobite opinion, and when Sir Alexander died suddenly in November he was accorded an anonymous epitaph:

If heaven be pleased when sinners cease to sin;
If hell be pleased when sinners enter in;
If earth be pleased to lose a truckling knave;
Then all be pleased – Macdonald's in his grave.[33]

Charles' journey to the Western Isles will be forever associated with Flora Macdonald, although her importance has been considerably exaggerated. Another Macdonald, Neil MacEachan, was of far greater service during the whole of this time, eventually following Charles into exile. His son was one day to become a Marshal of France and Duke of Tarentum. Finally, in September 1746, just over a year after he arrived, the Prince sailed for France, never to return. Alasdair MacMhaighstir records his parting from the Gaels.

> Farewell to the whole Clan Donald,
> Your devotion I will ever bless,
> Between Islands and Mainland,
> Loyal comrades in distress.
> Many a ben and sea and moorland,
> Risking death we have explored
> Sleuth hounds after for destruction.
> But our help was in the Lord.[34]

But the real song Charles left behind was altogether less sweet.

13

IT IS NO JOY WITHOUT CLAN DONALD

After the failure of the Rebellion the reaction was far more savage than it had been in 1716. For a time outrages and atrocities were commonplace. Captain John Fergusson, a Lowlander, committed some of the worst. He commanded HMS *Furnace* in a cruise through the Isles, ravaging the Clanranald territories of Eigg and Canna. On Eigg Dr John Macdonald and thirty-nine others were taken prisoner and severely abused. Those who survived the ordeal were eventually transported to Jamaica. Many others died, officially and unofficially. Neutrality, or the pretence of neutrality, was no defence. Old Glengarry and Old Clanranald were both thrown into prison. To prevent the Highlanders ever taking the government by surprise again new strongholds were built, including Fort George on the Moray Firth. To end an ancient martial tradition the government disarmed the clans and forbade the wearing of tartan, legislation embracing Whig and Jacobite without distinction. The proscription of Highland dress outraged the poet Duncan Ban MacIntyre, who was soon longing for the return of the Prince with a French army:

> When the men of Scotland indeed shall hear your trumpet,
> Quickly they'll assemble beneath thy waving banner;
> MacDonalds as of old, the boldest in the charge,
> Tailors of red-coats, though they won't repair them,
> With their keen-edged tempered broadswords, splitting skulls
> Asunder,
> For each check in their tartan a foe's head shall be severed.[1]

For some years the government certainly feared another rising and did its best to destroy the spirit of clanship. Although this was to have a long-term effect, in the short term the clans, surrounded by a hostile world, did their best to maintain ancient traditions. As late as 1750 a government agent in the Highlands reported that 'the most despicable creature of the name of McDonald looks upon himself as a gentleman of far superior quality and dignity than a man in England of £1000 a year'.[2] Within a short space of twenty years all this was to change. Clan Donald, contrary to Duncan Ban MacIntyre's hope, would never rise again.

Subject to increasing financial pressure the chiefs began to see their lands as a source of income rather than a cradle for warriors, and within a very short time Jacobites became landlords. Take one example. Archibald Macdonnell of Barisdale, a cadet of Glengarry, although attainted for his part in the '45 remained at liberty among his people in Knoydart until 1753. To the frustration of Mungo Campbell, appointed to manage the forfeited estate, Barisdale was able to roam the area in perfect liberty, collecting rents from his loyal tenants. He was eventually captured and imprisoned for a time. Finally pardoned by George III after agreeing to serve in the Seven Years War, he returned to Scotland in 1763. His first act was to apply for the restoration of his old estate, promising to improve an area inhabited by 'lazy and ignorant people'. An old Jacobite had been turned into a new landlord, the hallmark of which was the rejection of clanship and the Gaelic way of life.[3]

There were some, most notably Young Clanranald, who tried to hold back the tide. He was allowed to return home in 1754, and did his best to respect the old ways. But the estate was heavily burdened by debt, forcing him to increase rents. Even so, the problem became no easier by the time he died in 1766. He was the last Captain of Clanranald to live among his people on a regular basis. His widow took his young son, John, to live in Edinburgh, where they enjoyed an expensive lifestyle. More Lowland than Highland in outlook, the Clanranald chiefs now became absentee landlords. Here was the advent of the 'enervated drawing-room chief, whose fixed idea is to be an . . . English gentleman'.[4] This phenomenon was not entirely new. As early as the reign of Charles II Iain Lom had recognised the danger in his poem on Lord Macdonnell:

> You seem to me to be a long time in England, being
> ruined by gaming.
> I would prefer you in coat and plaid than in a cloak
> which fastens.
> And that you should walk in a sprightly manner in trews
> made of tartan cloth
> And visit for a spell in grassy Glenquoich.[5]

By the time Boswell and Johnson came to the Hebrides in 1773, rack rents and emigration were an established part of the Highland scene. Refusing to accept the new conditions, many of the old tacksmen, the gentry of the clan, were leading people across the Atlantic, like Moses seeking the Promised Land. Among the first to leave were the men of Glengarry, who eventually made new homes for themselves in Glengarry County in Canada. They were soon followed by many of the people of Clanranald. By 1771 the emigration from the lands of Macdonald of Sleat was so serious that it was thought he was likely to become a proprietor without tenants.[6] It is worth stressing that these migrants were the best of the clan, the most productive, the youngest, the officers in time of war. These people, many of whom could claim some blood relationship with the chiefs, however distant, were the twine that bound the clan together. What was left was little more than a fiction. Among the saddest Gaelic poems ever written is a ballad by John MacCodrum, the bard of Sleat. It is called 'Song to the Fugitive':

That did ravage MacDonald, it despoiled Morar, it wasted Knoydart, it wounded Clan Ranald: the going of the young ones, the going of the great ones, the going of the brave ones who would repay at time of pursuit; chiefs will be alone and their shoulders left without protection, without strength or support when oppression rears its head: your foes gleefully trampling you under their boots; oppressors will be strong when there is no one alive to deny them . . .

Depart now, my lads, to a country without want – set your backs to the land which has waxed excessive in rent for you – to the country of milk, to the country of houses, to a country where you may buy land to your will, to a country without scarcity, without blight or limit, where you will amass more than will last during your days: 'tis the wise manly soldier who would escape with his life and not stay on the field when he saw overwhelming odds . . .

Look around you and see the nobility without pity for poor folk, without kindness to friends; they are of the opinion that you do not belong to the soil, and though they have left you destitute they cannot see it as a loss; they have lost sight of every law and promise that was observed by the men who took this land from the foe; but let them tell me whether they will not lose their right to it, without means of saving it, when you go into exile.[7]

Dr Johnson arrived in the Highlands with an enthusiasm for the old ways, which met with no response from Sir Alexander Macdonald of

Sleat when the two men met at Armadale Castle. Johnson's view that Sir Alexander should dole out beef and whisky to his clan was hopelessly anachronistic, for all Highland estates were now firmly locked into the Lowland economy. Faced with servicing ever-increasing debts Sir Alexander and the other chiefs, as Johnson rightly observed, 'expect more rent, as they have less homage'.[8]

But what of a chief who tried to preserve something of the old style in the face of economic realities and a changing world? We only have to project a generation forward to the time of Alasdair Ranaldson, the fifteenth chief of Glengarry, to see the risks this would bring. In his efforts to maintain the antique dignity of a chief he became at once theatrical and absurd. His pride of race simply appeared to others, including Sir David Stewart of Garth, as arrogance and bad manners. Even his friend Sir Walter Scott could see he was out of place in the modern world.

> This gentleman is a kind of Quixote in our age, having retained, in their full extent, the whole feelings of clanship and chieftainship, elsewhere so long abandoned. He seems to have lived a century too late and to exist, in a state of complete law and order, like a Glengarry of old, whose will was law to his sept. Warm-hearted, generous, friendly, he is beloved by those who know him, and his efforts are unceasing to show kindness to those of his clan who are disposed fully to admit to his pretensions. To dispute them, is to incur his resentment, which has sometimes broken out in acts of violence which has brought him into collision with the law.[9]

His conceit involved him in an expensive and pointless legal dispute with Clanranald over the chieftainship of Clan Donald, which even the fair-minded Scott recognised as ridiculous.[10] If Glengarry was truly the Quixote of his day there was no room in his world for Sancho Panza. Living well beyond his means, he was forced to increase rents, driving still more people from their homes. Some of his people showed the ancient spirit of Clan Donald. When Glengarry's factor tried to evict Archibald Dhu Macdonnell from his farm at Kinlochnevis the old man armed himself with the broadsword his grandfather had carried at Culloden and called on the aid of his seven sons. Outraged by this act of defiance, Glengarry persisted. By 1817 a Lowland sheep farmer occupied Kinlochnevis.[11] These ongoing evictions from the Glengarry estates, and the threat they represented to the Highland way of life, outraged Stewart of Garth, who likened it to a form of extirpation. In the end, by his own admission, Glengarry squandered his heritage in pursuit of an empty fiction. At the time of his accidental death in 1828 he left his heir with a staggering debt for the time of £80 000. One by one the old Glengarry estates were sold off, until only Knoydart was left.

The Highland Clearances will forever be associated with the replacement of people by sheep followed by forcible emigration. But it was not really like that, at least to begin with. From the 1760s the Great Cheviot and the Linton, new and hardier breeds of sheep, began their steady advance into the Highlands, undermining a traditional farming economy based on black cattle. Lowland sheep farmers could afford to pay far higher rents than the local people. Many of the richer inland pastures were let to the sheep men, but the local people tended to be displaced, rather than removed altogether. The old farming communities were based on a shared use of land known as runrig. By the early nineteenth century this was giving way to crofting, small landholdings usually located in less fertile coastal areas. Those who refused to accept the new realities set out for New Worlds beyond the Oceans – of their own volition, it has to be stressed, and not by the will of the landlord. For the chiefs this had become a serious concern, for if they cared little for clan they had a healthy interest in profit. Before the end of the eighteenth century money, and lots of it, was found floating in the sea. The only trouble was it needed a plentiful supply of labour to bring it home.

Kelp, an alkaline ash obtained by burning seaweed, and used in the manufacture of soap and glass, had first been made in Scotland in the 1720s. Originally the industry had been confined to the Forth estuary, but by the 1760s it was well established in the Hebrides. At first it made little impact on the local economy, as southern manufacturers made heavier use of imported Spanish barilla. But once this source of supply was choked off things changed, and dramatically so. From 1793 until 1815, apart from brief interruptions, Britain was at war with France. As imports of barilla halted the demand for kelp increased. When profit margins began to soar what had been little more than a cottage industry became of major interest to the landlords, especially those owning estates with a long coastline. None were better placed to exploit the new economic realities than the chiefs of Sleat and Clanranald. The problem was that labour, of which kelp demanded a huge supply, was still haemorrhaging away to the Americas and elsewhere.

In 1799, Lord Macdonald of Sleat commissioned a report on his estates on Skye and North Uist with a view to maximising his income. Runrig was condemned as slovenly and careless: new, larger, inland farms were recommended, some for cattle and others for sheep. These were to be let to people with better agricultural knowledge, while the local people were to be moved to coastal crofts. These would not be large enough to support them, so they would be forced to supplement their incomes by making kelp, to the benefit of the landlord who owned the seaweed and claimed the profit. Rather than become seaweed serfs, whole communities made for the ships. Complaining bitterly about the disloyalty of his tenants and the activities of emigration agents, Lord Macdonald had no choice but to delay implementation of his scheme. To stop their tenants voting with their feet the landlords persuaded parliament to pass the Passenger Vessel Act in 1803. Supposedly an attempt to improve standards on emigration ships, this greatly increased the price of a transatlantic passage, well beyond the means of most ordinary people. With the loss of this outlet the population of the Highlands and Islands began a steady increase. This was further stimulated by the use of the potato, which could be grown on even the most marginal land, as the staple food crop. Here was a great disaster in the making.

Free from the threat of emigration, Lord Macdonald and Reginald George Macdonald of Clanranald benefited enormously from the kelp boom. From a price of £2 a ton in 1750 it reached a peak of £20 a ton in 1810.[12] Clanranald was at one point selling over 1000 tons a year, exceeded only by Lord Macdonald at 1200 tons. By 1809 Clanranald was earning £10 000 a year from kelp alone. This was almost pure profit as the labour force remained on a fixed wage, regardless of market conditions. Part of this wage was, of course, clawed back in rent, giving a combined annual income of over £17 000 on estates which only fifty years before had been worth £760 a year. Lord Macdonald did even better.

Neither Lord Macdonald nor Clanranald had any real interest in the traditional role of Highland chief, and did not spend their money like Alasdair Ranaldson in the pursuit of some antique fantasy. Their patterns of conspicuous consumption may have been different, but they were no less wasteful. Apart from the construction of Gothic castles, little of the excess profit was poured back into the Highlands and Islands. Both Lord Macdonald and Reginald of Clanranald seem to have been affected by an odd kind of blindness. It must have been clear that the kelp boom was born of artificial economic conditions. Indeed, even before the end of the Napoleonic Wars the price had started to fall. But no provision was made for the anticipated lean years; no attempt made to look for some kind of economic diversity. It is as if Pharaoh, having his dream interpreted by Moses, perversely decided to set nothing aside and use up his available surplus as quickly as possible. Moreover, a new kind of clansman had emerged, living at subsistence level and useful only for as long as the price of kelp remained high. With the end of the wars the bubble burst.

By 1828 kelp had slumped to £3 a ton, and was simply no longer worth gathering. The house of Clanranald, which had maintained itself for centuries by courage and force of arms was ironically destroyed by seaweed. Reginald George's estates were burdened with debts of almost £74 000. In an attempt to reduce expenditure he decided to end his long absence by settling in Arisaig. But while he paraded in tartans made of silk, the conditions of his tenants deteriorated still further. Sheep were introduced and over 800 people were removed from seven South Uist townships to make way for them. But matters were now beyond recall. Piece by piece the Clanranald lands were sold until, by 1836, only South Uist and Benbecula remained. Against the will of Reginald George, the estate trustees decided to sell the islands. In opposing this the Captain of Clanranald attempted to enlist the help of his chief tenants, but his people had lost all affection for him. When he proposed to settle in Benbecula in 1838 it was not considered safe for him to do so.[13] All that remained, with the exception of Castle Tioram, was sold to John Gordon of Cluny, one of the worst of the clearers. As a territorial and kin-based society the Macdonalds of Clanranald now ceased to exist in all but affection and memory.

By 1850 the Macdonalds of Keppoch and Glencoe had also gone. On the mainland only Glengarry was left, precariously poised on Knoydart. Lord Macdonald had survived the economic tidal wave that had overtaken the rest of Clan Donald, but he was bending under an ever-increasing burden of debt. Emigration, previously restricted, was now actively encouraged, but it was simply not happening fast enough. A bad situation was made infinitely worse with the onset of the Highland potato famine in 1845. The authorities acted quickly and the famine was accompanied by none of the horrors of the Irish holocaust. Lord Macdonald made his own limited efforts at famine relief, but with rent arrears mounting, his financial affairs slipped into a chaotic state, with debts amounting to an almost unbelievable £218 000.[14] In 1849 Godfrey William Wentworth, the fourth Lord Macdonald, initiated a policy of widespread removal. Those who agreed to go were offered assisted passage to Canada; those who refused were to be evicted. In the period up to 1856 some 2500 people were exported to Australia and Canada, a process often accompanied by heartbreaking scenes. Years later, Sir Archibald Geikie recorded an episode he witnessed on Skye when the crofters of Suishnish were removed to make way for sheep.

I had heard some rumours of these intentions, but did not realise that they were in the process of being carried into effect, until one afternoon, as I was returning from a ramble, a strange wailing sound reached my ears at intervals on a breeze from the west. On gaining the top of one of the hills on the south side of the valley, I could see a long and motley procession winding along the road that leads north from Suishnish. It halted at the point of the road opposite Kilbride, and there the lamentation became loud and long. As I drew nearer, I could see that the minister with his wife and daughter had come out to meet the people and bid them all farewell. It was a miscellaneous gathering of at least three generations of crofters. There were old men and women, too feeble to walk, who were placed in carts; the younger members of the community on foot were carrying there bundles of clothes and household effects, while the children, with looks of alarm, walked alongside. There was a pause in the note of woe as the last words were exchanged with the family of Kilbride. Everyone was in tears; each wished to clasp the hands that had so often befriended them, and it seemed as if they could not tear themselves away. When they set forth once more, a cry of grief went up to heaven, the long plaintive wail, like a funeral coronach, was resumed, and after the last of the emigrants had disappeared behind the hill, the sound seemed to re-echo through the whole wide valley of Strath in one prolonged note of desolation. The people were on their way to be shipped to Canada. I have often wandered since over the solitary ground of Suishnish. Not a soul is to be seen there now, but the greener patches of field and the crumbling walls mark where an active and happy community once lived.[15]

There were similar scenes after the Glengarry family decided to sell Knoydart, the last of their estates, in 1853 with vacant possession as one huge sheep farm. The local people were forcibly taken to the emigration ships, with no choice over where they were to be sent. Homes were destroyed, as some took to hiding in the hills. Allan Macdonnell, one of those evicted, a widower with four children, was one of the clansmen who had accompanied Alasdair Ranaldson to Edinburgh in 1822 to greet George IV.[16] Those who tried to remain built crude shelters; but these were repeatedly destroyed on the orders of Alexander Grant, factor to the Glengarry family. Father Coll Macdonald brought the plight of these people to the attention of Donald Ross, a lawyer and campaigner, who did his best to inform the public. Whatever public opinion might think, the law at this time was firmly on the side of the landlord.

Cut by cut the old Gaelic world of Clan Donald was dying, at a time when Queen Victoria and Prince Albert were creating a fashion for all things Highland. *The Illustrated London News* for November 1847 records the royal couple's voyage down the Western Isles:

> Dowart Castle, once the stronghold of Maclean of Dowart, appeared on the left and on the right the ancient fortresses of Ardtornish and Mingarry. The former belonged in remote periods to the Lords of the Isles, and the latter to the Maciains of Ardnamurchan. In one or both of them James IV and James V resided when visiting the Highlands to compel the submission of the refractory chiefs; nor have these wild shores and deserted promontories been since visited by the sovereign, until yesterday her Majesty surveyed them from the deck of the *Victoria and Albert*. The changes which have been wrought on that coast in the interval are striking enough, for few can help recognizing the distinction between the peaceful objects of Queen Victoria and the mission of her predecessors; or, observing, that lands which, in the sixteenth century, must have produced a numerous, hardy, and adventurous race of mountaineers, now supplied little else than black-faced sheep, and are entirely devoted to pasture.[17]

Eventually the people did fight back. Encouraged by the example of the Irish Land League, in 1881 the people of Braes on Skye demanded the return of some ancient grazing land from Lord Macdonald. When this was refused they went on a rent strike. This was followed in the spring of 1882 by the famous scuffle with the police known as the Battle of the Braes. Of little significance in itself, it made the Liberal government of William Gladstone, worried about the possible extension of Irish land agitation to Scotland, take note. The Napier Commission followed and crofters were later given some security of tenure. In fighting for their rights they had rallied under the slogan '*Is treasa tuath na tighearna*' – 'a people is mightier than a landlord'. As they were of the same blood as those who marched with the Lord of the Isles to Harlaw it might also be rendered, perhaps, as 'a clan is mightier than a chief'.

For Lord Macdonald and his descendants economic conditions became no easier, and in 1971 what was left of the Sleat estates and the once vast Clan Donald empire came on to the market. Part was bought by the Clan Donald Lands Trust and a new Clan Donald Centre was set up at Armadale Castle to remind the world of an ancient dignity.

Loch Finlaggan in the north of Islay is a lonely and windswept place. In standing among the ruins of what is left of the palace of the Lords of the Isles it is certainly possible to reflect, with the Bible and Shelley, on the vanity of all earthly power. Instead the simple words of the poet come to mind:

It is no joy without Clan Donald; it is no strength to be without them; the best race in the round world; to them belongs every goodly man . . .

For sorrow and sadness I have forsaken wisdom and learning; on their account I have forsaken all things: it is no joy without Clan Donald.

NOTES

⚜

FOREWORD

1. *The Book of Clanranald* p. 161 in *Reliquiae Celticae*, vol. II, 1894.
2. *Acts of the Lords of the Isles*, 1986.
3. J. M. MacDonell, *The MacDonells of Keppoch and Gargavach*, 1931.
4. The National Library of Scotland, *Yule Manuscript 3134*.

CHAPTER 1

1. MacInnes, J. 1972–4, pp. 520–1.
2. MacDonald, C. 1950, p. 15.
3. Lynch, M. 1991, p. 17.
4. *Annals of the Kingdom of Ireland by the Four Masters*. 1851, p. 453.
5. Ibid., p. 487.
6. O'Corrain, D. 1980, p. 178; Hudson, B. T. 1994, pp. 40–2.
7. O'Bergin 1970, pp. 291–4.
8. *Monro's Western Isles* etc. 1961, p. 43. See also Sellar, W. D. H. 1966.
9. McDonald, R. A. 1997, p. 29.
10. Ibid., p. 31; MacDonald, C. op. cit. p. 59.
11. Duffy, S. 1992, p. 106; Broderich, G. 1980, p. 32.
12. Moore, A. N. 1990, vol. 1, p. 103.
13. Anderson, A. O. (ed.) 1922, vol. II, pp. 112–3. King Edgar is wrongfully identified as King Malcolm.
14. Duncan, A. A. M. and Brown, A. L. 1956–7, p. 194.
15. Innes, C. (ed.) 1851, vol. II, p. 1.
16. The chronology is uncertain; but assuming Somerled was born sometime between 1100 and 1110 then the dispossession would fit in with the expedition of Magnus Barelegs. See Macdonald,

Hugh *Highland Papers* 1914 vol. I, p. 1; *The Book of Clanranald* op. cit. p. 155.

17. Gregory, D. 1975, p. 7.
18. Macdonald, A. and A. 1896–1904, vol. I, p. 38.
19. *Book of Clanranald* op. cit. p. 155. There is very little archaeological evidence of Norse settlement on the Argyll mainland. See Dawson, J. E. A. 1995.
20. *Highland Papers* I op. cit. p. 6.
21. Anderson, A. O. op. cit. II, pp. 264–5.
22. Duncan, A. A. M. 1975, p. 166.
23. Anderson, A. O. op. cit. II, p. 137.
24. Afreca was Ranghild's stepmother. Sellar, W. D. op. cit. p. 7.
25. McDonald, R. A. 1992.
26. Anderson, A. O. II, p. 223.
27. Munch, P. A. (trans.) 1874, p. 69.
28. Anderson, A. O. op cit. p. 231.
29. Clark, W. 1993, pp. 20–1.
30. *Acts of Malcolm* IV. See G. W. S. Barrow intro. p. 220.
31. *Book of Islay* 1895, p. 440.
32. This whole thesis is very convincingly set out by R. A. McDonald op cit. pp. 65–6. See also Cowan, E. J. 1990, p. 112.
33. Anderson, A. O. op. cit. p. 254; Munch, P. A. op. cit. p. 75.
34. Anderson, A. O. op. cit. pp. 257–8.
35. Kermack, W. R. 1957, pp. 48–9.
36. Mcdonald, R. A. op. cit. p. 141.
37. *Highland Papers* I op. cit. p. 9; *Book of Clanranald* op. cit. p. 155.
38. *Letters to the Argyll Family* 1839, p. 45. Also McDonald, R. A. 1991, pp. 7–8.
39. Macdonald, A. and A. vol. I, pp. 60, 513–4.
40. *Highland Papers* I op. cit. p. 10.
41. *Book of Clanranald* op. cit. p. 157. See also Scott, J. E. 1971, pp. 114–41. This author confuses Ranald MacSorley with Ranald, King of Man.
42. *Annals of Ulster* vol. II, p. 253.
43. *Annals of Tigernach – Continuation* 1898, p. 18.
44. Innes, C. (ed.) op. cit. Contains a reference to Walter Stewart obtaining Bute, although as both the date and the King Malcolm referred to are clearly wrong, this has to be treated with caution.
45. Barrow, G. W. S. and Royan, A. 1985, p. 167; Douglas-Simpson, W. 1939, p. 172; *Registrum Monasterrii de Passelet* 1832, p. 15.
46. Anderson, A. O. vol. II, op. cit. p. 232.
47. Ibid., p. 327.

48. *Registrum Monasterrii de Passelet* op. cit. p. 125; *Highland Papers* vol. III, 1920, p. 67.
49. Duncan and Brown op. cit. p. 198.
50. *Highland Papers* vol. I, op. cit. p. 12.
51. Reid, J. F. 1864, p. 378; Hewison, J. K. 1893–5, vol. I, p. 248.
52. McEwan, A. B. 1980, p. 6; Duncan and Brown op. cit. p. 198.
53. Duncan and Brown op. cit. p. 200.
54. McDonald, R. A. op. cit. pp. 84–5.
55. *The Saga of Hacon* 1894, p. 150.
56. *Annals of Loch Ce* vol. I, p. 377; Duffy, S. 1991, p. 68; McDonald, R. A. 1997, p. 94.
57. Macdonald, A. and A. op. cit. p. 73.
58. Sellar, W. D. H. 1988, p. 6.
59. *Calendar of Documents Relating to Scotland* 1881, vol. 1, p. 393.
60. O' Bergin, op. cit. poem 45.
61. *Registrum Monasterri de Passelet* op. cit. pp. 125–31. See also McKerral, A. 1948.
62. *The Saga of Hacon* op. cit. p. 340.
63. Cowan, E. J. op. cit. pp. 121–2.
64. Anderson, A. O. op cit. p. 608.
65. Ibid, p. 660.
66. *Acts of the Parliament of Scotland* vol. I, p. 424.
67. E. M. Barron 1934, among others, refers to Angus Og as 'Lord of the Isles', a title he only ever enjoyed in fiction.

CHAPTER 2

1. Barrow, G. W. S. 1976, pp. 25–6.
2. *Acts of the Parliament of Scotland* op. cit. vol. I, p. 447; Lamont, W. D. 1981, p. 160.
3. McDonald, R. A. 1997, p. 164; Barrow, G. W. S. op. 1976, pp. 79–80.
4. *Calendar of Documents Relating to Scotland* vol. II, p. 145.
5. *Rotulie Scotiae* vol. I, p. 21.
6. Lamont, W. D. op. cit. p. 160.
7. Gregory, D. op. cit. p. 67.
8. *Calendar of Documents Relating to Scotland* II p. 235–6.
9. *Highland Papers* I op. cit. pp. 15–16.
10. *Annals of Ulster* II op. cit. p. 393. Also W. D. Sellar 1981, 1986.
11. Duffy, S. 1991, pp. 311–2.
12. There is a reference in Fordun's *Chronicle* (p. 337) to a Donald of the Isles, defeated by Edward Bruce in Galloway in 1308. In Walter

Bower's later *Chronicle* he becomes Donald of Islay (pp. 343–5). In more recent accounts he has been transformed into Alexander of Islay, with what justification is not at all clear.

13. *Calendar of Documents Relating to Scotland* II op. cit. p. 320. This is an undated letter to a King Edward. Joseph Bain, the editor, suggests it was written in October 1301 to Edward I. A case has been made for 1310, in which case it would be to Edward II. This is possible, but it would mean that Angus was changing sides with bewildering rapidity. See MacEwan, R. A. 1984, p. 4.

14. *The Bruce* by John Barbour 1964, trans. p. 102.

15. Fordun II p. 335.

16. Barron, E. M. op. cit. p. 276.

17. Stanford Reid, W. 1960, pp. 13, 16.

18. R. A. McDonald (1997) argues that the traditional site for the battle is wrong and that it took place, rather, on the shores of Loch Etive. This could only have happened if Bruce had already cleared the Pass of Brander first, although this was the obvious place for an ambush. An advance along the difficult shores of Loch Etive north of Ben Cruachan in full view of the enemy galleys would have been military suicide. As for Loch Awe being a Campbell lake, the author ignores his earlier point that the Campbells had been eclipsed by the Macdougalls at this time. Even on an inland loch, a galley would offer the best mode of escape from slow-moving land forces. A simple glance at a map will show that there could never have been a 'Battle of Ben Cruachan'.

19. Barron, E. M. op cit. p. 364. He adds to the confusion by referring to Angus as Alexander.

20. *Acts of the Parliament of Scotland* op. cit. p. 459; *Liber de Melros* II p. 341; *Rotuli Scotiae* op cit. p. 121; *Calendar of Documents Relating to Scotland* IV p. 377.

21. Barrow, G. W. S. op. cit. p. 231. Also note 3.

22. I would like to thank Norman H. Macdonald of the Clan Donald Society for giving me his own views on this difficult problem.

23. John Barbour op. cit. p. 269.

24. MacDonald, C. M. op. cit. p. 73; Barrow G. W. S. op. cit. p. 346; Paterson, R. C. 1996, pp. 80–1.

25. Grant, A. 1988, p. 123; Roberts, J. L. 1997, p. 181. Gregory, D. op. cit. p. 25.

26. *Annals of Innisfallen* 1951, p. 429; *Annals of Loch Ce* op. cit. p. 595.

27. McDonald, R. A. 1997, p. 187.

28. *Highland Papers* I op. cit. p. 23.

29. Bower, Walter vol. VII, p. 111.

30. *Acts of the Lords of the Isles* pp. 1–2; *Calendar of Documents Relating to Scotland* III p. 213.

31. *Acts of the Lords of the Isles* pp. 3–4.

32. He is mentioned separately in the 1357 Treaty of Berwick as an ally of the English. *Calendar of Documents Relating to Scotland* III p. 305.

33. Grant, A. op. cit. p. 137, n45.

34. The conjecture that he fought at Poitiers in 1356 is based on a misreading of the sources. John of Islay is confused with Sir John de Isle, who was taken prisoner at the battle. John could not be both an ally of the English in the Berwick treaty and a prisoner of the Prince of Wales in the same year. See *Rotulie Scotie* I p. 817; *Syllabus of Rymer's Foedera* p. 393; *Calendar of Documents relating to Scotland* III p. 305.

35. Grant, A. op. cit. p. 126.

36. *Book of Clanranald* op. cit. p. 161.

37. Grant, A. op. cit. p. 126.

38. MacEwan, A. B. W. 1980, pp. 6–12.

CHAPTER 3

1. *Book of Clanranald* op. cit. p. 161.

2. *Highland Papers* I p. 24. Hugh Macdonald is referring to a general ceremony, rather than to the particular coronation of Donald of Islay.

3. Steer, K. A. and Bannerman, J. W. M. 1977, p. 205.

4. Caldwell, D. H. and Ewart, G. 1993. An excellent article on the archaeology of Finlaggan. Also Lamont, W. D. 1966, p. 27.

5. Boardman, S. 1996, p. 91.

6. Roberts, J. L. op. cit. p. 196.

7. *Registrum Episcopatus Moraviensis* 1837, p. 211.

8. *Highland Papers* I op. cit. pp. 32–3.

9. Curtis, E. 1927, pp. 175–6.

10. *Rotuli Scotiae* II pp. 155–6. A safe conduct was issued in the name of both to come to England.

11. Nicholson, R. 1974, p. 232.

12. Ibid., p. 233.

13. Macdonald, A. and A. vol. I op. cit. p. 142.

14. *Calendar of Documents Relating to Scotland* IV 1888, p. 144.

15. Ibid., p. 163.

16. Brown, M. 1994, p. 58; Nicholson, R. op. cit. p. 234.

17. Bower, Walter vol. VIII, 1987, p. 75.

18. Paterson, R. C. 1997, pp. 43–4.
19. Bower VIII op. cit. p. 77.
20. Marren, P. 1990, p. 92; Mackay, W. 1922, p. 23.
21. Thomson, D. 1976, p. 30.
22. Douglas Simpson, W. 1949, pp. 51–53.
23. Marren, P. op. cit. p. 93.
24. This margin first appears in a Lowland poem on Harlaw, and clearly is added for dramatic effect. See Ramsay, A. 1876, pp. 71–90.
25. Hugh Macdonald suggests that Mar's army was stronger than Donald's. As with Bower, his figures should not be taken too seriously. *Highland Papers* I p. 29.
26. Major, John. 1892, translation pp. 240–1.
27. Ibid., p. 348; W. Douglas Simpson op. cit. p. 57; *New Statistical Account of Scotland* vol. XII, 1845, p. 569 n. 1.
28. *Annals of Loch Ce* op. cit. vol. II, p. 137.
29. *Calendar of State Papers Relating to Scotland* vol. XII, p. 202.
30. Dixon, W. M. (ed.) 1910, pp. 223–7.
31. John Major op. cit.; Hector Boece 1941, p. 37.
32. Bower, op. cit. VIII, p. 77.
33. *Exchequer Rolls* vol. IV, p. 239.
34. Jupp, C. N. 1994, p. 62.
35. *Calendar of Scottish Supplications to Rome* 1934, p. 269.
36. Boardman, S. op. cit. 181, 2; Mcdonald, C. pp. 187.

CHAPTER 4

1. Gregory, D. op. cit. p. 33.
2. Brown, M. 1994, p. 58; C. McDonald op. cit. p. 193.
3. *Highland Papers* op. cit. I p. 39.
4. Bower, VIII op. cit. p. 261.
5. Nicholson, R. op. cit. p. 317.
6. *Annals of Ireland of the Four Masters* op. cit. p. 234; Brown, M. op. cit. p. 102.
7. Bower, vol. VIII, op. cit. p. 263.
8. Ibid., p. 265; *Highland Papers* I op. cit. p. 40.
9. Brown, M. op. cit. p. 139.
10. *Acts of the Lords of the Isles* op. cit. p. 37.
11. Innes, C. vol. II, p. 176.
12. Barron, E. M. 1930, p. 29; *The Mackintosh Muniments*, 1442–1820. 1903, pp. 1, 3. Donald Mackintosh later received confirmation of this charter from James III.
13. Stewart, John, of Ardvorlich 1974, p. 13.

14. Balfour, Sir James vol. I, 1824, p. 173.
15. On this whole question see McGladdery, C. 1990, p. 63.
16. *Highland Papers* I op. cit. p. 239.
17. McDonald, C. M. op. cit. p. 239.
18. Grant, I. F. 1969, p. 2.
19. *Auchinleck Chronicle*, 1829; McGladdery, C. op. cit. p. 239; Grant, A. 1981, pp. 170–2.
20. Donald Gregory op. cit. p. 40 says the details have been destroyed, but then claims it was a plot to depose the king.
21. *Acts of the Parliament of Scotland* II p. 42; *The Book of the Thanes of Cawdor* 1859, p. 25; Mackay 1914, p. 57.
22. Brown, M. 1998, p. 303.
23. Pittscottie, Robert Lindsay 1892, I p. 142.
24. *Rotuli Scotiae* II p. 402.
25. Ibid., p. 407.
26. *Acts of the Parliament of Scotland* II p. 108.
27. Paterson, R. C. 1997, p. 93.
28. Macdougall, N. 1982, p. 65.
29. *Calendar of Papal Letters* V p. 671.
30. *Annals of Ulster* III p. 213.
31. *Highland Papers* I p. 47.
32. Ibid., pp. 45–6.
33. *Acts of the Parliament of Scotland* II p. 108.
34. Ibid., p. 113.
35. Ibid., p. 115, 119.
36. Macdonald, A. and A. vol. I p. 262.
37. Maclean Bristol, N. 1995, p. 70; *Highland Papers* I pp. 49–50.
38. Angus is known to have had a brother, John, who died young. There is no evidence that he had a sister. John may have had a daughter by Elizabeth Livingstone, but she was not married to Mackenzie of Kintail. See Dunbar, J. 1981, p. 32.
39. *Exchequer Rolls* vol. X; Barron, E. M. 1930, pp. 46–7.
40. *Highland Papers* II 1916, p. 98.
41. *Scots Peerage* vol. I, p. 335 she appears as Mary, while in vol. V, she reappears as Margaret. Mackenzie, A. C. 1881, calls her first Mary and then Katherine.
42. *Acts of the Parliament of Scotland* III p. 247.
43. *Highland Papers* I p. 50.
44. Lesley, J. 1830, p. 34; Fraser, J. 1905, p. 108. See also Mackenzie, W. C. 1974, p. 99; Grant, I. F. op. cit. p. 140.
45. *Book of Clanranald* p. 163; *Calendar of Letters* etc. *Henry VIII* 1965 vol. XX, part II p. 18.

46. *Annals of Loch Ce* II p. 187.
47. Watson, W. J. (ed.) 1937, p. 85.
48. McDonald, C. M. op. cit. p. 275.
49. Watson, W. J. (ed.) op. cit. pp. 91–3.

CHAPTER 5

1. MacDougall, N. 1997, p. 101.
2. Register of the Great Seal XIII pp. 104, 200.
3. Gregory, D. op. cit. p. 59.
4. Gordon, R. 1809, p. 59.
5. *Annals of Ulster* III p. 383.
6. Ibid., p. 443.
7. MacDougall, N. 1997, p. 177.
8. Donald Gregory is confused on this point. He believes the cause of the change to be 'shrouded in obscurity' and then peers through the mist to spot the Earl of Argyll. But the age of majority in the sixteenth century was twenty-five not twenty-one. Op cit. p. 94 n. 2.
9. Cunningham, A. 1932, p. 54; Maclean Bristol, N. 1995, p. 79.
10. Watson, W. J. 1914–19, p. 215.
11. MacDonald, C. M. explains the point well, op. cit. p. 173.
12. Gregory, D. op. cit. p. 96.
13. *Acts of the Parliament of Scotland* II p. 263.
14. Mackenzie, W. C. 1974, pp. 118–9.
15. Macdonald, A. and A. op. cit. I p. 316.
16. Gregory, D. op. cit. p. 117.
17. Tytler, P. F. vol. V, 1841, p. 122.
18. Gregory, D. op. cit. p. 122; *Acts of the Lords of the Council* XXIX p. 128.
19. Macdonald, N. H. 1995, pp. 24, 25.
20. Steer, K. A. and Bannerman J. 1977, p. 212.
21. *Acts of the Lords of the Council*, 1501–04, p. 80.
22. Lamont, W. D. 1966, p. 35.
23. *Miscellany of the Spalding Club* vol. II, 1842, pp. 83–4.
24. *Acts of the Parliament of Scotland* II p. 333.
25. Macdonald, A. and A. vol. II, p. 253.
26. He was not, however, imprisoned, as is often alleged. See Cameron, J. 1998, p. 234.
27. Nicholson, A. 1930, p. 49.
28. Grant, I. F. 1981, p. 107.
29. Gregory, D. op. cit. p. 146.
30. Mackenzie, W. C. 1974, pp. 131–3.

CHAPTER 6

1. Paterson, R. C. 1997, p. 171.
2. *Letters and Papers* etc. *Henry VIII* vol. XX, part II, 1965, p. 18.
3. Sadler, Sir Ralph, vol. I, 1809, p. 192.
4. Jupp, C. N. 1994, p. 81. Also Hill, G. 1861, p. 361.
5. Mackay, D. N. 1922, p. 94.
6. MacDonald, C. 1889, p. 1.
7. Gregory D. op. cit. pp. 159–60; Macdonald, A. and A. op. cit. II p. 264.
8. Leslie, J. op. cit. p. 184.
9. Fraser, J. 1905, p. 184.
10. *Letters and Papers* etc. *Henry VIII* vol. XX, part II, 1965, p. 18; D. N. Mackay 1922, p. 100, n.55.
11. Cameron Lees, J. 1897, p. 45.
12. Mackay, W. 1914, p. 97.
13. *Letters and Papers* etc. *Henry VIII* vol. XIX, part II, p. 466.
14. Ibid., vol. XX, part II, pp. 54–5.
15. Ibid., p. 86.
16. Ibid., p. 135.
17. *Book of Clanranald* op. cit. p. 167.
18. *Letters and Papers* etc. *Henry VIII* vol. XIX, part I, p. 130.
19. Ibid., p. 50.
20. Leslie, J. op. cit. p. 185.
21. Gregory, D. op. cit. p. 183.
22. Leslie, J. op. cit. p. 254.
23. *Acts of the Parliament of Scotland* III p. 44.
24. Various accounts. See the *New Statistical Account of Scotland* vol. XX; Grant, I. F. 1981, p. 135; John Lorne Campbell *et al. The Scotsman* 10–30 July 1954; Macpherson, N. 1978, p. 500.
25. Scott's Diary for 25 August 1814 in Lockhart, J. G. 1902, pp. 279–81.
26. Miller, H. 1858, pp. 39, 44–5. See also James Wilson vol. I, pp. 235–6. Another trip in the 1840s, when a coin dating to the reign of Mary Queen of Scots was found in the cave. The remaining bones were finally buried by the local parish priest at Kildonnan shortly after Miller's visit.
27. *Register of the Privy Council, 1585–92.* 1881, pp. 341–2.
28. A point well made by John Lorne Campbell. *The Scotsman* 27 July 1954.
29. Sadler, Sir Ralph I p. 431.
30. Ibid., II p. 55–6.
31. *Register of the Privy Council* 1545–69, p. 251.
32. Ibid., pp. 272–3.

CHAPTER 7

1. On this whole subject see A. McKerral 1951 and G. A. Hayes-McCoy 1937.
2. Walsh, P. 1936, p. 31.
3. Cosgrove, A. 1993, pp. 574–5.
4. Hayes-McCoy, G.A. op. cit. p. 26.
5. Hill, J.M. 1993, p. 34.
6. Quoted in G. Hill 1873, p. 37; *Calendar of Letters and Papers, Foreign and Domestic* vol. VI, p. 645.
7. Hill, J. M. 1993, p. 34.
8. Bagwell, R. vol. I, 1885–90, p. 361; Gregory, D. p. 195.
9. Hill, G. 1873, p. 122.
10. Ibid., pp. 52–3.
11. Dawson, J. E. A. 1987, p. 115.
12. Hill, J. M. 1993, p. 43.
13. Dawson, J. E. A. 1987, p. 117.
14. Hill, G. 1861, p. 62; Macdonald, A. and A. op. cit. p. 676.
15. *Book of Islay* op. cit. pp. 62–5.
16. Webb, M. 1860, pp. 251–68.
17. Hill, J. M. 1993, p. 54; Hill, G. 1873, pp. 125–6.
18. Hayes-McCoy, G. A. 1937, p. 87.
19. Hill, G. 1873, p. 148n.
20. For the Glentasie campaign see G. Hill 1861, pp. 121–41; J. M. Hill 1991, pp. 129–138.
21. Brady, C. 1982–3, pp. 116–123.
22. Hill, G. 1873, p. 139.
23. Webb, M. 1860, p. 255.
24. Breathnach, C. 1992, p. 173.
25. On this see C. Brady 1982–3; H. Morgan 1988–9; C. Breathnach 1992.
26. Wright, G. N. 1823, pp. 39–40.
27. Dawson, J. E. A. 1987, p. 119.
28. *Calendar of State Papers Ireland* vol. I, 1860, p. 355.
29. Ibid., p. 393.
30. *Calendar of Carew Manuscripts,* 1515–1574. 1867, p. 449.
31. There appears to be some confusion here. A. and A. Macdonald say it was Angus and J. M. Hill says in was Donnell Gorme.
32. *Calendar of State Papers Ireland* I p. 539.
33. Gregory, D. op cit. p. 222.
34. *Calendar of State Papers Scotland.* Vol. XII, 1595–7, p. 343.
35. Ibid., pp. 507, 511.

CHAPTER 8

1. Cowan, E. J. 1979 I p. 34.
2. *Register of the Privy Council* III, 1578–85, pp. 505–6.
3. Ibid., p. 506.
4. *Register of the Privy Council* III p. 739.
5. Gordon, R. 1813, p. 187.
6. He was the son or grandson, it is not clear which, of Archibald the Clerk who led the clan during the minority of Donald Gormeson, Donald Gorme Mor's father. A. and A. Macdonald III p. 29.
7. *History of the Feuds and Conflicts of the Clans*, pp. 59–66. This is an anonymous work, apparently written during the reign of James VI and first published in 1764.
8. Mackay, D. N. 1922, p. 161.
9. The Maclean hostages were never harmed.
10. *Calendar of State Papers Ireland* III p. 478.
11. *Calendar of State Papers Scotland* IX, 1586–88, p. 629.
12. Gordon, R. op. cit. p. 191.
13. *Calendar of State Papers Scotland* VIII p. 79.
14. *Acts of the Parliament of Scotland* III pp. 461–7.
15. *Register of the Privy Council* IV, 1585–93, pp. 290–1.
16. *Pitcairn's Criminal Trials* II, 1833, pp. 224–30, 227, 228–9.
17. Gregory, D. op. cit. p. 242.
18. *Register of the Privy Council* V, 1592–99, p. 321.
19. *The Warrender Papers* vol. II, 1931–2, pp. 429–30.
20. See E. J. Cowan 1984–6, p. 269.
21. *James I* 1918, p. 269.
22. *Acts of the Parliament of Scotland* IV p. 160.
23. *Calendar of State Papers Scotland* XIII part I, p. 191.
24. *Pitcairn* III 1835, p. 67.
25. *Calendar of State Papers Scotland* XIII part I, pp. 259–62; Calderwood, D. vol. V, 1844, p. 726.
26. *Calendar of State Papers* XIII pp. 261–2.
27. Gregory D. op. cit. p. 289 and many others.
28. Lamont, W. D. 1966, p. 47.
29. *Calendar of State Papers Scotland* XIII p. 1085.
30. Gordon, R. op. cit. p. 244.
31. Ibid., pp. 244–5. Also I. F. Grant 1981, p. 191.
32. Macdonald, N. H. 1995, p. 41.
33. Gregory, D. op. cit. p. 303.
34. See Macdonald, K. 1890, pp. 11–24.
35. *Macbeth* Act I, Scene II, lines 10–14.

36. *Register of the Privy Council* VII, 1604–7, p. 465.
37. Ibid., pp. 749–50.
38. *Calendar of State Papers Scotland* XII pp. 201–211; *Miscellany of the Maitland Club* IV, 1847, pp. 42–48
39. Cowan, E. J. 1979, p. 152.
40. We need mention only one example. W. C. Mackenzie 1974 argues on p. 233 that James, by his order to exterminate the Macleods of Lewis, alienated Highland people from the Stewarts for all time. Only a few pages later the Statutes of Iona are said to have created a permanent bond between the Highlanders and the Stewarts!
41. Stevenson, D. 1994, p. 31.
42. *Highland Papers* II, 1920, p. 115.
43. Calderwood, D. vol. VII, p. 200.
44. Stevenson, D. 1994, p. 1.
45. *Highland Papers* III p. 200.
46. *Register of the Privy Council* X, 1613–1616, p. 759.
47. He was later charged with the murder of Malcolm Macphee and others, but suffered no ill consequences, presumably because of the support of the Campbells.
48. *Register of the Privy Council* XI, 1616–19, p. 468.

CHAPTER 9

1. Gregory, D. op. cit. p. 407; Cowan, E. J. 1984–6, p. 294.
2. *Register of the Privy Council*, second series I, 1625–7, p. 35.
3. *Historical Manuscripts Commission* VI p. 489.
4. Shaw, F. J. 1977, pp. 44–47; MacInnes, A. I. 1993, p. 46.
5. Campbell, J. L. 1953, p. 115. Also Giblin, C. 1964, pp. 24, 45, 62. This provides further proof, if any is needed, of how overstated the Statutes of Iona are.
6. *Register of the Privy Council*, second series V, 1633–35, p. 464.
7. Paterson, R. C. 1998, p. 17.
8. *Hamilton Papers* vol. I, 1880, pp. 12–13.
9. Historical Manuscripts Commission, supplementary report. Duke of Hamilton XXI, 1932, p. 50.
10. Baillie, R. vol. I, 1841–2, p. 93.
11. Knowler, W. (ed.) vol. II, 1732, p. 187.
12. Hill, G. 1873, pp. 254, 444.
13. Stevenson, D. 1994, p. 67.
14. Knowler op. cit. II p. 187.
15. Ibid., p. 266.
16. Stevenson, D. 1994, p. 73.

17. Gilles, W. A. 1980, p. 147; Mackenzie, A. M. Notes to *Orain Iain Luim* pp. 233–4; Macpherson, D. M. 1879, p. 372; Sinclair, A. 1880, p. 98; Macdonald, A. and A. op. cit. II p. 209.
18. *Orain Iain Luim* 1964, p. 11.
19. Stevenson, D. 1981, p. 61.
20. Stevenson, D. 1982, pp. 3–8; 1994, pp. 82–3.
21. Black, R. 1972–4, p. 225.
22. Baillie, R. op cit. p. 74.
23. O'Danachair 1959–60, pp. 61–7.
24. Gordon, Patrick, of Ruthven 1844, p. 63.
25. *Book of Clanranald* op. cit. p. 179.
26. Gordon op. cit. p. 64.
27. Ibid., p. 94.
28. Spalding, J. vol. II, 1828, p. 294.
29. Baillie, R. vol. II, p. 263.
30. Forbes-Leith, W. 1909, pp. 366–7.
31. Baillie op. cit. II p. 263.
32. *Orain Iain Luim* op. cit. pp. 20–5.
33. Maclean, J. A. Unpublished PhD Aberdeen 1939, p. 29.

CHAPTER 10

1. Baillie, R. op. cit. p. 263.
2. Fraser, J. op. cit. p. 289.
3. *Orain Iain Luim*, intro. pp. xxxv– xxxvi.
4. Gordon op. cit. pp. 123–4.
5. *Orain Iain Luimm* pp. 26–7. My own account (1998, pp. 114–7) is based largely on David Stevenson's brilliant reconstruction of Auldearn. 1994 chapter 7.
6. Cowan, E. J. 1977, p. 214.
7. Watson, W. J. ed. vol. II, 1927, p. 75.
8. Wishart, G. 1893 translation p. 138.
9. Buchan, J. 1996 ed. p. 131.
10. McKechnie, H. 1938, p. 171.
11. *Book of Clanranald* op. cit. p. 203.
12. Matheson, A. 1958, p. 27.
13. Stevenson, D. 1994, p. 223.
14. Maclean, J. A. op. cit. pp. 65–7.
15. Ohlmeyer, J. 1993, p. 174.
16. Montereul, J. de 1898, I pp. 193, 199; II p. 50.
17. Stevenson, D. 1994, p. 231.
18. Turner, Sir James 1829, p. 45.

19. Gordon op. cit. p. 263; Campbell, A. 1885, p. 222.
20. Ibid., p. 91.
21. *Orain Iain Luim* p. 35.
22. Black, R. op. cit. p. 231; Loder, J. 1935, pp. 143–4.
23. Firth, C. H. 1895, p. 310; 1899, pp. 111–2.
24. Ibid., 1895, p. 188.
25. *Register of the Privy Council*, third series vol. III, 1669–72, p. 552.
26. Ibid., 1669–72, pp. xxvi, 222, 312; Fraser, J. op. cit. p. 462.
27. *Register of the Privy Council* third series, vol. I 1661–4, pp. 1, 55.
28. *Orain Iain Luim* p. 83.
29. Maclean, J. A. op. cit. pp. 187–8.
30. Lord Macdonnell is named as the instrument of vengeance and the episode is dated to the early seventeenth century. On the Keppoch murders see Campbell, A. 1942–50, pp. 167–75.
31. Maclean, J. A. op. cit. p. 196, n. 2.
32. Hopkins, P. 1986, p. 32.
33. *Orain Iain Luim* p. 43. The boar's head is the badge of the Campbells.

CHAPTER 11

1. *Fountainhall Historical Notices* vol. II, 1848, pp. 553–4.
2. Macinnes, A. I. 1996, p. 44.
3. McBane, D. 1728, pp. 76–77.
4. Maclean, J. A. op. cit. p. 240.
5. Ibid., p. 236.
6. Ibid., p. 242; Macinnes, A. I. op. cit. p. 44.
7. Lord Macdonnell died childless in 1680. As the title was reserved to heirs male rather than heirs general it passed with his death. Ranald, his cousin, succeeded as tenth chief of Glengarry. Because of Ranald's advanced age, management of the clan's affairs passed to his son, Alasdair Dubh.
8. Philip, J. 1888, pp. 124–5.
9. The editor of Philip's poem is unfamiliar with the Highland name Coll, which he takes to be an abbreviation for the rank of colonel. Hence, Coll of the Cows becomes, rather absurdly, Colonel of the Cows! Ibid., p. 127 fn.
10. Ibid., p. 129.
11. McBane, D. op. cit. p. 79.
12. *Orain Iain Luim* op. cit. p. 219.
13. Hopkins, P. 1986, p. 200; McDonald, A. 1998, p. 21.
14. National Library of Scotland, *Yule Manuscript 3134* contains

Cannon's order. John Campbell of Glenorchy was created Earl of Breadalbane by Charles II.

15. He seems to have held Coll of Keppoch more culpable, omitting Maciain altogether from his petition for compensation laid before parliament.

16. Zee, von der, H. and B. 1988, reprint p. 352.

17. Mackay, Hugh 1833, p. 18.

18. *Leven and Melville Papers* 1843, p. 394.

19. Ibid., p. 585.

20. *Papers Illustrative of Political Conditions in the Highlands*, 1845, p. 101.

21. Hopkins, P. 1986, p. 227; Fergusson, W. 1968, p. 19.

22. Hopkins, P. 1986, p. 22; Cunningham, A. 1919, p. 41; Riley, P. W. J. 1979, p. 69. John Prebble apparently fails to see the logical inconsistency. 1968, p. 142.

23. Drummond, J. 1842, p. 309.

24. *Papers Illustrative* etc. op. cit. pp. 35–7.

25. Hopkins, P. 1986, p. 100.

26. *Papers Illustrative* etc. p. 49.

27. The religious affiliations of the Glencoe people has been the subject of heated debate. See Fergusson, W. 1967, 1968 (ii) and Prebble, J. 1967. While not absolutely conclusive, it is almost certain that, like most of Clan Donald, they were Catholic. They were certainly regarded as Catholic martyrs by the church. See Forbes-Leith, W. 1909, I p. 171; Blundell, O. 1917, pp. 203–4.

28. *Papers Illustrative* etc. p. 62. Macinnes, A. 1992, p. 17 says Argyll 'gleefully' informed Dalrymple of the news. The sources do not reveal Argyll's state of mind, gleeful or otherwise.

29. Buchan, J. 1933, p. 107. Macdonald, D. J. 1965, p. 112 says that Argyll and Breadalbane neglected their 'orders', but suggests that Argyll may have positioned his forces to the south of Rannoch Moor, to what purpose is not clear. No evidence is cited for this proposition.

30. Macdonald, A. and A. op. cit. II pp. 213–4.

31. *Gallienus Redivivus* 1695, pp. 4–5.

32. Hopkins, P. 1986, p. 336. Hopkins provides the best account by far of the events surrounding the massacre, although his prose tends to be leaden.

33. *Gallienus Redivivus* op. cit. p. 9.

34. *Breadalbane Papers* in the Scottish Record Office. GD/112/39/159/2.

35. *Calendar of State Papers Domestic 1694–5*, p. 506.

36. Macaulay, Lord 1953, III pp. 409–11. Buchan, J. p. 108 says that the Argyll regiment were all Breadalbane men, which was never claimed, even at the time.

CHAPTER 12

1. Baynes, J. 1970, p. 18.
2. MacDonald, C. 1889, p. 110.
3. Campbell, D. 1886, p. 241.
4. Murray, K. (ed.) 1908, p. 275.
5. Ibid., p. 283n.
6. MacDonald, Sileas 1972, p. 39.
7. *Book of Clanranald* op. cit. p. 249.
8. Mitcheson, R. 1970, p. 31.
9. Macdonald, A. and A. op. cit. II p. 350.
10. Devine, T. M. 1994, p. 15.
11. *More Culloden Papers* 1927, III p. 141,
12. Mackenzie, W. C. 1932, p. 49.
13. Murray, John. 1898, p. 151.
14. Ibid., p. 155.
15. MacDonald, Alexander. 1924, pp. 71–3.
16. Ibid., p. 79. The images invoked at the conclusion are found in the Macdonald arms.
17. *Culloden Papers* 1815, p. 207.
18. Ibid., pp. 405–6.
19. Prebble, J. 1967, p. 262.
20. See A. Livingstone *et al*. 1984, pp. 216–9.
21. Johnstone, James 1958, p. 87. So much for the contention that Highlanders were afraid of cavalry.
22. Forbes, R. (ed.) 1834, p. 88.
23. Campbell, J. L. (ed.) 1933, p. 209.
24. Bailey, G. B. 1996, pp. 170–1.
25. Most recently, as far as I can determine, by a Macdonald in search of his roots. See Macdonald, S. 1994, p. 167.
26. *Celtic Magazine* vol. II, 1887. The author identified only as 'J. M. W. S.' says the stain on the military reputation of Clan Donald will forever be uneffaced.
27. Campbell, J. L. 1933, p. 179.
28. *Lockhart Papers* 1817, vol. II, p. 510; Home, J. 1802, pp. 233–4 fn.
29. Tomasson, K. and Buist, F. 1978, p. 141. A small flaw in an otherwise excellent book. With some 800 men in total, the Macdonald

regiments were only 100 short of the combined strength of the Camerons and the Atholl Brigade.

30. Charles, G. 1817, vol. II, p. 297.
31. Leask, J. C. and McCance, H. M. 1915, p. 50.
32. Seaton, B. G. and Arnot, J. G. (eds.) 1928–9, p. 37.
33. Paton, H. (ed.) 1895–6, p. 239.
34. MacDonald, Alexander. 1924, p. 103.

CHAPTER 13

1. Campbell, J. L. 1933, p. 209.
2. *The Highlands of Scotland in 1750*, 1898, pp. 51–2.
3. Maclean, M. 1991, p. 24.
4. Macdonald, A. and A. op. cit. II p. 719.
5. *Orain Iain Luim* op. cit. p. 125.
6. Paton, H. op. cit. III p. 259.
7. Matheson, W. (ed.) 1938, pp. 199– 203.
8. Johnson, Samuel 1996, edit. p. 83.
9. Diary entry 14 February 1826, Lockhart, J. G. vol. VIII, 1902, pp. 203–4.
10. Those who wish to follow this debate might enjoy the highly partisan J. Riddel 1821. The copy held by the National Library of Scotland has been inscribed by Alasdair Ranaldson himself.
11. Prebble, J. 1969, pp. 140–1.
12. Gray, M. 1951–2, p. 198.
13. Stewart, A. Unpublished Edinburgh University PhD thesis 1982, p. 577.
14. Hunter, J. 1976, p. 62.
15. Geikie, A. 1904, pp. 225–7.
16. Ross, D. 1853, p. 16. Also Mackenzie, A. C. 1881, p. 2.
17. Bray, E. 1996.

SELECT BIBLIOGRAPHY

DOCUMENTARY AND NARRATIVE SOURCES

Acts of the Lords of the Council in Public Affairs, 1501–1554 (ed.) R. K. Hanny, 1932.

Acts of the Lords of the Isles, 1336–1493, (eds) J. Munro and R. W. Munro, 1986.

Acts of the Parliament of Scotland.

The Auchinleck Chronicle (ed.) T. Thomson, 1829.

The Albermarle Papers, 2 vols. (ed.) C. S. Terry.

Alison, J. N. (ed.) *The Poetry of Northeast Scotland*, 1976.

Anderson, A. O. (ed.) *Early Sources of Scottish History*, 2 vols, 1922.

Ane Breve Chronicle of the Earldom of Ross, 1850.

Annals of Connacht (ed. and trans.) A. M. Freeman, 1944.

Annals of Innisfallen (ed. and trans.) S. MacAirt, 1951.

Annals of Ireland by the Four Masters (trans.) O'Connellan, 1846.

Annals of the Kingdom of Ireland by the Four Masters, (ed. and trans.) J. O'Donovan, 1851.

Annals of Loch Ce (ed. and trans.) W. M. Hennessy, 1871.

Annals of Tigernach – Continuation (ed. and trans.) W. Stokes, in *Revue Celtique*, 18, 1898.

Annals of Ulster (ed. and trans.) B. Maccarthy, 1887–1901.

Argyll Family, Letters to, The Maitland Club, 1839.

Baillie, Robert, *Letters and Papers*, 3 vols, 1841–2.

Balfour, Sir James, *Historical Works*, 4 vols, 1824.

Barbour, John, *The Bruce*, (ed. and trans.) A. A. H. Douglas, 1994.

Bergin, O. (ed.) *Irish Bardic Poetry*, 1970.

Blakie, W. B. (ed.) *The Origins of the 'Forty-Five*, 1975.

Boece, H., *The Chronicles of Scotland*, Bellenden translation, (ed.) E. C. Batho and W. Husbands, 1941.

The Book of Clanranald, in *Reliquae Celticae*, vol. II, (eds) A. MacBain and J. Kennedy, 1894.

The Book of Islay (ed.) G. Gregory Smith, 1895.

Bower, Walter, *Scotichronicon,* vols 6, 7, 8 variously edited, 1991–9.

The Breadalbane Papers, manuscripts in the Scottish Record Office.

Burnet, Gilbert, *History of my Own Life and Times*, (eds) O. Airey and H. C. Foxcroft, 1897–1902.

Calderwood, David, *A History of the Kirk of Scotland*, vols V and VII, 1844–5.

Calendar of Carew State Papers, 1515–1574, 1867.

Calendar of Documents Relating to Scotland, 4 vols, (ed.) R. Bain, 1881–88.

Calendar of Letters and Papers, Foreign and Domestic of the Reign of Henry VIII, 1965 reprint.

Calendar of Scottish Supplications to Rome, 1418–1422 (eds) E. R. Lindsay and A. I. Cameron, 1934.

Calendar of State Papers Domestic, William and Mary, 1694–5 (ed.) W. J. Hardy, 1906.

Calendar of State Papers Relating to Ireland, variously edited, 1860–87.

Calendar of State Papers Relating to Scotland, variously edited, 1860–1969.

Cameron, A. I. (ed.) *The Scottish Correspondence of Mary of Lorraine*, 1927.

Campbell, J. L. (ed. and trans.) *Highland Songs of the Forty-Five*, 1933.

Campbell, J. L. (ed.) 'The letter sent by Iain Muidertach Twelfth Chief of Clanranald, to Pope Urban VIII', in the *Innes Review*, vol. IV, pp. 110–6, 1953.

Charles, G., *History of the Transactions in Scotland*, 2 vols, 1817.

The Chronicle of Man and the Sudreys (ed. and trans.) P. A. Munch, 1874.

Collectanea de Rebus Albanicus, Iona Club, 1848.

Culloden Papers, 1625–1748, 1815.

More Culloden Papers, vols III and IV, (ed.) D. Warrant, 1927.

Dalrymple, Sir John, *Memoirs of Great Britain and Ireland*, 1771–88.

The Dewar Manuscripts (ed.) J. Mackechnie, 1964.

Dickinson, W. C. *et al.*, *Source Book of Scottish History*, 1952.

Dixon, W. M. (ed.) *The Edinburgh Book of Scottish Verse, 1300–1900*, 1910.

Drummond, John, *The Memoirs of Sir Ewan Cameron of Locheil*, 1842.

Exchequer Rolls of Scotland, vols IV, V and X, (ed.) G. Burnett, 1880–87.

Firth, C. H. (ed.) *Scotland and the Commonwealth*, 1895.

Firth, C. H. (ed.) *Scotland and the Protectorate*, 1899.

Forbes, R., *The Lyon in Mourning*, (ed.) H. Paton, 1895.

Forbes-Leith, W., *Memoirs of Scottish Catholics*, 2 vols, 1909.

Fordun, John, *Chronicle of Scotland*, (trans.) F. J. Skene, 1872.

Fountainhall Historical Notices, 1661–1683, 2 vols, 1848.

Fraser, James, *Chronicle of the Frasers. The Wardlaw Manuscripts* (ed.) W. Mackay, 1905.

Gallienus Redivivus or, Murther Will Out etc. Charles Leslie, 1695.

Geikie, Archibald, *Scottish Reminiscences*, 1904.

Genealogical Collections Concerning Families in Scotland made by Walter Macfarlane, 2 vols, (ed.) W. Clark, 1900.

Gordon, Robert, *A Genealogical History of the Earldom of Sutherland*, 1813.

Gordon, Patrick, of Ruthven, *A Short Abridgement of Britane's Distemper*, 1844.

The Hamilton Papers (ed.) S. R. Gardiner, 1880.

Henderson, A., *The Edinburgh History of the Late Rebellion*, 1752.

Highland Papers vol. I (ed.) J. R. N. Macphail, 1914.

Highland Papers vol. II (ed.) J. R. N. Macphail, 1916.

Highland Papers vol. III (ed.) J. R. N. Macphail, 1920.

Highland Papers vol. IV (ed.) J. R. N. Macphail, 1934.

The Highlands of Scotland in 1750, anonymous, intro. by A. Lang, 1898.

Historical Manuscripts Commission Eleventh Report, Appendix Part VI. *Manuscripts of the Duke of Hamilton*, 1887.

Historical Manuscripts Commission Supplementary Report on the Manuscripts of the Duke of Hamilton, XXI, 1932.

The Historie and Life of King James the Sext, anonymous, 1825.

The History of the Feuds and Conflicts among the Clans etc., anonymous, 1764.

Home, John, *History of the Rebellion in the Year 1745*, 1802.

Innes, C. (ed.) *Origines Parochiales Scotiae*, 1851.

James VI and I, *Basilikon Doron*, in *The Political Works of James I*, intro. C. H. McIlwraith, 1918.

Jenner, H. (ed.) *Memoirs of the Lord Viscount Dundee*, 1903.

Johnson, Samuel, *A Journey to the Western Islands of Scotland*, (ed.) I. McGow, 1996.

Johnstone, James, Chevalier de, *A Memoir of the 'Forty-Five*, 1958.

Knowler, W., *The Earl of Strafforde's Letters and Papers*, 1739.

Leask, J. C. and McCance, H. M., *The Regimental Records of the Royal Scots*, 1915.
Lesley, Bishop John, *The History of Scotland from the death of King James I* etc., 1830.
Leven and Melville Papers, 1689–1691, 1843.
Lockhart, J. G., *The Life of Sir Walter Scott*, vols IV and VIII, 1902.
Lockhart, George, of Carnwath, *The Lockhart Papers*, 2 vols, 1817.
Liber de Melrose, 2 vols, 1837.

McBane, Donald, *The Expert Sword-Mans Companion*, 1728.
MacCodrum, John, *The Songs of John MacCodrum*, (ed.) W. Matheson, 1938.
MacDonald, Alexander, *Poems* (ed. and trans.) A. and A. Macdonald, 1924.
MacDonald, Hugh, 'History of the Macdonalds', in *Highland Papers* I, 1914.
MacDonald, Sileas, *Poems and Songs* (ed.) C. O'Baoill, 1972.
Mackay, Hugh, *Memoirs of the War* etc., 1833.
Mackenzie, A., *The Highland Clearances*, 1881.
Major, John, *A History of Greater Britain*, 1892.
Martin, Martin, *A Description of the Western Islands of Scotland circa 1695*, 1994.
The Melrose Papers, 2 vols, 1837.
Miller, Hugh, *The Cruise of the Betsy*, 1858.
Miscellany of the Maitland Club, vol. IV, 1847.
Miscellany of the Spalding Club, vol. II, 1842.
Monro's Western Isles of Scotland and the Genealogies of the Clans (ed.) R. W. Monro, 1961.
Murray, Lord George, 'Marches of the Highland Army', in *Jacobite Memoirs of the Rebellion of 1745* (ed.) R. Forbes, 1834.
Murry, John, of Broughton, *Memorials* (ed.) R. F. Bell, 1898.

The New Statistical Account of Scotland.

Orain Iain Luim. Songs of John MacDonald, Bard of Keppoch (ed.) A. M. MacKenzie, 1964.
The Orkneyinger Saga (trans.) G. W. Dasent, 1894.

Papers Illustrative of Political Conditions in the Highlands of Scotland from the Year 1689 to 1696, 1845.
Paton, H., *The Mackintosh Muniments, 1442–1820*, 1903.

Philip, James, *The Grameid* (ed. and trans.) A. D. Murdoch, 1888.

Pitcairn, Robert, *Criminal Trials in Scotland*, 3 vols, 1833–5.

Pittscottie, Robert Lindsay of, *Historie and Cronicles of Scotland* (ed.) A. J. G. Mackay, 1894.

Ramsay, A., *The Ever Green. A Collection of Scots Poems*, 1876.

Records of Inverness, 2 vols, (eds) W. Mackay and H. C. Boyd, 1911, 1924.

Register of the Great Seal of Scotland, 1882.

The Register of the Privy Council of Scotland, variously edited, 1877–1933.

Registrum Episcopatus Moraviensis, 1837.

Registrum Monasterii de Passelet, 1832.

Ross, D., *The Glengarry Evictions*, 1853.

Rotuli Scotiae, vols I and II, 1824, 1829.

Sadler, Sir Ralph, *State Papers and Letters*, 3 vols, 1809.

The Saga of Hacon, (trans.) G. W. Dasent, 1894.

Sinclair, John, Master of, *Memoirs of the Insurrection in Scotland in 1715*, 1858.

Spalding, John, *History of the Troubles*, 2 vols, 1828.

Syllabus of Rymer's Foedera (ed.) T. D. Hardy, 1869–1885.

Thomson, D., *An Introduction to Gaelic Poetry*, 1976.

Turner, Sir James, *Memoirs of his own Life and Times*, 1829.

The Warrendar Papers (ed.) A. I. Cameron, 1931–2.

Watson, W. J., 'Classic Gaelic Poetry', in *Transactions of the Gaelic Society of Inverness*, vol. 29, 1914–19, pp. 194–235.

Watson. W. J., 'Unpublished Gaelic Poetry', in *Scottish Gaelic Studies*, vol. II, 1927, pp. 75–91.

Watson, W. J., *Scottish Verse from the Dean of Lismore*, 1937.

Wilson, J., *Voyage Round the Coasts of Scotland and the Isles*, 1842.

Wishart, George, *The Memoirs of James Marquis of Montrose* (trans.) A. D. Murdoch and H. F. Morland Simpson, 1893.

Wyntoun, Andrew of, *The Original Chronicle* (ed.) F. J. Amours, 1903.

Yule Collection 3134, The National Library of Scotland.

SECONDARY WORKS

Adam, F., *The Clans, Septs and Regiments of the Scottish Highlands*, 1970.

Anon., *Historical and Genealogical Account of the Clan and Family of Macdonald*, 1819.

Argyll, An Inventory of Ancient Monuments, vol. I *Kintyre*, 1971.

Bagwell, R., *Ireland Under the Tudors*, 3 vols, 1885–90.

Baillie, G. B., *Falkirk or Paradise!* 1996.

Bannerman, J., 'The Lordship of the Isles', in *Scottish Society in the Fifteenth Century*, (ed.) J. M. Brown, 1977 pp. 209–240.

Barron, E. M., *Inverness and the Macdonalds*, 1930.

Barron, E. M., *The Scottish War of Independence*, 1934.

Barrow, G. W. S., *The Kingdom of the Scots*, 1973.

Barrow, G. W. S., *Robert Bruce*, 1976.

Barrow, G. W. S., *The Anglo-Norman Era in Scottish History*, 1980.

Barrow, G. W. S., *Kingship and Unity. Scotland, 1000–1306*, 1981.

Barrow, G. W. S. and Royan, A., 'James Fifth Steward of Scotland', in *Essays on the Nobility of Medieval Scotland*, (ed.) K. J. Stringer, 1985, pp. 166–90.

Baynes, J., *The Jacobite Rising of 1715*, 1970.

Beveridge, E., *Coll and Tiree*, 1903.

Black, R., 'Colla Coitach', in *Transactions of the Gaelic Society of Inverness*, vol. 48, 1972–4, pp. 201–43.

Black, R., 'The Genius of Cathal MacMhuirich', in *Transactions of the Gaelic Society of Inverness*, vol. 50, 1976–80, pp. 327–66.

Blundell, O., *The Catholic Highlands of Scotland*, 1917.

Boardman, S., *The Early Stewart Kings, Robert II and Robert III, 1371–1405*, 1996.

Brady, C., 'The Killing of Shane O' Neil: Some new Evidence', in *Irish Sword*, vol. 15, 1982–3, pp. 116–23.

Bray, E., *The Discovery of the Hebrides. Voyages to the Western Isles, 1745–1883*, 1996.

Breathnach, C., 'The Murder of Shane O' Neil', in *Eriu*, vol. 53, 1992, pp. 159–75.

Bremner, R. C., *The Norsemen in Alba*, 1923.

Broderich, G., 'Irish and Welsh Strands in the Genealogy of Godred Crovan', in *Journal of the Manx Museum*, vol. 8, 1980, pp. 32–8.

Brown, A. L., 'The Cistercian Abbey of Saddell, Kintyre', in the *Innes Review*, vol. 20, 1969, pp. 130–7.

Brown, M., *James I*, 1994.

Brown, M., *The Black Douglases*, 1998.

Buchan, J., *The Massacre of Glencoe*, 1933.

Buchan. J., *The Marquis of Montrose*, 1996.

Byrne, K., *Colkitto! A Celebration of Clan Donald of Colonsay*, 1997.

Caldwell, D. H. and Ewart, G., 'Finlaggan and the Lordship of the Isles: An Archaeological Approach', in *The Scottish Historical Review*, vol. 72, 1993, pp. 146–66.

Cameron, J., *James V–the Personal Rule, 1528–1542*, 1998.

Cameron Lees, J., *The History of the County of Inverness*, 1897.

Campbell, A., 'The Keppoch Murders', in *Transactions of the Gaelic Society of Inverness*, vols 39–40, 1942–50, pp. 167–175.

Campbell, A., *Records of Argyll*, 1885.

Campbell, D., *The Lairds of Glenlyon*, 1886.

Campbell, J., 'Glencoe – A Plot that Misfired', in the *Clan Campbell Newsletter*, no. 16, 1988, pp. 14–16.

Chambers, R., *History of the Rebellion of 1745–6*, 1869 edn.

Clark, A. M., *Murder Under Trust or the Topical MacBeth and other Jacobean Matters*, 1981.

Clark, W., *The Lords of the Isles Voyage*, 1993.

Clarke, A., 'The Earl of Antrim and the First Bishops' War', in *Irish Sword*, vol. 6, 1963–4, pp. 108–15.

Cosgrove, A., *The New History of Ireland*, vol. II, 1993.

Cowan, E. J., 'Clanship, Kinship and the Campbell Acquisition of Islay', in *The Scottish Historical Review*, vol. 58, 1979, pp. 132–57.

Cowan, E. J., 'Fishers in Drumlie Waters: Clanship and Campbell expansion in the time of Gilleasbuig Grumach', in the *Transactions of Gaelic Society of Inverness*, vol. 54, 1984–6, pp. 269–312.

Cowan, E. J., 'Norwegian sunset–Scottish dawn: Hakon IV and Alexander III', in *Scotland in the Reign of Alexander III*, (ed.) N. H. Reid, 1990.

Cowan, E. J., *Montrose. For Covenant and King*, 1995.

Creggan, E. R., 'The changing role of the house of Argyll in the Scottish Highlands', in *History and Social Anthropology* (ed.) I. M. Lewis, 1968.

Cunningham, A., 'The revolution government in the Highlands', in *Scottish Historical Review*, vol. 16, 1919, pp. 29–51.

Cunningham, A., *Loyal Clans*, 1932.

Curtis, E., *Richard II in Ireland*, 1927.

Dawson, J. E. A., 'Argyll: the enduring heartland', in *The Scottish Historical Review*, vol. 64, 1995, pp. 75–98.

Dawson, J. E. A., 'Two kingdoms or three? Ireland in Anglo-Scottish relations in the middle of the sixteenth century', in *Scotland, and England, 1286–1815* (ed.) R. A. Mason, 1987.

Dawson, J. E. A., 'The fifth earl of Argyll, Gaelic lordship and political power in sixteenth century Scotland', in *The Scottish Historical Review*, vol. 67, 1988, pp. 1–27.

Devine, T. M., *Clanship to Crofters' War*, 1994.

Donaldson, G., *Scotland from James V to James VII*, 1969.

Douglas Simpson, W., *The Earldom of Mar*, 1949.

Dow, F. D., *Cromwellian Scotland, 1651–1660*, 1979.

Dressler, C., *Eigg – The Story of an Island*, 1998.

Duffy, S., 'The "Continuation" of Nicholas Trevet: a new source for the Bruce Invasion', in *Proceedings of the Royal Irish Academy*, vol. 91, 1991.

Duffy, S., 'The Bruce brothers and the Irish Sea world', in *Cambridge Medieval Celtic Studies*, 21, 1991, pp. 55–86.

Duffy, S., 'Irishmen and Islemen in the kingdoms of Dublin and Man', in *Eriu*, vol. 43, 1992, pp. 93–133.

Duncan, A. A. M. and Brown, A. L., 'Argyll and the Isles in the earlier Middle Ages', in *Proceedings of the Society of Antiquaries of Scotland*, vol. 90, 1956–7, pp. 192–220.

Duncan, A. A. M., *Scotland, the Making of the Kingdom*, 1975.

Dunbar, J., 'The Lordship of the Isles', in *The Middle Ages in the Highlands*, Inverness Field Club, 1981.

Dunn, J. A., *History of Renfrew*, n. d.

Fergusson, W., *Scotland, 1689 to the Present*, 1968.

Fergusson, W., 'Religion and the Massacre of Glencoe', in *The Scottish Historical Review*, vol. 46, 1967, pp. 82–7, followed up in vol. 47, 1968, pp. 203–9.

Fergusson, W., *Scotland's Relations with England*, 1979.

Fyfe, J. G., *The Massacre of Glencoe*, 1948.

Giblin, C. (ed.), *Irish Franciscan Mission to Scotland, 1619–1646*, 1964.

Gilles, W. A., *In Famed Breadalbane*, 1980.

Goodare, J., 'The Statutes of Iona in context', in *The Scottish Historical Review*, vol. 77, 1998, pp. 31–57.

Gordon Seton, B. and Arnot, J. G., *The Prisoners of the '45*, 3 vols, 1928–9.

Grant, A., 'The Revolt of the Lord of the Isles and the death of the Earl of Douglas', in *The Scottish Historical Review*, vol. 60, 1981, pp. 169–74.

Grant, A., 'Scotland's "Celtic Fringe" in the late Middle Ages: the Macdonald Lords of the Isles and the Kingdom of Scotland', in A. Grant and R. R. Davies (eds) *The British Isles, 1100–1500*, 1988.

Grant, I. F., *The Lordship of the Isles*, 1935.

Grant, I. F., *Angus Og of the Isles*, 1969.

Grant, I. F., *The Macleods. The Making of a Clan*, 1981.

Grant, I. F. and Cheape, H., *Periods in Highland History*, 1987.

Gray, M., 'The kelp industry in the Highlands', in *The Economic History Review*, vol. 4, 1951–2, pp. 197–208.

Gregory, D., *History of the Western Highlands and Islands of Scotland*, 1975.

Grieve, S., *The Book of Colonsay and Oronsay*, 2 vols, 1923.

Grumach, D., *The House of Islay*, 1962.

Hanham, H. J., 'The problem of Highland discontent', 1880–1885, in the *Transactions of the Royal Historical Society*, fifth series, vol. 19, 1969, pp. 21–65.

Hewison, J. K., *The Isle of Bute in the Olden Time*, 2 vols, 1893–5.

Hayes McCoy, G. A., *Scots Mercenary Forces in Ireland*, 1937.

'Highland Battles and Highland Arms', in *The Celtic Magazine*, vol. 2, 1877, pp. 470–7, by 'J.M.W.S.'

Hill, G., 'Shane O' Neil's expedition against the Antrim Scots, 1565', in *The Ulster Journal of Archaeology*, vol. 9, 1861, pp. 122–41.

Hill, G., 'The MacQuillins of the Route', in *The Ulster Journal of Archaeology*, vol. 9, 1861, pp. 57–60.

Hill, G., 'Notices of Clan Iain Vor, or the Clan Donnell Scots', in *The Ulster Journal of Archaeology*, vol. 9, 1861, pp. 301–17.

Hill, G., *An Historical Account of the Macdonnells of Antrim*, 1873.

Hill, J. M., 'Shane O' Neil's Campaign Against the MacDonnells of Antrim, 1564–5', in *Irish Sword*, vol. 18, 1991, 129–38.

Hill, J. M., 'The Distinctiveness of Gaelic Warfare, 1400–1750', in *The European History Quarterly*, vol. 22, 1992, pp. 323–45.

Hill, J. M., *Celtic Warfare, 1595–1763*, 1993, i.

Hill, J. M., *Fire and Sword. Sorley Boy MacDonnell and the Rise of Clan Iain Mor*, 1993, ii.

Hill, J. M., 'The rift within Clan Iain Mor: the Antrim and Dunyveg MacDonnells, 1590–1603', in *The Sixteenth Century Journal*, vol. 24, 1993 iii, pp. 865–79.

Holden, R. M., 'The first Highland Regiment. The Argyllshire Highlanders', in *The Scottish Historical Review*, vol. 3, 1906, pp. 27–40.

Hopkins, P., 'Glencoe: An English historian on a very Scottish subject', in *The Seventeenth Century in the Highlands*, The Inverness Field Club, 1980, pp. 150–71.

Hopkins, P., *Glencoe and the End of the Highland War*, 1986.

Hudson, B. T., *Kings of Celtic Scotland*, 1994.

Hunter, J., *The Making of the Crofting Community*, 1976.

Hunter, J., *The Last of the Free*, 1999.

Hunter Marshall, D. W., *The Sudreys in Early Viking Times*, 1929.

Jupp, C. N., *The History of Islay from the earliest times to 1848*, 1994.

Kelly, B. W., *The Fate of Glengarry or the Extirpation of the MacDonnells*, 1905.

Kermack, W. R., *The Scottish Highlands. A Short History*, 1957.

Kinvig, R. H., *History of the Isle of Man*, 1944.

Lamont, W. D., *The Early History of Islay*, 1966.

Lamont, W. D., 'Alexander of Islay, Son of Angus Mor', in *The Scottish Historical Review*, vol. 60, 1981, pp. 160–9.

Lee, M., *Government by Pen. Scotland under James VI and I*, 1980.

Lee, M., *Great Britain's Solomon: James VI and His Three Kingdoms*, 1990.

Lenman, B., *The Jacobite Risings in Britain, 1689–1746*, 1984.

Linklater, M., *Massacre: the Story of Glencoe*, 1982.

Linklater, M. and Hesketh, C., *For King and Conscience. John Graham of Claverhouse, Viscount Dundee*, 1989.

Livingstone, A., Aikman, C. and Hart, B. S., *Muster Roll of Prince Charles Edward Stuart's Army, 1745–6*, 1984.

Loder, J. de vere, *Colonsay and Oronsay in the Isles of Argyll*, 1935.

Lynch, M., *Scotland. A New History*, 1991.

Macaulay, Lord, *The History of England*, Everyman edition, 4 vols, 1953.

MacAuly, J., *Birlinn. Longships of the Hebrides*, 1996.

MacDonald, Angus and Archibald, *Clan Donald*, 3 vols, 1896–1904.

McDonald, A., *The Macdonalds of Glencoe*, 1998.

MacDonald, C., *Moidart; or among the Clanranalds*, 1889.

MacDonald, C. M., *The History of Argyll*, 1950.

MacDonald, D. J., *Slaughter Under Trust. Glencoe, 1692*, 1965.

MacDonald, D. J., *Clan Donald*, 1978.

MacDonald, K., 'A modern raid in Glengarry and Glenmoriston, and the burning of the church of Gilliechrist', in *Transactions of the Gaelic Society of Inverness*, vol. 15, 1890, pp. 11–24.

MacDonald, K., *MacDonald Bards from Medieval Times*, 1900.

MacDonald, N. H., *The Clan Ranald of Lochaber. A History of the MacDonalds or MacDonells of Keppoch*, n.d.

MacDonald, N. H., *The Clan Ranald of Knoydart and Glengarry*, 1995.

McDonald, R. A., 'Death and burial of Somerled of Argyll', in *West Highland Notes and Queries*, November 1991, pp. 6–9.

McDonald, R. A., 'Somerled of Argyll: A new look at an old problem', in *The Scottish Historical Review*, vol. 71, 1992, pp. 3–22.

McDonald, R. A., 'Images of Hebridean Lordship in the late twelfth and early thirteenth centuries: the Seal of Raonall MacSorley', in *The Scottish Historical Review*, vol. 74, 1995, pp. 129–43.

McDonald, R. A., *The Kingdom of the Isles. Scotland's Western Seaboard, 1100–c1336*, 1997.

Macdonald, S., *Back to Lochaber*, 1994.

MacDonell, J. M., *The MacDonells of Keppoch and Gargavach*, 1931.

Macdougall, N., *James III*, 1982.

Macdougall, N., *James IV*, 1997.

MacEwan, A. B. W., 'The Death of Reginald, Son of Somerled', in *West Highland Notes and Queries*, September 1980, pp. 3–7.

MacEwan, A. B. W., 'Alexander de Yle, Lord Of Lochaber and his Son Alasdair Carrach', in *West Highland Notes and Queries,* December 1980, pp. 6–12.

MacEwan, A. B. W., 'The English fleet of 1301', in *West Highland Notes and Queries*, August 1984, pp. 3–7.

McGladdery, C., *James II*, 1990.

Macinnes, A. I., 'Scottish Gaeldom, 1638–1651: the vernacular response to the Covenanter dynamic', in *New Perspectives on the Politics and Culture of Early Modern Scotland* (eds) J. Dwyer, R. A. Mason and A. Murdoch, n.d. (circa 1982).

Macinnes, A. I., 'Repression and conciliation: the Highland dimension, 1660–1688', in *The Scottish Historical Review*, vol. 65, 1986, pp. 167–95.

Macinnes, A. I., 'The Massacre of Glencoe', in *The Historian*, vol. 35, 1992, pp. 16–18.

Macinnes, A. I., 'Crown, Clans and Fine: the "civilizing" of Scottish Gaeldom, 1587–1638', in *Northern Scotland*, vol. 13, 1993, pp. 31–55.

Macinnes, A. I., *Clanship, Commerce and the House of Stewart, 1603–1788*, 1996.

Macinnes, J., 'West Highland Sea Power in the Middle Ages', in *Transactions of the Gaelic Society of Inverness*, vol. 48, 1972–4, pp. 518–56.

Macinnes, J., 'Poetry and historical tradition', in *The Middle Ages in the Highlands*, The Inverness Field Club, 1981.

Mackay, D. N., 'Clan warfare in the old Highlands', in *Transactions of the Gaelic Society of Inverness*, vol. 29, 1914–19, pp. 67–80.

Mackay, D. N., *Clan Warfare in the Scottish Highlands*, 1922.

Mackay, W., *Urquhart and Glenmoriston*, 1914.

Mackay, W., *The Battle of Harlaw – Its True Place in History*, 1922.

McKechnie, *The Lamont Clan, 1235–1935*, 1938.

Mackenzie, A., *History of the MacDonalds and Lords of the Isles*, 1881.

Mackenzie, A., *History of the Macleods*, 1889.

Mackenzie, A., *History of the Mackenzies*, 1894.

Mackenzie, W. C., *The Western Isles: Their History, Traditions and Place Names*, 1932.

Mackenzie, W. C., *The Highlands and Islands of Scotland*, 1937.

Mackenzie, W. C., *History of the Outer Hebrides*, 1974.

McKerral, A., *Kintyre in the Seventeenth Century*, 1948.

McKerral, A., 'West Highland mercenaries in Ireland', in *The Scottish Historical Review*, vol. 30, 1951, pp. 1–14.

McKerral, A., 'A chronology of the abbey and castle of Saddell, Kintyre', in *Proceedings of the Society of Antiquaries of Scotland*, vol. 86, 1951–2, pp. 115–121.

Maclean, A., *A MacDonald for the Prince*, 1990.

Maclean, J. A., *The Sources, particularly the Gaelic Sources, for the History of the Highlands in the Seventeenth Century*, unpublished PhD thesis, Aberdeen, 1939.

Maclean, J. A., *History of the Island of Mull*, 2 vols, 1923–5.

Mclean, M., *The People of Glengarry. Highlanders in Transition, 1745–1820*, 1991.

Maclean Bristol, N., 'The Macleans from 1560–1707: A reappraisal', in *The Seventeenth Century in the Highlands*, The Inverness Field Club, 1980.

Maclean Bristol, N., *Warriors and Priests. The History of Clan Maclean, 1300–1570*, 1995.

Maclean Bristol, N., *Murder Under Trust. The Crimes and Death of Sir Lachlan Mor Maclean of Duart, 1558–1598*, 1999.

Maclean Sinclair, A., *The Clan Gillean*, 1899.

Macleod, R. C., *The Island Clans During Six Centuries*, n. d.

Macleod, R. H., *Flora MacDonald*, 1995.

MacMillan, S., *Bygone Lochaber*, 1971.

MacNeill, E., 'Chapters in Hebridean history', in *The Scottish Review*, vol. 39, 1916, pp. 254–76.

MacNeill, E., *Phases in Irish History*, 1919.

McNeill, P. and Nicholson, R. (eds.), *An Historical Atlas of Scotland, c400–c1600*, 1975.

Macpherson, N., 'Notes on antiquities from the island of Eigg', in *Proceedings of the Society of Antiquaries of Scotland*, vol. 12, 1878, pp. 577–97.

Matheson, A., 'Traditions of Alasdair MacColla', in *Transactions of the Gaelic Society of Glasgow*, vol. 5, 1958, pp. 9–93.

Metcalfe, W. M., *A History of the County of Renfrew*, 1905.

Mitchell, D., *A Popular History of the Highlands and Islands*, 1900.

Mitchison, R., 'The Government of the Highlands, 1707–1745', in R. Mitchison (ed.) *Scotland in the Age of Improvement*, 1970.

Moore, A. W., *A History of the Isle of Man*, 2 vols, 1900.

Moore, A. W., 'The Connection between Scotland and Man', in *The Scottish Historical Review*, vol. 3, 1906, pp. 393–409.

Morgan, H., 'The end of Gaelic Ulster: a thematic interpretation of events between 1534 and 1610', in *Irish Historical Studies*, vol. 26, 1988–9, pp. 8–32.

Munro, J., 'The Earldom of Ross and the Lordship of the Isles', in J. R. Baldwin (ed.) *Firthlands of Ross and Sutherland*, 1986.

Murray, K. (ed.) *A Military History of Perthshire*, 1908.

Murren, P., *Grampian Battlefields*, 1990.

Nicholson, A., *History of Skye*, 1930.

Nicholson, R., *Scotland, the Later Middle Ages*, 1974.

O'Corrain, C., 'Review of "Studies of Dalriada by John Bannerman"', in *Celtica*, vol. 13, 1980, pp. 168–82.

O'Danachair, C., 'Montrose's Irish Regiments', in *Irish Sword*, vol. 4, 1959–60, pp. 61–7.

Ohlmeyer, J., *Civil War and Restoration in the Three Stuart Kingdoms. The Career of Randal MacDonnell, Marquis of Antrim, 1609–1683*, 1993.

Paterson, R. C., *For the Lion. A History of the Scottish Wars of Independence, 1296–1357*, 1996.

Paterson, R. C., *My Wound is Deep. A History of the Later Anglo Scots Wars, 1380–1560*, 1997.

Paterson, R. C., *A Land Afflicted. Scotland and the Covenanter Wars, 1638–1690*, 1998.

Paul, J. B. (ed.) *The Scots Peerage*, vol. I, 1904.

Power, R., 'Magnus Barelegs' expeditions to the west', in *The Scottish Historical Review*, vol. 65, 1986, pp. 107–32.

Prebble, J., *Glencoe*, 1967.

Prebble, J., *Culloden*, 1968.

Prebble, J., 'Religion and the Massacre of Glencoe', in *The Scottish Historical Review*, vol. 47, 1968, pp. 203–9.

Prebble, J., *The Highland Clearances*, 1969.

Prebble, J., *The King's Jaunt. George IV in Scotland, 1822*, 1988.

Reid, J. E., *History of the County of Bute*, 1864.

Richards, E., *A History of the Highland Clearances*, 2 vols, 1982, 1985.

Riddel, J., *A Vindication of Clanranald of Glengarry*, 1821.

Riley, P. W. J., *King William and the Scottish Politicians*, 1979.

Rixon, D., *The West Highland Galley*, 1998.

Roberts, J. L., *Lost Kingdoms. Celtic Scotland and the Middle Ages*, 1997.

Robertson, C. M., 'Topography and traditions of Eigg', in *Transactions of the Gaelic Society of Inverness*, 1897–8.

Robertson, J. I., *The First Highlander. Major-General David Stewart of Garth*, 1998.

Scott, J. E., 'Saddell Abbey', in *Transactions of the Gaelic Society of Inverness*, vol. 56, 1969–70, pp.114–41.

Scott, W. W., 'John of Fordun's description of the Western Isles', in *Scottish Studies*, vol. 23, 1979, pp. 1–13.

The Scotsman, July 1954.

Sellar, W. D. H., 'The origins and ancestry of Somerled', in *The Scottish Historical Review*, vol. 45, 1966.

Sellar, W. D., 'MacDonald and MacRuari Pedigrees in MS 1467', in *West Highland Notes and Queries*, vol. 28, March 1986, pp. 3–15.

Shaw, F. J., 'Landownership in the Western Isles in the seventeenth century', in the *Scottish Historical Review*, vol. 56, 1977, pp. 34–48.

Smout, T. C., *History of the Scottish People*, 1970.

Smyth, A. P., *Warlords and Holy Men. Scotland AD 80–1000*, 1989.

Stanford Reid, W., 'Sea power in the Anglo-Scottish War, 1296–1328', in *The Mariner's Mirror*, vol. 46, 1960, pp. 7–23.

Steer, K. A., and Bannerman, J. W. M., *Late Medieval Monumental Sculpture in the West Highlands*, 1977.

Stevenson, D., *Scottish Covenanters and Irish Confederates*, 1981.

Stevenson, D., *Highland Warrior, Alasdair MacColla and the Civil Wars*, 1994.

Stewart, J., *The Camerons*, 1974.

Stewart, J. A., *The Clan Ranald: History of a Highland Kindred*, unpublished PhD thesis, Edinburgh, 1982.

Storrie, M., *Islay–Biography of an Island*, 1997.

Thomson, D. S., *The Companion to Gaelic Scotland*, 1983.

Tomasson, K. and Buist, F., *The Battles of the '45*, 1978.

Tytler, P., *History of Scotland*, vols. III–VI, 1841.

Walsh, P., 'Scots Clann Domhnaill in Ireland', in *The Irish Ecclesiastical Record*, vol. 48, 1936, pp. 23–42.

Watson, W. J., 'The Macdonald bardic poetry', in the *Transactions of the Gaelic Society of Inverness*, vol. 36, 1931–3, pp. 138–158.

Webb, M., 'The clan MacQuillin of Antrim', in the *Ulster Journal of Archaeology*, vol. 8, 1860, pp. 251–68.

Williams, R., *The Lords of the Isles. The Clan Donald and the Early Kingdom of the Scots*, 1984.

Wright, G. N., *A Guide to the Giant's Causeway*, 1823.

Young, D., 'Clanship to Clearance', in *West Highland Notes and Queries*, vol. 16, April 1997, pp. 5–14.

Young, G. V. C., *The History of the Isle of Man Under the Norse or Now through a Glass Darkly*, 1981.

Zee, von der, Henri and Barbara, *William and Mary*, 1988.

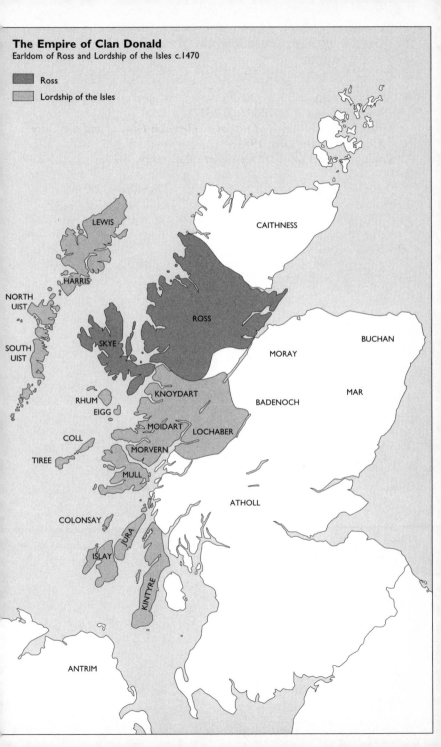

The Empire of Clan Donald
Earldom of Ross and Lordship of the Isles c.1470

- Ross
- Lordship of the Isles

LEWIS

CAITHNESS

HARRIS

NORTH UIST

ROSS

BUCHAN

SOUTH UIST

SKYE

MORAY

MAR

KNOYDART

BADENOCH

RHUM

EIGG

MOIDART

LOCHABER

COLL

MORVERN

TIREE

MULL

ATHOLL

COLONSAY

JURA

ISLAY

KINTYRE

ANTRIM

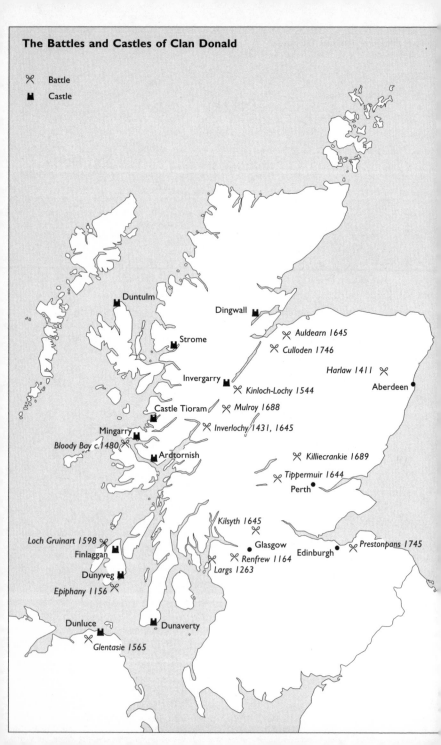

The Battles and Castles of Clan Donald

⚔ Battle

🏰 Castle

Duntulm

Dingwall

Strome

Auldearn 1645

Culloden 1746

Harlaw 1411

Aberdeen

Invergarry

Kinloch-Lochy 1544

Castle Tioram

Mulroy 1688

Mingarry

Inverlochy 1431, 1645

Bloody Bay c.1480

Ardtornish

Killiecrankie 1689

Tippermuir 1644

Perth

Kilsyth 1645

Loch Gruinart 1598

Glasgow

Finlaggan

Renfrew 1164

Prestonpans 1745

Edinburgh

Dunyveg

Largs 1263

Epiphany 1156

Dunluce

Dunaverty

Glentasie 1565

INDEX